DECISIONS OF THE ATLANTA CAMPAIGN

OTHER BOOKS IN THE COMMAND DECISIONS IN AMERICA'S CIVIL WAR SERIES

Decisions at Stones River: The Sixteen Critical Decisions That Defined the Battle
Matt Spruill and Lee Spruill

Decisions at Second Manassas: The Fourteen Critical Decisions That Defined the Battle
Matt Spruill III and Matt Spruill IV

Decisions at Chickamauga: The Twenty-Four Critical Decisions That Defined the Battle
Dave Powell

Decisions at Chattanooga: The Nineteen Critical Decisions That Defined the Battle
Larry Peterson

DECISIONS
OF THE
ATLANTA CAMPAIGN

The Twenty-One Critical Decisions That Defined the Operation

Larry Peterson

Maps by Tim Kissel

COMMAND DECISIONS
IN AMERICA'S CIVIL WAR

The University of Tennessee Press / Knoxville

First Edition.

Library of Congress Cataloging-in-Publication Data

Names: Peterson, Lawrence K., author. | Kissel, Tim, cartographer.
Title: Decisions of the Atlanta Campaign : the twenty-one critical decisions that defined the operation / Larry Peterson ; maps by Tim Kissel.
Description: First edition. | Knoxville : The University of Tennessee Press, [2018] | Series: Command decisions in America's Civil War | Includes bibliographical references and index. |
Identifiers: LCCN 2018054718 (print) | LCCN 2018055893 (ebook) | ISBN 9781621904731 (kindle) | ISBN 9781621904748 (pdf) | ISBN 9781621904724 | ISBN 9781621904724 (pbk.)
Subjects: LCSH: Atlanta Campaign, 1864. | Command of troops—Case studies.
Classification: LCC E476.7 (ebook) | LCC E476.7 .P48 2018 (print) | DDC 973.7/371—dc23
LC record available at https://lccn.loc.gov/2018054718

To Kathleen,
my wife and partner
for many, many years

CONTENTS

ILLUSTRATIONS

Figures

Maps

PREFACE

Like many amateur and professional historians today, I found the Civil War fascinating from the time I was in grade school. I continued to study the conflict while progressing through the educational system. A short career as a National Park Service ranger continued to whet my appetite for more knowledge about the Civil War, especially with the NPS managing so many of its battlefields. However, when I decided to publish a biography of my ancestor, Confederate Brig. Gen. Alfred J. Vaughan Jr., the serious work began. Some eighteen years of research later, by the time of the publication of that biography, I understood more of the scope and impact of the Civil War.[1]

My interest in the Atlanta Campaign arose as I researched Vaughan. At the beginning of the Civil War, Vaughan, a graduate of the Virginia Military Institute, commanded the Thirteenth Tennessee Infantry at the Battles of Shiloh and Perryville and was acting brigade commander at the Battles of Richmond, Kentucky, Stones River, and Chickamauga. Vaughan earned a promotion to brigadier general after the death of his brigade commander at the Battle of Chickamauga. He commanded Vaughan's Brigade during the Atlanta Campaign until he lost his left foot to a cannon shell on July 4, 1864, while on the Smyrna Line. The injury ended Vaughan's field service.[2]

I spent quite a bit of time and effort tracing Vaughan's movements during the Atlanta Campaign. This research stimulated my interest in this lengthy expedition, which included thrusts, feints, flanking maneuvers, and battles. Already involved, I continued to examine why a campaign so important to both sides resulted in the eventual capture of Atlanta. I wondered if the outcome could have been different.[3]

Over many years, I have made multiple visits to the sites of the Atlanta Campaign, and I have been fortunate in communicating with and digesting the opinions of a number of professional historians in person and by correspondence. These efforts helped me distill the critical decisions of the Atlanta Campaign. Seeing significant locations associated with the fighting continued to solidify my understanding of the terrain and the physical obstacles each side faced.

After considerable study, it became obvious to me that, as in any military campaign, key commanders on both sides made decisions that contributed significantly to the outcome. Eventually I compiled a list of these critical decisions of the Atlanta Campaign.[4]

The major premise of this study is that once you know what happened, the next step is determining why an event happened. Understanding the critical decisions is the vehicle for asking and answering this question.

The Atlanta Campaign did not unfold as the result of random chance. Events evolved as they did due to decisions that Union and Confederate officers at all levels of command made in response to orders from their superiors. These judgments were reached before, during, and after battles and other movements. However, of all the decisions made during the fighting, only twenty-one critical decisions shaped the Atlanta Campaign. My criterion for a critical decision is that it shaped not only the events immediately following it but also the events from that point on. The critical decisions of the Atlanta Campaign may be classified as strategic, operational, tactical, organizational, personnel, and logistical.

These choices were made at all levels of command. Army, corps, and division commanders were responsible for some of them, and brigade commanders made a few others. Sometimes an organizational decision proved to be a critical decision.

The chart below represents the decisions hierarchy. At the bottom are the many important decisions. Above those are a lesser number of important decisions, while at the top are the very few critical decisions.

Be very careful to not classify as a critical decision an important choice made in reaction to a critical decision. Other considerations are the fog of battle, weather, and just plain luck or the lack thereof, all of which can affect these decisions.

For ease of presentation and understanding, the critical decisions are presented in the same format. A brief chronology ties all of them together. For each critical decision, the situation as it appeared to the decision-maker is

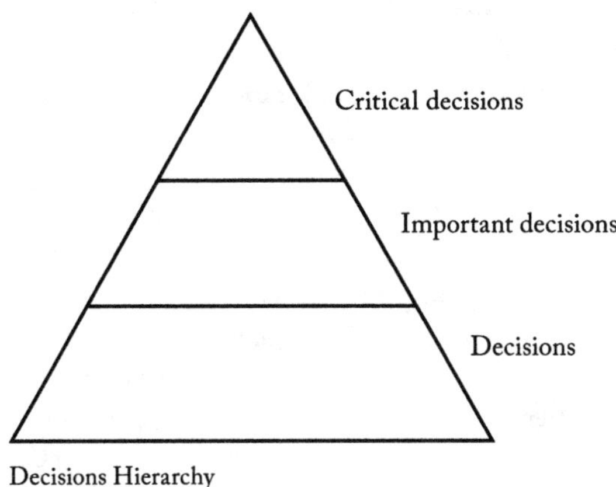

Decisions Hierarchy

described. An examination of the available options and ultimate decision follows, along with a brief review of the result(s) or impact of that decision. Finally, the impact that selecting another option might have had on the Atlanta Campaign is discussed. Here, readers can interject their own views of how events might have occurred had one of these alternate decisions been chosen.

While the above concept sounds easy to understand and evaluate, through this series of books we have discovered otherwise. For example, most everyone who has any knowledge of the Civil War is familiar with the Battle of Gettysburg. So we ask this question: What critical decision did Gen. Robert E. Lee make on the third day of the battle, July 3, 1863? The overwhelming response is that he ordered Pickett's Charge. However, this answer is incorrect! Early on July 3, Lee had three options: remain on the battlefield and attack, remain on the battlefield on the defense, or retreat. Lee made the critical decision to remain and attack. Following his orders, the results were fighting on Culp's Hill and the famous Pickett-Pettigrew-Trimble Charge. This example indicates that one must be very careful not to confuse a resulting action with the actual critical decision.

The next comment often made is that the critical decisions are already common knowledge and obvious. But where can you find information about them? Chances are that it would require a considerable amount of thought and study to define all of these choices. Books about Civil War battles and campaigns often mention these critical decisions and group them with other important but non-critical decisions. Where else will you find such judgments listed and discussed in chronological order?

Another matter brought to our attention is that books like this one present little, if any, new material. This is true: this series is not about discovering previously unreported portions of a battle, or the newly discovered actions or thoughts of a few commanders. The Atlanta Campaign has been well documented almost since it occurred. However, evolving scholarship has been incorporated into this work when relevant. Closely reviewing Maj. Gen. James McPherson's retreat back to Snake Creek Gap and failure to sever the Western and Atlantic Railroad doesn't change the outcome. That McPherson was new to army command doesn't change the outcome; it merely provides an explanation of why he may have so acted. Our attempt is to indicate how this action directly affected the outcome of the Atlanta Campaign.

If the reader has previous knowledge of the Atlanta Campaign, it may be helpful to better understand the critical decisions. However, it is important to note that this work is not another history of the Atlanta Campaign. As stated above, this book is the story of why events happened, not of the events themselves. It is my hope that the reader might then apply this line of reasoning to gain insight into other battles and campaigns. Note that the many, many important decisions at all levels of command were made as the result of the critical decisions.

There seems to be a new trend to label the Atlanta Campaign the North Georgia Campaign. The latter name may be more correct, but the Atlanta Campaign has been known as such for some 150-plus years. Thus I will continue to utilize that more recognized appellation. In a similar circumstance, the Revolutionary War Battle of Bunker Hill was actually fought on Breed's Hill. Even though the engagement is incorrectly labeled, historians have long accepted its name, and revisionists have not been able to change it.

The introduction briefly updates the reader on events of the Civil War leading to the situation for both sides in the spring of 1864. Chapters covering actions prior to and during the Atlanta Campaign then present the critical decisions as follows:

> Chapter 1, "Decisions Made Prior to the Atlanta Campaign, December 16, 1863–May 7, 1864," describes the initial seven critical decisions that had profound effects on the fighting.
>
> Davis Appoints Johnston to Command the Army of Tennessee
> Lincoln Appoints Grant General-in-Chief of all Union Armies
> Grant Attaches Himself to the Army of the Potomac as an Advisor
> Grant Appoints Sherman to Command in the West

Sherman Strengthens and Improves His Railroad Supply Line
Johnston Decides to Defend the Dalton Area from Attack
Davis Orders Reinforcements to Johnston

Chapter 2, "The Snake Creek Gap Turning Movement, May 8–May 13, 1864," discusses the three critical decisions reached between the opening of the campaign and the Battle of Resaca.

Sherman Orders McPherson to Sever the Railroad at Resaca
Sherman Fails to Support McPherson's Turning Movement
McPherson Fails to Capture Resaca

Chapter 3, "Retreat, Retreat! May 14 to June 7, 1864," examines the three critical decisions concerning Resaca, Cassville, and the Hell Hole fighting in and around Dallas and Pickett's Mill.

Sherman Outflanks Johnston at Resaca
Johnston Plans to Attack near Cassville
Sherman Decides to Leave the Railroad

Chapter 4, "Attack! June 8–June 27, 1864," considers the attempts to change the strategy of the campaign with two more critical decisions.

Johnston Decides Not to Order His Cavalry to Sever Sherman's Supply Line
Sherman Orders a Direct Attack on the Kennesaw Mountain Line

Chapter 5, "New Plans, June 28 to July 22, 1864," addresses two critical decisions Sherman made as his armies moved closer to the city of Atlanta. During this same period of time, Davis made one critical decision, as did Hood, his new commander.

Sherman Makes Atlanta His Objective
Sherman Decides to Destroy the Railroads Supplying Atlanta

Davis Appoints Hood to Command the Army of Tennessee
Hood Orders a Flank Attack against McPherson

Chapter 6, "Finishing the Campaign, July 23 to September 2, 1864," covers the two critical decisions that eventually caused Sherman's success in the Atlanta Campaign and Hood's failure.

Sherman Destroys the Railroad, Not Hardee
Sherman Ends the Pursuit of Hood, Captures Atlanta

Chapter 7, "Aftermath and Conclusions," summarizes the critical decisions' effects.

The reader needs to be aware of two sets of abbreviations that appear throughout this book. First, I rely on officer rank abbreviations used during the Civil War, not those currently in use. During the war *lieutenant colonel* was abbreviated *lieut. col.*, and the other ranks were similarly abbreviated. I employ these short forms in this work.

As you read, you will notice the Union and the Confederacy often used similar methods to identify units, but their schemes diverged in many places, too. Therefore, some explanatory comments are appropriate.

Both sides used the same method to identify units at the company, battalion, and regimental level. Companies were identified by a letter—e.g., A Company. Regiments were identified by a number—e.g., Eighth (8th) Illinois, Ninth (9th) Indiana. Above the regimental level, the Union and Confederate armies identified their units differently.

The official designations of Union brigades, divisions, and corps were numeric and began with a capital letter. Some examples include First Brigade, First Division, Third Corps or Brig. Gen. Charles R. Wood's First Brigade, Brig. Gen. Peter J. Osterhaus's First Division, and Maj. Gen. John A. Logan's Fifteenth Corps. Many publications use roman numerals to designate a corps —e.g., III Corps. However, examine the *Official Records* and you will find that this form of designation was not used in the Civil War. When referring to a brigade or division belonging to or commanded by an individual, lowercase letters are used, so that Wood's brigade, Osterhaus's division, and Logan's corps would all be correct designations.

While early in the war the Confederacy used a numbering and a name system for unit designations, as the war progressed the numbering system was used less and the name system was most commonly used. Thus the official designations of Confederate brigades, divisions, and corps were the commanders' names followed by Brigade, Division, or Wing (later Corps). Examples include Vaughan's Brigade, Cheatham's Division, and Hardee's Corps.

The Confederate system sometimes can be confusing. Depending on the situation, a unit could have its name changed immediately upon change of command or retain the old commander's name out of respect. This was the situation with Vaughan's Brigade after a wound had removed Vaughan himself from the war.

Lowercase letters are used when referring to a brigade, division, or corps commanded by an individual. For example, Vaughan's Brigade becomes Brig. Gen. Alfred Vaughan's brigade when the commander himself is under discussion. The same rule holds for Maj. Gen. Benjamin F. Cheatham's division and Maj. Gen. William J. Hardee's corps, for example. As with any matter pertaining to the Civil War, there are always exceptions.

As many readers will already be aware, there is nothing better than being able to walk the ground of a battlefield and to study the terrain on which each army fought and traveled. While many books attempt to explain the situation and environment of a battle or campaign, they simply cannot do justice to the view the commanders and men on the field actually saw. Because having "boots on the ground" is so significant to understanding the Atlanta Campaign, appendix I provides a driving tour of locations that offer greater insight into where and why many of the critical decisions were made. Please note that this appendix does not offer a tour of the entire Atlanta Campaign. Rather, it offers a tour of the locations where select critical decisions were made between Chattanooga and Atlanta. Appendix I also offers the reader a brief description of events pertinent to each decision site, as well as quotes from decision-makers. As mentioned at the beginning of the driving tour, each stop is optional.

Although available elsewhere, the orders of battle for the Union and Confederate armies appear in appendices II and III. This is a matter of convenience—the reader won't have to search elsewhere to keep track of who belonged under whose command. Note these appendices do not designate army corps with Roman numerals, as they were not so used until long after the Civil War.

ACKNOWLEDGMENTS

There are times when an author wonders if his work is worth the effort. What I have discovered through my interactions with the many current and bygone Civil War historical organizations over the years is not only a source of information and guidance, but also a source of great personal reward, as I now count many of their historians, volunteers, and staff as friends. I truly thank them all, those listed here as well as others whom I may have failed to mention, for sharing their time and expertise with me.

My thanks to Ken Padgett, "Mr. Resaca," for his personal assistance and guidance in developing the history of the Battle of Resaca with me. His efforts and those of the Friends of Resaca have led to the successful opening of that state historic site. Thanks to James Wooten, former manager of Pickett's Mill Battlefield State Historic Site, who was so instrumental in interpreting the "Hell Hole" battles for me. Also thanks to Melvin Dishong for his hospitality and instruction on the actions at Pine Mountain.

It is so unfortunate that the Friends of Civil War Paulding County have recently disbanded after so many years of dedication to preserving the history there, especially the "Hell Hole" fighting. I was pleased to be the only member from Colorado! Thanks to members among whom were Wayne Willingham, Hugh Walters, Danny Echols, and Connie Tibbits for the many hours they devoted to my research. Their local knowledge and works were and are nothing short of stupendous.

The other organization which was and is so foundational for anyone interested in the Atlanta Campaign is the Georgia Battlefields Association (GBA). Longtime president Colonel Charles Crawford (USAF retired) has spent countless hours driving me to the many sites involved in the campaign and introduced me to numerous helpful historians and individuals. Additionally, the annual GBA tour remains an incredible source of information on the Atlanta Campaign. In addition to Charlie, tour guides Ed Bearss, National Park Service Historian Emeritus, and Jim Ogden, longtime historian at Chickamauga and Chattanooga National Military Park, have shared countless details on the campaign for GBA members like me. Thanks to all the past and present officers and members of that organization, including former-president the late Charlie Geiger, who was such a ready resource. The annual GBA tour is definitely valuable for those wishing to brush up on their knowledge of the campaign and other Civil War Georgia actions (www.georgiabattlefields.org).

Special thanks to Dr. Stephen Davis for mentoring me and providing so many constructive comments as a reader for the manuscript. His vast knowledge of the campaign kept me on track.

My longtime friend, cohort, and mentor Colonel Matt Spruill (US Army retired), has also donated countless hours to refining my knowledge of the Civil War and helped to enhance my writing skills. Our collaboration on this series has been a constant source of satisfaction and good conversation (with apologies to his wife, Kathy).

I also extend my thanks to Scot Danforth, director of the University of Tennessee Press, and his staff, among whom are Thomas Wells, Jon Boggs, Tom Post, Stephanie Thompson, and Linsey Perry. Kudos to copyeditor Elizabeth Crowder who made the manuscript readable.

Thanks to the American Battlefield Trust (formerly the Civil War Trust), most ably managed by their president, James Lighthizer, along with David Duncan and the staff, whose many tours and leaders have shed yet more light on this campaign. If you are not a member, please consider supporting this wonderful organization (www.battlefields.org).

Finally, thanks to my wife, Kathleen, who has tolerated and supported my efforts to learn and write about the Civil War, knowing all along which side won!

Larry Peterson
Evergreen, Colorado

INTRODUCTION

THE SITUATION PRIOR TO THE ATLANTA CAMPAIGN

Many factors caused the American Civil War, which began after years of argument and debate. It is beyond the scope of this book to dwell extensively on the history and causes of the war. This introduction is meant to provide the reader with a brief review of events prior to the Atlanta Campaign.

For the sake of simplicity we will assume that the two major causes of the Civil War were states' rights and the propagation of slavery into the newly created states. Attempts to solve these problems by means of congressional acts such as the Missouri Compromise and the Compromise of 1850 temporarily placated the Southern states.[1]

After Abraham Lincoln's election in November 1860, the Deep South concluded that the new president would resist the further expansion of slavery. The region's states began holding conventions to vote on secession from the United States. After voting to withdraw from the Union and form the Confederate States of America (CSA), they began capturing former US facilities located within the new Confederacy, specifically forts and arsenals. Only Fort Pickens and Fort Sumter remained in Federal hands. After the CSA fired on and captured Fort Sumter near Charleston, South Carolina, on April 12, 1861, President Lincoln responded by requesting seventy-five thousand volunteers to help protect these facilities.[2]

In the Eastern Theater, after the Battle of Bull Run, or First Manassas, on July 21, 1861, where the Union forces eventually fled from the field, the war settled into a stalemate. President Lincoln appointed Maj. Gen. George B. McClellan to command what became the Army of the Potomac. A master of organization, McClellan built this army into a large, well-equipped, well-supplied force. In 1862 he conducted a massive operation to capture Richmond. These efforts began by utilizing the navy to transport the general's large army to a landing at Fort Monroe, near Norfolk. McClellan then marched up the Virginia Peninsula intent on capturing Richmond. Initial Federal success was foiled when, at the Battle at Seven Pines or Fair Oaks, the retreating Confederate commander, Gen. Joseph E. Johnston, was wounded. Gen. Robert E. Lee replaced Johnston and went on the offensive, fighting a series of battles called the Seven Days Battles.

McClellan's men retreated as a result. From August 28 to August 30, 1862, Lee's troops soundly defeated Maj. Gen. John Pope's Army of Virginia at the Second Battle of Bull Run. The Confederate general then conducted an invasion into Maryland in September. Though outnumbered, Lee fought to a draw at the Battle of Antietam, the bloodiest day of fighting in American history. He retreated into Virginia afterward. Utilizing this victory, President Lincoln issued the Emancipation Proclamation and replaced McClellan with Maj. Gen. Ambrose Burnside. Burnside planned to attack Richmond by first crossing the Rappahannock River at Fredericksburg, but Lee's forces repulsed him there. Burnside's infamous Mud March after the battle ended his term in command.[3]

Meanwhile, in the Western Theater, things were going much better for the Union. Confederate Maj. Gen. Leonidas Polk violated Kentucky's neutrality by capturing the commanding heights overlooking the Mississippi River at Columbus. Union Brig. Gen. Ulysses S. Grant immediately captured Paducah. Shortly thereafter and with help from the navy, Grant captured the two Confederate forts guarding the Tennessee and Cumberland Rivers, Forts Henry and Donelson, respectively. This triumph opened up large parts of the Confederate interior or Heartland. Grant then proceeded south, traveling up the Tennessee River to Pittsburg Landing, near a small church called Shiloh. While Grant and his Army of the Tennessee waited for reinforcements from Maj. Gen. Don Carlos Buell's Army of the Ohio, Confederate troops under the overall command of Gen. Albert S. Johnston planned to attack before that assistance arrived. Here, on April 6, 1862, the Confederates launched a surprise assault and pushed the Union line back significantly by the day's end. Instead of sealing their victory the next day, the Southern soldiers came under assault from Grant, whom Buell had strongly reinforced during the night. Shortly thereafter, Union soldiers captured Corinth, Mississippi, an important railroad junction.[4]

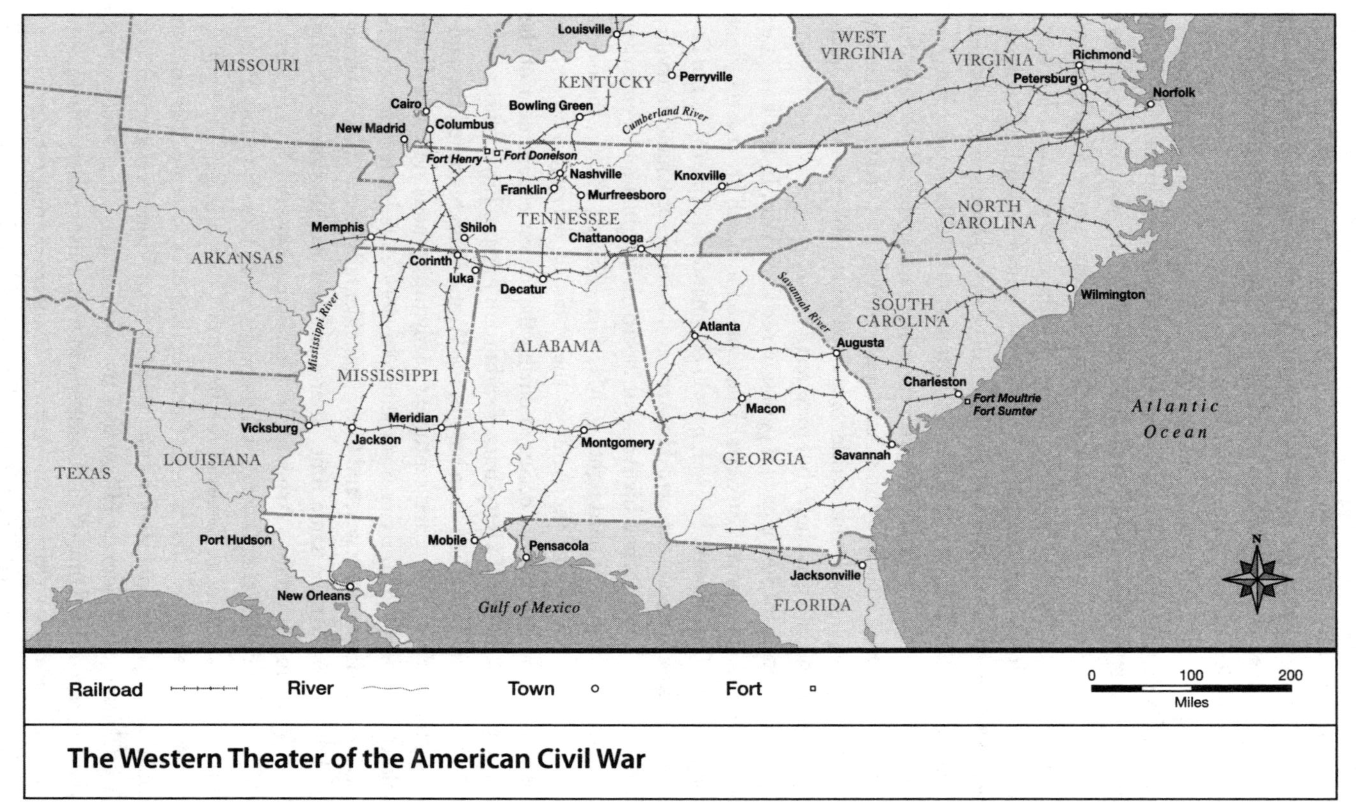

The Western Theater of the American Civil War

Now under the command of Gen. Braxton Bragg, this Confederate army, soon to be designated the Army of Tennessee, made a foray into Kentucky. Bragg's troops combined forces with Maj. Gen. Edmund Kirby Smith's small army in the Kentucky Campaign of 1862. Smith won the most complete victory of the war at the Battle of Richmond, Kentucky, on August 30. Unfortunately, Confederate success in the state faltered after the Battle of Perryville on October 8; Bragg won the battle but realized that he was now badly outnumbered. He retreated in terrible drought conditions to the Murfreesboro, Tennessee, area, where his army regrouped. Now in command, Maj. Gen. William S. Rosecrans led his Army of the Cumberland from Nashville, which had been captured soon after the fall of Fort Donelson, to confront Bragg at the Battle of Stones River near Murfreesboro, Tennessee. Early on December 31, 1862, Bragg engineered a surprise attack against Rosecrans that almost cut the Union supply line. After a day of rest, on January 2, a hastily organized grouping of Union artillery repulsed an attack by the Confederate right. Bragg had no real choice but to retreat.[5]

The year 1863 marked a pivotal period in the Civil War. In the East, Lee sent Lieut. Gen. Thomas "Stonewall" Jackson on a march around the right flank of Maj. Gen. Joseph Hooker, now in command of the Army of the Potomac. Jackson's troops defeated Hooker's at the Battle of Chancellorsville. Emboldened, Lee marched his Army of Northern Virginia into Pennsylvania. After three days of hard fighting, Maj. Gen. George Meade, the newly appointed commander of the Army of the Potomac, defeated Lee and his men. This Confederate loss occurred during the largest engagement of the entire war, the Battle of Gettysburg, fought from July 1 to July 3, 1863.[6]

Meanwhile, Grant had been busy in the West. He orchestrated the campaign that led to the siege and capture of nearly thirty thousand Confederate soldiers at Vicksburg. The city was the final major Confederate defense protecting the Mississippi River, and Grant coincidentally received its surrender on July 4, 1863. At the same time, after a brilliant flanking move by Maj. Gen. William Rosecrans's Army of the Cumberland around Bragg's Army of Tennessee during the Tullahoma Campaign, from June 23 to July 3, 1863, Rosecrans fell to Bragg's forces at the Battle of Chickamauga. The fighting occurred just south of Chattanooga from September 18 to September 20, and Lieut. Gen. James Longstreet's two divisions from Virginia assisted Bragg. A final stand on Snodgrass Hill, under the command of Maj. Gen. George Thomas, saved the Army of the Cumberland from further destruction. This was the only major victory for the Army of Tennessee during the war.[7]

Lincoln then placed Grant in overall command of the Western Theater. He relieved Rosecrans and placed the Army of the Cumberland under the command of Thomas, the "Rock of Chickamauga." Thomas was penned up in Chattanooga under a semi-siege by Bragg. Thomas was eventually augmented by Maj. Gen. William T. Sherman's Army of the Tennessee, both now under the personal direction of Grant, later augmented by two divisions from the East under the command of Maj. Gen. Joseph Hooker. Once resupplied, and after two days of fighting on November 24 and 25, Grant routed the Confederates at the Battle of Chattanooga or Missionary Ridge. Federals pushed the enemy soldiers back to Dalton, Georgia, where they spent the winter.[8]

As 1864 opened, the scene was set for further conflict. President Lincoln appointed Grant general-in-chief of all Union armies. In the Eastern Theater, Maj. Gen. George G. Meade faced Lee, who was continuing to protect the Confederate capital of Richmond, Virginia. In the Western Theater, Grant appointed Sherman to command the three armies constituting the Military Division of the Mississippi, created in October 1863. The Armies of the Tennessee, Cumberland, and Ohio were rested and refitted in preparation for the upcoming campaign. Likewise, the Confederate Army of Tennessee received a new commander, Gen. Joseph E. Johnston, who refitted, reequipped, and ordered furloughs for some of his men. Significant changes in all of these armies soon resulted from critical decisions that would affect the upcoming Atlanta Campaign.[9]

The capture of Chattanooga provided the Union high command with an excellent jumping-off point to maneuver farther into Georgia and the Deep South. So far, both areas were largely untouched by the war. The closest target other than Johnston's army was the important railroad hub and manufacturing city of Atlanta. Only some 130 miles southeast, its capture would be a significant blow to Southern independence. Obviously, once the Union captured Atlanta, the Federal military could conduct forays to other Deep South locations, further disrupting the dwindling Confederate resources. Atlanta's vulnerability was not lost on the Confederate high command, which knew that the city had to be protected at all costs.[10]

The Union commander of the Military Division of the Mississippi would have to confront two major problems. While capturing Chattanooga was a significant victory for the Union, a significant supply line had to be established, expanded, maintained, and protected to keep the city adequately supplied with the necessities a force the size of Sherman's required. As Sherman's command marched southeast toward Atlanta, his supply line would continue to lengthen. In contrast, his opponent's would decrease, favoring the Confederacy. As will be seen, Sherman expended great effort on this issue.[11]

The weather was another problem the Union and Confederate commands would confront. In Georgia, the typical hot, sultry summer days would adversely affect soldiers, often causing both heat stroke and heat exhaustion. Men in this condition were unavailable for any military duties. The rain would be even more pronounced, quickly rendering the available roads difficult to travel on foot or by wagon. Even worse, the roads could become so muddy that practical movement of both men and wagons would be impossible. In spite of these difficulties, the stage had been set for what would soon be labeled the Atlanta Campaign.[12]

CHAPTER 1

DECISIONS MADE PRIOR TO THE ATLANTA CAMPAIGN, DECEMBER 16, 1863–MAY 7, 1864

If you have bypassed the preface, please direct your attention there and read the definition of a critical decision in order to more fully understand the discussions in this book.

Prior to what would eventually be designated the Atlanta Campaign, seven critical decisions formed the initial action. Had these decisions not been made, the campaign might have taken a much different form. Prior planning is usually necessary to ensure the desired outcome.

Davis Appoints Johnston to Command the Army of Tennessee

Situation

After the Battle of Chickamauga, Gen. Braxton Bragg quarreled with his officers and reduced the number of troops maintaining a semi-siege around Chattanooga. He sent reinforcements including Longstreet's divisions to confront Maj. Gen. Ambrose Burnside's Ninth Corps at Knoxville. While Bragg kept reducing his force at Chattanooga, Grant continued to increase his presence. This measure helped Grant rout Bragg's Army of Tennessee off both Lookout Mountain and Missionary Ridge on November 24 and 25,

1863. After this debacle Bragg realized that he could no longer effectively command. On November 28, 1863, he ended a routine telegraph message to the adjutant general of the Confederacy, Gen. Samuel Cooper, with a request to be relieved from command. Cooper replied on November 30 and granted the request. Bragg stepped down the next day, following orders to transfer command of the army to the senior officer present, Lieut. Gen. William J. Hardee.

Hardee had generally given a solid performance as a corps commander, and he was known and respected for his book on tactics published prior to the war. Officers on both sides of the conflict had read his work. When given his new command, Hardee surprised President Davis by thanking him for his confidence yet stating, "Feeling my inability to serve the country successfully in this new sphere of duty, I respectfully decline the command, if designated to be permanent." Davis had no choice but to make the critical decision of considering and appointing a replacement commander. Obviously, the new leader of the Army of Tennessee would have a huge impact on the war's course in the Western Theater.[1]

President Jefferson Davis, a former senator, secretary of war, and plantation owner, had also served as a colonel during the Mexican-American War. Based on this prior experience, he firmly believed he could manage the day-to-day Confederate military situation while president of the Confeder-

President Jefferson Davis, CSA.
Library of Congress.

acy. Therefore, he meddled in military matters that should not have directly concerned him. He should have let senior military commanders manage the armies and fighting while he observed their overall achievements.[2]

Options

In naming a replacement for Bragg, President Davis had two options: He could appoint the new commander from the ranks of his full generals. Alternatively, he could ignore seniority and appoint the new commander from the ranks of the available lieutenant or major generals.[3]

Option 1

Davis believed that he was limited to selecting the new commander from the short list of his full generals, all graduates of West Point. This limitation was of his own volition; it was not necessarily incumbent upon him. Only two men apparently received serious consideration, Gens. P. G. T. Beauregard and Joseph E. Johnston, but Davis disliked both. Beauregard had demonstrated command success beginning with the Battle of Bull Run (First Manassas), and he could certainly be an aggressive commander. However, Davis had quickly wearied of Beauregard's penchant for espousing grandiose, unrealistic strategies for the Confederacy.[4]

General Joseph E. Johnston, CSA.
Library of Congress.

Johnston was born in Virginia on February 3, 1807. He graduated from West Point in the class of 1829 (a classmate of Robert E. Lee's) and served with great distinction during the Seminole and Mexican-American Wars. Johnston was appointed quartermaster general with the staff rank of brigadier general on June 28, 1860. As the highest-ranking officer to leave the Union army, he felt that he would be the ranking general officer when he offered his services to the Confederacy. Jefferson Davis didn't agree. He placed Johnston, a former staff officer, junior to former line officers Samuel Cooper, Albert Sidney Johnston, and Robert E. Lee. In November 1861, Johnston railed at Davis for ranking him inappropriately in seniority. This did not endear the general to the Confederate president. Further, Johnston's constant retreating during Maj. Gen. George B. McClellan's 1862 Peninsula Campaign had not demonstrated an aggressive posture. Yet Johnston presented a good physical appearance as compared to Bragg, and he was much better than Bragg at instilling morale in his troops.[5]

Gen. Robert E. Lee must also have been briefly considered to command the Western Theater. His appointment would give that theater and the Army of Tennessee a proven successful commander who would maximize the available resources. However, Davis was not yet sufficiently concerned to realize how badly the Confederacy was faring in the Western Theater. He tended to focus more on the Eastern Theater, where he resided. Two problems were associated with Lee's potential transfer. Lee had made it abundantly clear that he had no interest in going west, stating that he was unfamiliar with the territory and the officers within the various commands. In addition, if Lee were assigned to the West, another general would necessarily need to be appointed to replace him. Who would that be?[6]

Option 2

Davis had the option of elevating one of the lieutenant or major generals available, but none seemed to stand out. Moreover, the appointment of one of these officers over other more senior generals would likely cause more unneeded dissent within the Army of Tennessee. As previously noted, Hardee had indicated his reluctance to accept permanent army command (perhaps as, at this time, he was engaged to be married). Maj. Gen. Richard Taylor or Lieut. Gen. Edmond Kirby Smith could be considered for the position, but both already held commands elsewhere. Maj. Gen. Patrick Cleburne had exhibited outstanding divisional command. However, he had politically disqualified himself by proposing the use of slaves in the Confederate armies, and he had no experience at corps command, much less at army command.[7]

Decision

After weighing these options, on December 16, 1863, Davis made the critical decision to appoint Johnston as the new commander of the Army of Tennessee.[8]

Results/Impact

The result of this critical decision was that Johnston allowed Sherman to reach the gates of Atlanta, one of the three most important cities of the Confederacy. This important railroad hub was eventually lost, as well as the munitions and other supplies manufactured there that were all but irreplaceable.[9]

Johnston was a commander who worked diligently to make sure that his men were well fed, clothed, and supplied with ammunition. Further, he attempted to support his troops with wagons and to rebuild the artillery. His men reciprocated by marching and fighting hard for him. Johnston truly had the ability to provide leadership to the Confederate army. He tended toward the not uncommon belief that the enemy significantly outnumbered him, even when it was not true. Such disparity was usually the case, and all Rebel armies were typically outnumbered. Commanders had to utilize their available troops wisely. As Johnston tended not to understand that the Confederacy normally lacked reinforcements, he generally reacted to Sherman's movements rather than taking the initiative. It would be difficult for any general to win a campaign this way. Johnston's past record did not indicate that he would reasonably change his strategy and bring on an engagement. He continually refused to believe that reinforcements were unavailable, and he would not waiver from his belief that cautious Fabian retreat was the best reaction to the Union advance. While that approach certainly saved his army to fight another day, it did not save Atlanta from being captured. Whether another officer appointed in his place would have been more effective is anyone's guess. Aggressive fighter John Bell Hood was later assigned the temporary rank of general to replace Johnston, but he, too, was unsuccessful.[10]

Although some will argue that Davis had no choice but to select Johnston for this command, this contention is not true. Davis limited his own choices. As commander, Johnston strongly influenced the first part of the Atlanta Campaign, and for whatever reason, he failed to successfully conduct any offensive actions resulting in Confederate victory.[11]

Alternate Decisions and Scenarios

Had Davis considered some of his more junior generals for command of the Army of Tennessee, he might not have suffered the headaches engendered by

Johnston's continuous retreating, his lack of communication with the Confederate government, and his continual demand for more soldiers. One can only speculate on the results of a different appointment.[12]

In retrospect, what might have taken place had President Davis selected someone else to command this army? Beauregard had demonstrated command success beginning with the Battle of Bull Run, or First Manassas, and he certainly could be an aggressive leader. However, as previously mentioned, Davis had quickly tired of Beauregard's penchant for espousing grandiose, unrealistic strategies for the Confederacy. That Davis relieved Beauregard of command after the Battle of Shiloh, when he had taken unauthorized leave from his post, indicated he would not favor Beauregard to lead what had become the Army of Tennessee.[13]

An analysis of available lieutenant generals was not promising for Davis. After Bragg resigned from command of the Army of Tennessee, Hardee received a temporary appointment in his place. Hardee then notified President Davis that he was not interested in permanent command of the troops. Yet when Davis later appointed Hood to this position, Hardee sought to resign, believing that he was a better, senior, and more experienced candidate. Had President Davis again offered Hardee the command upon relieving Johnston in July 1864, and had Hardee accepted it, what might have resulted? Hardee might have stalled Sherman longer, fighting only segments of the Union general's forces. It is possible he might have kept Sherman from capturing Atlanta until after the November elections. However, as Sherman was quite aware of the presidential election and its implications for continuing the war, he probably would not have been delayed significantly. Hardee would not have squandered his men unnecessarily. He might have kept the Army of Tennessee more intact and able to fight after Atlanta fell, and Hardee was experienced with supplying his men.[14]

John Bell Hood was not available at this time, as he was convalescing as a major general in Richmond. While other eastern generals, including Lieut. Gen. James Longstreet, might have effectively served as commander, Gen. Robert E. Lee was hesitant to release them to his detriment. Longstreet had demonstrated poor independent command ability after his service at the Battle of Chickamauga, which indicated a low probability of success had he been appointed commander.[15]

Had Lee been transferred to the Western Theater while his Army of Northern Virginia, perhaps commanded by Longstreet, defended Richmond from the Union armies in the Eastern Theater, the Civil War might have taken an interesting turn. Under Lee's direct command, Confederate troops might have outfoxed Sherman and delayed his advance on Atlanta. Staving off the capture of Atlanta until after the Northern presidential election in November might have given the Confederacy a chance to negotiate a truce. Peace might have led to the South's eventual independence. However, Lee would likely have demanded his return to the Army of Northern Virginia after Grant/Meade crossed the Rapidan in early May 1864. While Davis may have considered this option unlikely, it was an option nevertheless.[16]

Lincoln Appoints Grant General-in-Chief of all Union Armies

Situation

The second critical decision of the Atlanta Campaign, and the first from the Union perspective, was President Abraham Lincoln's appointment of a general-in-chief of all the Union armies, with the newly reestablished rank of lieutenant general. Ironically, Lincoln's choice may actually have prolonged the Civil War.[17]

As of early 1864, President Lincoln, the quintessential politician and commander in chief, had tired of seeking a competent general to command the Army of the Potomac and enhance the Union war effort. Further, Lincoln had concluded that he needed someone to command all of the Union armies

President Abraham Lincoln, USA.
Library of Congress.

in order to effectively coordinate the superior Federal military resources. So far, this need for one leader controlling all armies and operations had gone unmet. Lincoln had long realized that Maj. Gen. Henry Halleck had not measured up to expectations as general-in-chief.[18]

Options

At this time President Lincoln had three options. He could continue to accept the status quo by retaining Halleck as general-in-chief, leaving Grant to command the Military Division of the Mississippi and Maj. Gen. George Meade to command the Army of the Potomac. As another option, Lincoln could promote Grant to general-in-chief of all the Union armies. Finally, instead of promoting Grant, the president could transfer him east to command the Army of the Potomac.[19]

Option 1

Lincoln's first option was to simply maintain the status quo, leaving Grant in command of the Military Division of the Mississippi and Meade in command of the Army of the Potomac. Lincoln would then remain an active commander in chief and the de facto general-in-chief. Meade had disappointed the president by failing to pursue Lee's Army of Northern Virginia as it retreated after the Battle of Gettysburg. Nonetheless, Meade's army had soundly defeated Lee's. In all likelihood, Meade would be able to at least force Lee and his army to remain in defense of Richmond. Grant, a more effective general, could then continue personally conducting operations in the Western Theater. Hopefully, he would continue his successes there as well. Once the Union dominated the Western Theater, the concentration of additional Federal troops in the Eastern Theater should ensure eventual victory in the region.[20]

Option 2

Lincoln could also turn over Union operations to a newly designated general-in-chief of all Union armies, reestablishing the rank of lieutenant general to place one such officer in overall command of all Union armies. Allowing a competent general to oversee Union strategy would relieve Lincoln of the day-to-day operations which he preferred, and benefit from a more coordinated effort against the Confederacy. Based upon his success in the Western Theater, Grant was certainly a good candidate for this position. This option ought to provide a much more efficient utilization of the Union armies. Grant was not a political general, and Lincoln undoubtedly found this quality refreshing.[21]

Lieutenant General Ulysses S. Grant, USA.
Library of Congress.

Grant was born on April 27, 1822. He entered the United States Military Academy for the free education, disliked it, but graduated in 1843 nevertheless. After leaving West Point, Grant was assigned to the Jefferson Barracks near Saint Louis, where he met and fell in love with his roommate's sister, Julia Dent. He subsequently served in the Mexican-American War, receiving several commendations, and as a first lieutenant, he spent many years in garrison duty in the East. Grant and Julia finally married in 1848. Assigned to the West in 1852, Grant left his growing family, grew despondent, and turned to alcohol. In 1854 he was forced to resign to avoid a court-martial. Grant then failed both as a farmer and real estate broker, events that led to his move to Galena, Illinois. There, he worked as a clerk in his father's leather goods store. Upon the outbreak of the Civil War, Grant quickly volunteered for military service. He was soon appointed colonel of the Twenty-First Illinois, and with the support of Congressman Elihu B. Washburne of Illinois, Grant was promoted to brigadier general shortly thereafter. This was good news for Grant, and he proved to be a natural commander. Grant then successfully completed three separate campaigns in the West. No other Union general could equal his record of success.[22]

Option 3

Rather than promoting Grant, Lincoln could also transfer him to command the Army of the Potomac. This measure would provide new leadership to that army from a general who had been successful so far. Grant's transfer might also be the means of Federal troops' finally moving to and capturing Richmond—a serious political blow to the Confederacy. In addition, this option would probably keep Lincoln actively involved in the Union war effort. However, a new commander for the Military Division of the Mississippi would be required as a result.[23]

Decision

On February 29, 1864, Lincoln signed into law the bill Congress had passed to reestablish the grade of lieutenant general. Grant received orders to Washington, DC, to accept the commission.[24]

Results/Impact

This promotion formally occurred on March 9, 1864. Lincoln and Grant's first meeting helped establish a working relationship that led to eventual Union victory. Grant knew which generals could be trusted to follow their orders, and he would place these men in the correct positions to carry out his orders. Interestingly, Lincoln's critical decision by Lincoln may actually have lengthened the Civil War.[25]

As will be discussed below, President Lincoln's appointing Grant general-in-chief resulted in Maj. Gen. William T. Sherman's appointment to command the Military Division of the Mississippi, and to plan and execute what became the Atlanta Campaign. Under Grant's leadership the Union went on to win the war. Lincoln, letting Grant control operations on multiple fronts, had placed his best fighting general where he could do the most good for the Union. With its significant advantage in manpower and other resources of war, the Union likely would have won regardless of the actions of some of its senior commanders. If the campaign had not been conducted in as timely a manner as Sherman managed it under Grant's orders, the Confederacy with its Army of Tennessee might have held off Federal forces and forced the Union into a temporary truce. The truce might eventually have become permanent, effectively allowing the Confederacy to win its war for independence.[26]

Alternate Decision and Scenario

Selecting another option might have produced some very interesting results. Specifically, what if President Lincoln had left Grant in charge of the Military Division of the Mississippi and its armies, feeling comfortable that Meade, having defeated Lee at Gettysburg, would at least hold Lee in check? Grant would then have had the opportunity to continue his success in the West. More specifically, had Grant been left in charge in the West, he would undoubtedly have initiated the Atlanta Campaign. With Grant in command, would there have been any doubt as to the outcome of the turning movement at Snake Creek Gap / Resaca?

Grant would probably have dispatched the Army of the Tennessee, still commanded by Sherman, his favorite subordinate, to pass through Snake Creek Gap in order to capture the railroad at Resaca. Grant reasonably would have accompanied Sherman to ensure the attack's success. He probably would have ordered additional assistance for Sherman to increase the odds in his favor. These actions suggest that Johnston would have been trapped above Resaca. In addition, Grant would have outmaneuvered Johnston's army, fighting until it was badly damaged, forced to surrender, or thoroughly dispersed. Without his supply line, Johnston's army simply would have quickly ceased to be a fighting force. Had Grant, like Maj. Gen. James B. McPherson, failed to trap Johnston at Resaca, he probably would have assaulted Johnston there without regard to casualties. Either of these events would have considerably shortened the Atlanta Campaign. Grant would have been able to capture Atlanta and other Confederate cities at his discretion, months earlier than Sherman did. Then he also could have dispatched parts of his forces to assist Meade, and/or he could have been appointed to command Meade's army, possibly allowing for the capture of Richmond and an end to the war in 1864. Although speculative, Lincoln's decision to appoint Grant to lieutenant general might well have extended the war by removing Grant from direct command in the West.[27]

Grant Attaches Himself to the Army of the Potomac as an Advisor

Situation

At the beginning of 1864, the Union faced a somewhat grim situation. In the East, despite the Army of Northern Virginia's 1863 defeat at Gettysburg, Lee still held Meade's Army of the Potomac in check while protecting the Confederate capital at Richmond. Since Grant had captured Vicksburg when Lee was defeated at Gettysburg, much of the Confederate West was under Union control. Yet a large part of the Northern population was against the war, with its continued loss of thousands of soldiers due to combat and disease.[28]

Most Union citizens were surviving economically, but the same was not true within the Confederacy. The lack of foreign goods, which the Union naval blockade kept away from Southerners, made everyday life a struggle. So, too, did the high inflation caused by competition for what goods were still produced within the Confederacy. Many Southerners, just like their Northern counterparts, wanted the war to end.[29]

Both sides were quite aware that, within the Union, the presidential election would take place in November 1864. If President Lincoln could be defeated in his bid for reelection, a newly elected candidate might agree to a temporary truce. Many on both sides of the conflict accepted that a truce would end the fighting and eventually lead to recognition of the Confederacy and its independence. Grant knew that Lincoln's future and his own hinged on the successes of the Union armies he now commanded. He knew something had to be done to attain success on the battlefield and demonstrate the Union's capability of winning the war.[30]

Options

Once Grant was appointed general-in-chief of all Union armies, he knew he was expected to formulate a plan for a coordinated Union movement against the Confederacy. Grant's proposed plan included four options for his role in the war effort. His first alternative was to remain in direct command of the Military Division of the Mississippi while monitoring the other armies and generals. Another option was for Grant to relocate to the Eastern Theater, a politically necessary move, and accompany Maj. Gen. George Meade's Army of the Potomac in an advisory role. In addition, Grant could take command of the Army of the Potomac while monitoring the other armies. As a final option, Grant could remove himself from direct command and oversee Federal operations from Washington, DC, or another location.[31]

Option 1

Grant could remain in command of the Military Division of the Mississippi while also commanding and overseeing all Federal armies and operations. His friend and immediate subordinate Sherman heartily endorsed this particular option, fearing that Grant would get caught up in Washington, DC, politics if located there. If Grant chose this option, he would reasonably be able to build on his previous successes in the Western Theater while leaving Meade to hold Lee in check.[32]

Option 2

Grant's second option was to go east, accompanying Meade, commander of the Army of the Potomac, as an advisor. Realistically, Grant would direct

Meade's maneuvering and fighting, with Meade issuing orders to move the Army of the Potomac according to Grant's wishes.[33]

Option 3

Grant could also go east and assume command of the well-worn Army of the Potomac. In doing so, he would provide this army with the successful leadership it had thus far lacked. Grant's success in the Western Theater might provide the required direction for the Army of the Potomac to move upon and capture Richmond, dealing the Confederacy a formidable political blow.[34]

Option 4

Grant's final option was to locate himself, logically in Washington, DC, but perhaps elsewhere, to maintain control and supervise Union operations of all armies in the field. Unencumbered by direct command, Grant could ensure that each unit would be properly commanded, supported, supplied, and maneuvered against the Rebels. While this choice was administratively sound, Grant preferred to remain in the field. This option would allow his unlimited concentration on each Union army or force. It would also result in more focused utilization of Federal resources.[35]

Decision

Grant opted to attach himself to the Army of the Potomac. While overseeing other Union operations, he would direct Meade and his army as it maneuvered against Lee.[36]

Results/Impact

Grant's plan was to keep Meade, an experienced officer with a quick temper, in command of the Union Army of the Potomac while accompanying it himself in an advisory capacity. As the first step in Grant's eventual five-part plan, Meade would pursue Lee's army wherever it moved. The costly and somewhat ineffective Overland Campaign resulted, including the Battles of the Wilderness and Spotsylvania Court House. Second, to assist Meade, political general Maj. Gen. Benjamin "Beast" Butler (his notorious treatment of Confederate women in New Orleans earned him the nickname) would advance his thirty-thousand-man Army of the James and attempt to capture Richmond. Butler and his troops were located in southeastern Virginia, and they would move up the south bank of the James River to City Point, near Petersburg. Third, to eliminate a source of sustenance for the Confederacy, Grant assigned Maj. Gen. Franz Sigel's nine-thousand-man column to move south up the

Shenandoah Valley and destroy the foodstuffs there. This measure would also divert Lee's attention. The fourth part of Grant's plan involved attacking the only viable Confederate army in the Western Theater, the Army of Tennessee, located at Dalton, Georgia. Finally, Grant proposed that Maj. Gen. Nathaniel Banks, another political general, advance from New Orleans to Mobile with his force of ten thousand men. However, Banks first had to complete an operation up the Red River into the Trans-Mississippi. Grant opposed this operation, but Lincoln had ordered it previously, and the general had no choice but to comply.[37]

This critical decision resulted in Sherman's becoming commander of the Military Division of the Mississippi (discussed in detail below). His leadership would directly impact what became the Atlanta Campaign.[38]

However, Grant's 1864 plan of attack proved mostly unsuccessful. Even with the help of Butler's force, and in spite of Grant's personally directing field operations in Virginia, Lee once again stymied the Federals' quest for Richmond. After the very bloody battles of the Overland Campaign, the best Grant could accomplish was the siege of Petersburg. This offensive reduced and eventually eliminated supplies flowing into Richmond.[39]

Sigel's march south up the Shenandoah Valley was rebuffed at the Battle of New Market on May 15. Grant immediately replaced Sigel with Maj. Gen. David Hunter, who proceeded up the valley before being defeated at Lynchburg. Lee then ordered Lieut. Gen. Jubal Early and two divisions to the valley. Early advanced to the defenses of Washington, DC, before retreating. Finally, Grant appointed one of his favorite generals, career officer Maj. Gen. Philip Sheridan, to the task. Sheridan defeated Confederates in the Shenandoah Valley in September and October, finally bringing success to that operation.[40]

The fourth part of Grant's plan, the Atlanta Campaign, was partially successful. It resulted in the surrender of Atlanta but not, as Grant had originally ordered, the destruction of the Confederate Army of Tennessee. As noted, this event contributed to Lincoln's reelection and the war's continuation to Union victory. This part of Grant's strategy would be followed to its ultimate success.[41]

The fifth part of Grant's plan, Banks's Red River Campaign, accommodated Lincoln's specific desire, but it was a disaster. It prevented reinforcements for Sherman during his initial movement toward Atlanta, or for an advance on Mobile.[42]

Alternative Decisions and Scenarios

Grant's other choices for his 1864 operational plan could have moved him in many directions. As discussed above, had he remained in command of the armies of the Military Division of the Mississippi, he would have begun the campaign just as Sherman had. But Grant probably would have successfully cut off Johnston at Resaca via the Snake Creek Gap turning movement or maneuver. Thus, he would have defeated Johnston right at the beginning of the campaign, potentially shortening the war.[43] Had Grant taken command the Army of the Potomac, he might have further augmented it at the expense of one or more of western armies in order to crush Lee with overwhelming numbers. Doing just the reverse, Grant might have detached some units from Meade to further augment the western armies in the hope that, together, they might overrun a good part of the Confederate West. Meade would have been left to simply hold Lee in place.[44]

Grant Appoints Sherman to Command in the West

Situation

In the fourth part of his plan for operations in 1864, Grant ordered that Johnston's Army of Tennessee be defeated or rendered ineffective. He also directed Federal troops to capture as much Confederate territory as possible while simultaneously destroying important infrastructure. Grant knew that the commander of the Military Division of Mississippi and its three armies had to be someone he could trust to act independently to accomplish this important objective.[45]

Options

Grant had three options for his replacement. One logical successor, Maj. Gen. George Thomas, was the senior general of the department and commander of the Army of the Cumberland. Another option was Grant's trusted friend Maj. Gen. William T. Sherman, commander of the Army of the Tennessee. Other possible candidates included Maj. Gen. John Schofield, commander of the Army of the Ohio, and Maj. Gen. Joseph Hooker, commander of the new Twentieth Corps.[46]

<u>Option 1</u>

Maj. Gen. George Thomas was the senior general in the department and Grant's logical successor. A career soldier, Thomas had saved the Army of the Cumberland at the Battle of Chickamauga after Maj. Gen. William S. Rosecrans had fled to Chattanooga, earning the sobriquet "the Rock of Chickamauga." Thomas was willing to fight, but only when he felt he had the necessary men and supplies. Unfortunately for Thomas, Grant, another longtime career

Major General William T. Sherman, USA. Library of Congress.

soldier, disliked him, especially as he felt Thomas was insufficiently aggressive on the offense and Grant desired an aggressive field commander for the operations against Johnston. That Thomas was a native of Virginia also led to speculation as to his true motives.[47]

<u>Option 2</u>

Although not the senior officer in this division, Grant's trusted friend Sherman, commander of the Army of the Tennessee, was certainly in contention for the position. Sherman had earned Grant's respect and was a reasonably aggressive commander emulating Grant himself.[48]

William Tecumseh Sherman graduated from the United States Military Academy in 1840. After thirteen years in the army, he resigned as a captain in the commissary department. Sherman tried banking in California and speculation in Kansas but was unsuccessful. With help from influential friends, in 1859 he was appointed the superintendent of a newly established military academy in Louisiana. When Louisiana seceded, Sherman resigned and became president of a streetcar company in Saint Louis. Unlike many of his peers, he had not fought in the Mexican-American War and thus lacked combat experience. Quickly promoted to colonel and then brigadier general, Sherman performed well at the Battle of Bull Run. After the battle, however, he soon showed signs of panic, requesting additional men to potentially fight greatly exaggerated numbers of Confederates. Saved by Halleck, Sherman went on to serve under Grant, whose steady influence provided the proper guidance that he needed. Grant quickly came to rely on Sherman, who became his right-hand man and supporter.[49]

Option 3

Grant had two other commanders available to head this department. Maj. Gen. John Schofield was the commander of the Army of the Ohio. However, as this army was nothing more than the Twenty-Third Corps augmented by a division of cavalry, Schofield realistically could only claim experience at the corps level. Additionally, his only prior combat experience was in the Battle of Wilson's Creek, a Union loss. Another commander present, Maj. Gen. Joseph Hooker, had demonstrated failure as commander of the Army of the Potomac when Lee defeated him at Chancellorsville. Hooker had been sent west with two corps to help relieve Grant at Chattanooga, and he now commanded the combined Twentieth Corps. Grant apparently considered the other corps commanders too inexperienced or otherwise lacking the credentials of a Thomas or a Sherman.[50]

Decision

On March 18 Grant made the fourth critical decision of what was to be the Atlanta Campaign, appointing Sherman commander of the Military Division of the Mississippi.[51]

Results/Impact

Sherman conducted an aggressive campaign and ultimately captured much of northern Georgia and, in particular, Atlanta. The results were very favorable for himself, as well as for Lincoln, Grant, and the Union effort. Although Sherman's conquest of Atlanta was successful, he failed to destroy the Rebel Army of Tennessee or render it harmless. After refitting, Sherman destroyed much of Atlanta and launched his famous March to the Sea.[52]

Alternate Decisions and Scenarios

As previously discussed, Grant had the option of remaining in the West. Had he done so, he would probably have better organized and superintended the advance through Snake Creek Gap to Resaca, thereby ensuring the capture of the railroad at or near that location (these events will be explored in greater detail in the discussion of Critical Decision 9). Also, by remaining in the

East, Grant, after the Overland Campaign, essentially would have remained in a stalemate with Lee's Army of Northern Virginia around Petersburg. Grant would have been conducting a siege for nine months while there was so much more potential for further success in the West.[53]

Had Grant remained in command of the Military Division of the Mississippi, the Atlanta Campaign as we know it likely would have been conducted much differently. Grant lost almost fifty-five thousand men in one month during the Overland Campaign, and he probably would not have hesitated to launch a similar attack on Johnston. Johnston's strategy of remaining largely on the defense might then have been more successful. Unlike Grant, Sherman chose maneuver over assault. In the Atlanta Campaign, Sherman's one attempt at defeating Johnston by direct assault at Kennesaw Mountain quickly failed, forcing him to disengage before the battle became too costly.[54]

If Grant had decided to appoint someone other than Sherman to command the West, what might have resulted? In Grant's absence, Thomas would have been the only reasonable alternative commander for the Western Theater. Although personal issues had arisen between Grant and Thomas, Grant's concern about Thomas was his "slowness." Yet, as he had proven at the Battle of Chickamauga, Thomas could and would fight. Thomas was already known for his demands for sufficient troops and supplies. Once he had these necessities, as he later demonstrated at the Battle of Nashville, he would take decisive action. Had Thomas assumed command of the West, it is reasonable to expect that he would have cautiously carried out the Atlanta Campaign in a similar manner as Sherman, but possibly without assaulting the Kennesaw Line. As a result, the campaign would probably have ended little differently than it ultimately did.[55]

Sherman Strengthens and Improves His Railroad Supply Line

Situation

As soon as Grant selected him to command the Military Division of the Mississippi, Sherman began preparing for what would become the Atlanta Campaign. Since Grant had tasked him with pursuing Johnston's Army of Tennessee and capturing as much enemy territory as possible, Sherman knew that the movement of supplies for his combined armies had to dramatically improve before he could move south. His three armies were the Army of the Tennessee, now commanded by Maj. Gen. James B. McPherson, consisting of 24,380 men; the Army of the Cumberland, commanded by Maj. Gen. George Thomas, consisting of 72,938 men; and the Army of the Ohio, commanded by Maj. Gen. John Schofield, consisting of 12,805 men. These armies' total manpower came to 110,123 officers and men, along with 254 cannon. Sherman was told he would need a minimum of 130 railroad boxcars daily (or an equivalent number of wagons), each carrying 10 tons of supplies, to provision his combined armies as they moved south. The maximum capability of the railroads involved was 65 to 85 boxcars per day.[56]

Sherman's railroad line of supply began in Louisville, where supplies could be shipped by rail or boat. The Louisville and Nashville Railroad brought supplies south to Nashville. There, supplies were transferred to the Nashville and Chattanooga Railroad and delivered to Fortress Rosecrans at Murfreesboro (the railroad ran through it) and Chattanooga. At Chattanooga the supplies would be transferred to the Western and Atlantic Railroad, then delivered to Sherman's armies as they advanced south. The railroad had the advantage of being able to reliably transport large amounts of supplies during rainy weather. An obvious option for Sherman was to use the railroads to Chattanooga, and specifically the existing Western and Atlantic Railroad from Chattanooga south to Atlanta. However, this dependence came with some problems. First, the railroad at that time was incapable of transporting enough supplies, ammunition, men, horses, etc. to meet the needs of Sherman's armies. In addition, as Sherman moved south, his supply line would only lengthen as Johnston's line, utilizing the same railway, would decrease in length.[57]

Options

Logically, Sherman would use the railroad as a major means of provisioning his soldiers. He had three options for making an operationally effective supply line: utilize the railroads in their present state and augment them with wagons; increase the railroads' ability to supply his armies; or improve the railroads' efficiency by combining them with additional methods of supply.[58]

Option 1

Sherman's first option was to utilize the railroads as best he could in their present condition. He could transport what additional supplies were needed using quartermaster wagons. Sherman would have to requisition thousands of wagons, and he would have to organize their comings and goings. A road or series of roads following his armies would also need to be constructed and maintained. Any period of rain would quickly reduce these roads to mud, significantly slowing down the rate and dependability of supply. Moreover, transporting supplies would require thousands of horses and mules, and even more to be relief animals. Yet the singular advantage of wagons was that they could go directly to Sherman's armies; they were not totally dependent on the railroad.[59]

Option 2

Another option was for Sherman to order improvements enhancing the railroads' ability to provide adequate supplies to maneuvering soldiers. The tracks would have to be significantly strengthened by adding sidings for trains to pass each other. Bridges would also need to be reinforced. The entire route would have to be guarded and protected from Confederate raiders, so numerous guard stations would have to be constructed and staffed with troops who would patrol the length of the railroad under Union control. Furthermore, the daily schedule of trains' arrivals and departures would have to be closely monitored. Sherman could not reasonably move far from the railroad. Johnston, facing a similar supply situation, was well aware of this fact.[60]

Option 3

A third option would be to greatly improve the existing railroads' ability to provide necessary supplies, then supplement these improvements with protocols for moving men, beef, and civilians via other means. This plan would entail significant management of the railroads, and it would require enforcing other methods of transportation to Chattanooga.[61]

Decision

Sherman made the critical decision to strengthen and improve the railroads as his supply line. He augmented his choice with orders restricting certain movements to better utilize the railroads.[62]

Results/Impact

As previously noted, to supply the necessary items for 110,000 men and 45,000 horses and mules, Sherman's supply officers had calculated that he needed 130 boxcars per day to bring supplies from his warehouses in Louisville, Nashville, and Chattanooga to his operating front. In order to increase and maintain these supplies, Sherman commandeered extra boxcars and engines from other railroads. To make the railroad fully operational, he appointed competent men such as Col. William W. Wright to head the Railroad Construction and Repair Corps, and Lieut. Col. Adna Anderson to be in charge of scheduling. Most importantly, Sherman supported these officers' decisions. To increase the supply capability, Sherman ordered incoming troops to march to the front near Ringgold, and he forbade civilians from riding the supply trains. By means of these hardheaded policies he increased his ability to supply his forces, at one point moving 195 boxcars in a day. Further,

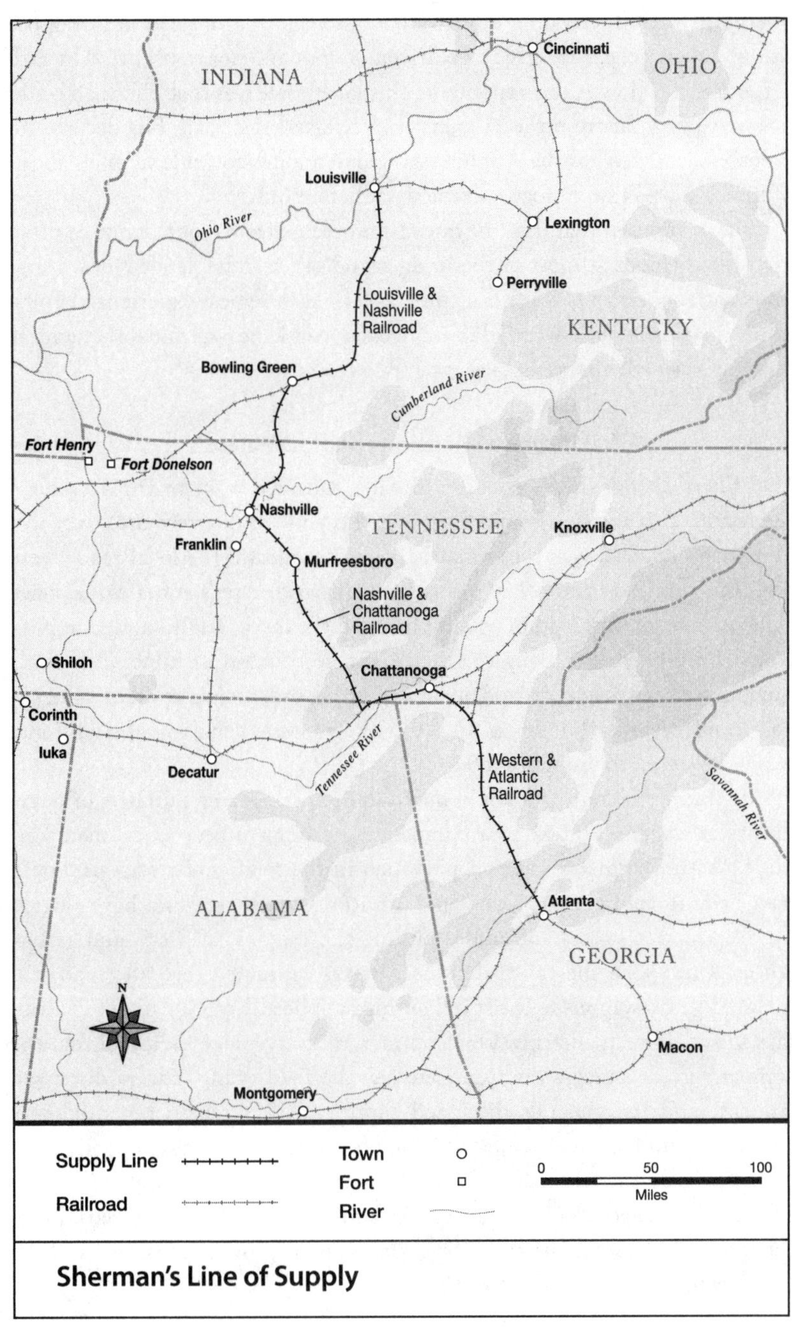

Sherman's Line of Supply

Sherman ordered returning units to march to the front instead of riding the trains. Likewise, cattle were to be driven on foot and not transported by rail. Of course, the downside to supplying this large force was that Sherman could not move very far from the Western and Atlantic Railroad. His decision to prepare adequately for the Atlanta Campaign and to stockpile supplies ahead of time allowed him to focus on the work before him.[63]

Sherman knew that this line must be protected from Confederate raiding. He posted troops at most of the bridges and other strategic locations, using units with enlistments ready to expire, as well as other less experienced units. Johnston continuously worried that Sherman would be a formidable enemy as long as his supply line remained intact.[64]

Alternate Decisions and Scenarios

Had Sherman not increased the railroad's capacity, what might have been the result? This decision would have forced the use of quartermaster wagons. While the railroad was somewhat immune from rain, the local roads were not. The teamsters and other men of the quartermaster's corps would have assumed a huge workload in wading through the mud. Additionally, supplies would have been less likely to reach their destination on time. The roads might have been macadamized or corduroyed in order to make them more usable in wet weather, but doing so would likely have taken as much additional work as moving the supplies required.[65]

Replacing the railroad would have required staggering numbers of quartermaster wagons. It took approximately 25 wagons to keep 1,000 men supplied. With Sherman's 100,000-plus men in the field, 2,500 wagons would have been in continuous movement. Additional wagons would have carried the feed for the horses and mules pulling the wagons, artillery, and ambulances. Even with the railroad in use, it was estimated that Sherman still required 5,000 wagons to assist in hauling supplies. It was a truly Herculean task to supply such an army. One common military adage indicated that the company grade officers discussed tactics, the field grade officers discussed strategy, and the generals discussed supply. Had Sherman not diligently worked to build up and maintain his supply line, he would have quickly been forced to retreat to where his men could have been properly supplied. When the general moved off of the railroad in and around Dallas, he received further proof of the immense task of using wagons to provision his men and the inability to keep up with supplies.[66]

Johnston Decides to Defend the Dalton Area from Attack

Situation

After his appointment to command the Army of Tennessee, Gen. Johnston traveled to Dalton, where he assumed command on December 27, 1863. He immediately began improving the army's condition. Johnston significantly reformed the supply of foodstuffs, clothing, and weapons. He offered amnesty for soldiers who had deserted, and he established a system of rotating furloughs. To his credit, Johnston enticed back thousands of soldiers who had, legally or otherwise, gone home; they returned upon hearing of the change of command. His initial reports to Richmond were quite the opposite of the fairly positive report of inspection conducted at President Davis's request by one of his aides, Col. Joseph C. Ives. Johnston stated the need for more and better food, blankets, clothing, and horses, among other items. He also began requesting reinforcements.[67]

While attending to his army's condition, Johnston did not initially revise his line of defense from what he found upon arriving at Dalton. The army had halted there after its defeat on Lookout Mountain and Missionary Ridge. Rocky Face Ridge provided a significant barrier west and north of Dalton, and the few gaps through it could easily be defended. Johnston was concerned with defending Crow Valley east of Rocky Face Ridge, through which the East Tennessee and Georgia Railroad passed to join the Western and Atlantic Railroad at Dalton. Crow Valley needed to be fortified, and Johnston made sure that it was. Undefended, this valley would provide Sherman an easy approach into Dalton. Johnston rightly deduced that Sherman would not seriously attack Rocky Face Ridge.[68]

Options

Johnston had four options for better protecting his army and the Confederacy from Sherman's inevitable movement south toward Atlanta and other important Southern cities. First, Confederate troops could retreat to more suitable defensive ground, perhaps near Resaca. Another option was for Johnston and his men to increase the cavalry reconnoitering of Union movements. Alternatively, Johnston could remain at Dalton and shore up his defenses, or he could take the offensive in some form or manner.[69]

Option 1

Johnston could consider retreating to more defensible ground. While Rocky Face Ridge provided an ideal defensive location, Crow Valley and points east

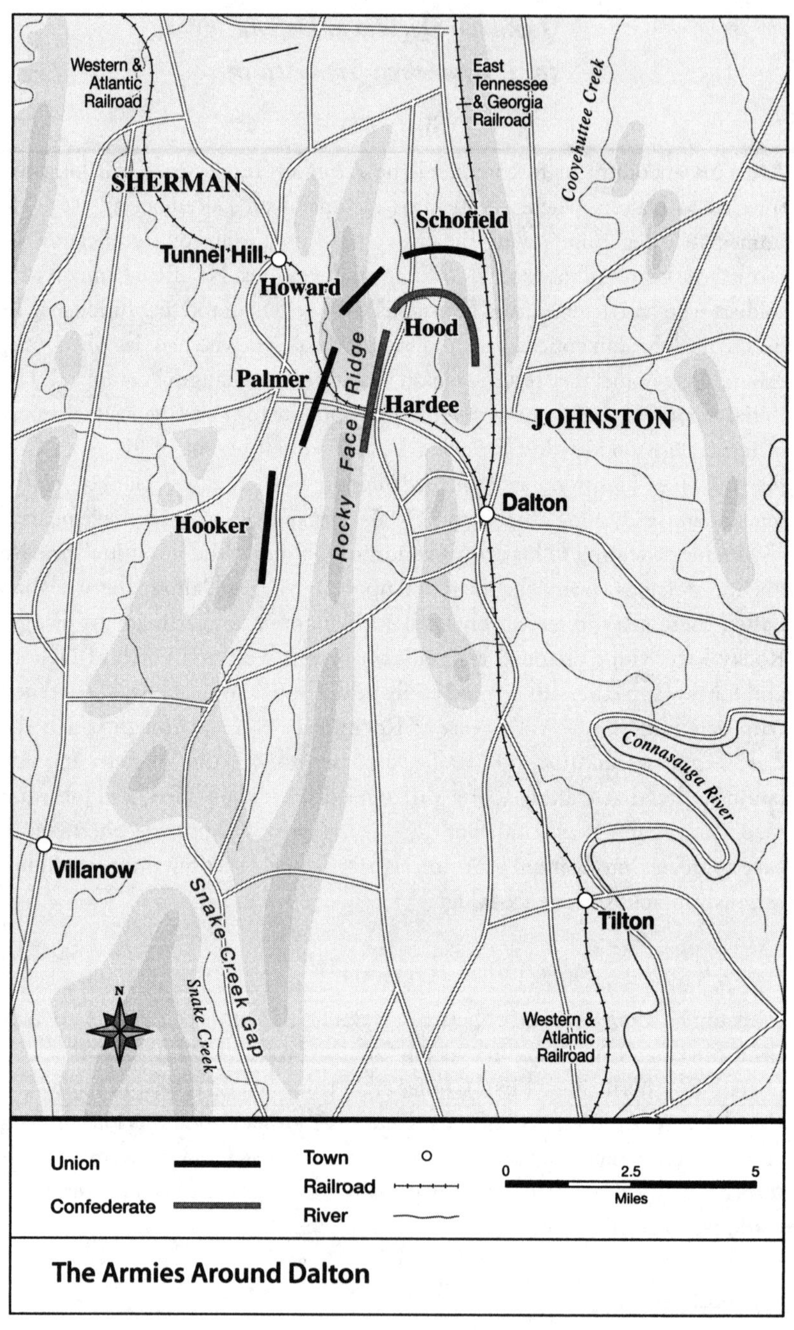

The Armies Around Dalton

Rocky Face Ridge, Mill Creek Gap. *Harpers Weekly.*

were more vulnerable. Locations farther south might provide more uniformly defensible terrain and a better position for Johnston. However, this choice would have negative political ramifications; the Confederacy might believe Johnston was retreating without a fight.[70]

Option 2

Another option was assigning some elements of cavalry, led by officers experienced in scouting, to become the Confederate army's eyes and ears. Johnston knew that he had to present a strong front to Sherman, and that he needed to protect his army from being outflanked. West of Dalton, several mountainous ridges ran north to south, with several passages or gaps in each one. The important manufacturing town of Rome, Georgia, was located southwest of Dalton on a natural pathway into Alabama. Several iron foundries critical to the Confederacy were located in Rome. A railroad ran from Kingston to Rome, and it needed to be protected from a Union advance. Limited as it was, Johnston's cavalry could scout more to the southwest toward Rome, as well as to the north and east. These lookouts would ensure that Johnston and his army would not be turned or outflanked.[71]

Option 3

To defend against an assault by Sherman, Johnston had the option of remaining at Dalton and reinforcing three locations on its east side: Crow Valley, Potato Hill, and Mount Hamilton.[72]

Option 4

Although this option was against Johnston's inclination to go on the offense, President Davis strongly favored attacking Sherman and his armies before they took to the field. The odds were against Johnston. However, an aggressive movement might catch a portion of the Union armies unprepared to resist an assault.[73]

Decision

Johnston focused his efforts on maintaining the Rebel presence at Dalton and reinforcing and expanding his defensive works.[74]

Results/Impact

Johnston's focus on digging in and reinforcing the area around Dalton had several ramifications. The general's failure to adequately monitor the region for movements by various Federal forces makes his decision particularly critical. This oversight allowed Sherman to devise his initial plan of attack. As a result, Johnston was almost turned via Snake Creek Gap and cut off from his supply line at Resaca. President Davis's critical decision to provide reinforcements to Johnston (discussed in the next critical decision) indirectly saved the general and his army from potential disaster.[75]

Johnston's defensive strategy resulted in part from his belief that he had to contend with an enemy force twice the size of his own army. Even as he fortified his works, he continually called for reinforcements, as well as for horses, food, and all the accoutrements of war. Given this perceived disparity in manpower, Johnston felt compelled to wait for Sherman to make the first move. He told the Confederate government in Richmond that he would first defeat the initial Union attack, then go on the offensive. This reactionary posture of defense would set the tone for the upcoming campaign. The matter is still debatable, and Johnston's supporters maintain he was simply waiting for the opportunity to attack Sherman's units in piecemeal fashion. However, based on Johnston's performances on the Virginia Peninsula in 1862 and in

Mississippi in 1863, he appeared unlikely to go on the attack. President Davis quickly became worried that Johnston might not be offensive minded.[76]

In fairness to Johnston, he inherited a situation he neither chose nor favored. He considered the defenses around Dalton ill chosen, and he was not overly pleased with the Dalton defensive works. However, Johnston knew that if he ordered his army to fall back to a more defensible location, perhaps around Resaca, he would be roundly criticized for abandoning yet more Confederate soil. As a result, this option was not politically viable.[77]

Alternative Decision and Scenario

In addition to fortifying Dalton, Johnston could have maintained constant cavalry patrols providing daily intelligence on the movements of the Union armies in the area and beyond. Certainly, the various gaps should have been monitored to prevent Federal movements such as McPherson's march through Snake Creek Gap, which will be discussed below, from surprising Johnston. More rigorous observation would have given Johnston more time to correctly react to Sherman's tactical moves.[78]

Davis Orders Reinforcements to Johnston

Situation

Johnston was convinced that his Union opponent greatly outnumbered him. While this was true, Sherman was burdened by having to protect his supply line, which more and more of his men would have to defend as he advanced south.[79]

The Confederacy knew from the beginning of the war that it would never field superior numbers of troops. President Davis's penchant for keeping each individual army within its assigned department compounded this obstacle. His practice did not support the transferring of units to threatened areas, and it minimized cooperation between departments. Commanders on both sides constantly struggled to find reinforcements. Naturally, each department commander believed that his department was critical to the war effort and deserving of protection. As a result, these leaders were loath to loan any of their troops to another department, perhaps never to see them again, perhaps to have them reduced by combat or other losses. Department commanders routinely exaggerated their opponents' numbers while downplaying their own numbers to build on their individual needs for help. Though aware of Davis's policies and tendencies, Johnston nonetheless frequently requested more reinforcements.[80]

Johnston, knowing the campaign season was about to start, simply waited for Sherman to make the first move. Since he knew the Union general would act soon, he once again petitioned Richmond for reinforcements. Johnston also contacted Lieut. Gen. Leonidas Polk, commander of the Army of Mississippi, seeking help if McPherson's army maneuvered toward Rome as predicted.[81]

Options

At this time President Davis had three options: He could refuse to send Johnston any reinforcements. He could also send Johnston large reinforcements at the expense of another department. Finally, Davis could assemble men spared from several departments and order them to support Johnston.[82]

Option 1

Davis had more to be concerned with than northern Georgia and Atlanta. He was responsible for defending the entire Confederacy from Union invasion, and he simply did not have unlimited troops to be detailed wherever necessary. Essentially, all of Davis's armies were on their own to defend their assigned departments. No department commander was likely to give his units or armies away to a neighboring one. Therefore, by his own prior decisions, Davis was constrained in reassigning his soldiers, who were scattered about the Confederacy. To maintain proper defenses throughout the South, Davis's first option was to order Johnston to utilize his own available manpower. No other reinforcements were readily available.[83]

Option 2

It was obvious to all concerned that a Union advance south from Chattanooga would occur when the weather finally permitted. While Johnston's soldiers did not come close to being the numerical equal of Sherman's, the Confederacy did not have unlimited manpower available for reassignment. However, this particular situation promised to be one of grave concern to the Confederate government. Sherman simply could not be allowed to advance unopposed into northern Georgia. Therefore, Davis could help block Sherman's advance by sending Johnston whatever troops were available. Ordering reinforcements might have ramifications elsewhere, but there was virtually no doubt that Sherman would advance south into northern Georgia. Priority had to be placed on resisting this advance. All available means of stopping it were required, with reinforcements being the most beneficial way to do so.[84]

Option 3

Davis's third option was to forward to Johnston what small portions of his other departments' manpower could be spared. Though diminished, these other departments could remain intact. This plan might result in Johnston's receiving a smaller number of reinforcements, but any support would be beneficial.[85]

Decision

President Davis ordered some garrison troops to Johnston, and he also ordered Maj. Gen. Leonidas Polk to send Johnston those units of his Army of Mississippi that he could spare. Polk cooperated and immediately dispatched Brig. Gen. James Cantey's brigade to Rome as initial reinforcements for Johnston, while preparing additional units to follow. Davis agreed that northern Georgia/Atlanta had to be defended and that Sherman was most likely headed toward that city, intent on its capture.[86]

Results/Impact

Cantey's Brigade initially reinforced Johnston at Rome, and Johnston then ordered the troops to march north from Rome to Resaca. This movement literally saved the day for Johnston. As we will see, McPherson, after marching through Snake Creek Gap, sighted Cantey's troops near Resaca and fell back to the gap, foiling Sherman's plan to cut Johnston's supply line at Resaca. This action resulted in a longer campaign, as discussed below.[87]

Under further orders, Polk eventually put into motion almost all of his Army of Mississippi to reinforce Johnston. This augmentation by the equivalent of an additional corps was of immediate benefit.[88]

Alternate Decisions and Scenarios

Had President Davis not ordered Polk to send reinforcements for Johnston, Cantey's Brigade would not have been at Resaca when McPherson moved toward it through Snake Creek Gap. Had McPherson not seen Cantey's men (although troops from the Georgia Home Guard had earlier been stationed there), he might not have called off his advance. McPherson would then have been more likely to seize the railroad (this will be discussed in more detail below). Under these circumstances, the Atlanta Campaign might have proceeded more rapidly toward Federal success. Each of these critical decisions shaped the campaign.[89]

Had Johnston received reinforcements in addition to Polk's army, we must wonder whether he would have remained on the defensive. He seemed inclined to react to his opponent. However, as we will see later on, Johnston would occasionally take the tactical and strategic initiative.[90]

CHAPTER 2

THE SNAKE CREEK GAP TURNING MOVEMENT, MAY 8–MAY 13, 1864

In coordination with Lieut. Gen. Ulysses S. Grant, Maj. Gen. William T. Sherman launched his campaign against Gen. Joseph E. Johnston on May 8, 1864. While Sherman ordered supporting attacks on Johnston's Dalton lines, his main effort was to send Maj. Gen. James B. McPherson's Army of the Tennessee through Snake Creek Gap to cut Johnston's railroad supply line at or near Resaca. Had this turning movement been successful, the ramifications would have been enormous—the war could possibly have ended months earlier. Unfortunately for the Union, Sherman's efforts failed, extending what became known as the Atlanta Campaign until September 2. Three critical decisions prompted this extension.[1]

Sherman Orders McPherson to Sever the Railroad at Resaca

Situation

Sherman had demonstrated that he would rather succeed by maneuver than by direct attack. Consequently, he did not expect a decisive result from his probes of Rocky Face Ridge. Both the difficult terrain and Johnston's strongly reinforced position along the ridge reduced the likelihood of a successful assault.[2]

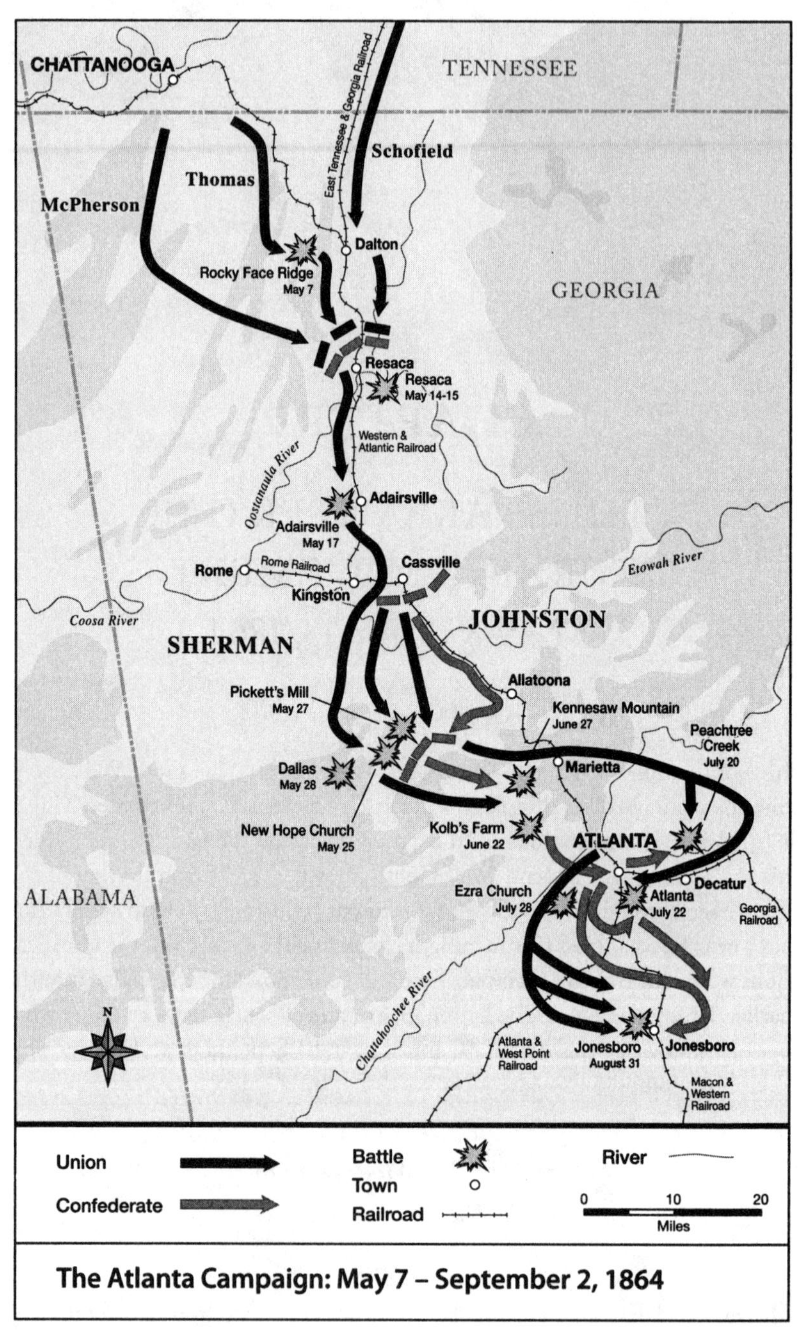

The Atlanta Campaign: May 7 – September 2, 1864

Johnston had decided to strengthen his position around Dalton and await Sherman's predicted advance. Johnston ordered fortifications all along Rocky Face Ridge, to the west of Dalton, and also in Crow Valley, located northeast of Dalton. He was fully committed to protecting the city. Though Johnston ordered occasional cavalry patrols, he remained largely unaware of any maneuvering by Sherman, other than against his lines at Dalton. Sherman quickly realized the inherent strength of Johnston's well-fortified lines, and he wisely decided against ordering a direct assault by his armies. The measure would be too costly. Instead, the Union general searched for other options to possibly avoid the heavy casualties that assaulting Johnston's lines along Rocky Face Ridge and Crow Valley would bring.[3]

Options

In planning how to open the campaign, Sherman had four options: First, he could attack the Crow Valley entrenchments of the Confederates while providing diversionary assaults against Rocky Face Ridge. Another choice was to cut Johnston's supply line at or near Resaca via Snake Creek Gap. Alternatively, Sherman could cut the railroad supplying Johnston at some point farther south of Resaca, or he could direct his armies to outflank Johnston altogether and move south toward Rome or another location.[4]

Option 1

An attack into Crow Valley, northeast of Dalton, would avoid an offensive on the highly defensible terrain of Rocky Face Ridge. However, attacking the Crow Valley entrenchments would come at a high cost for Sherman, as the defense always held the advantage by this time in the war. Johnston had fortified Crow Valley in anticipation of an attack there, ensuring that Sherman could only achieve success with such an assault with horrific casualties. Yet Sherman held roughly a two-to-one advantage in manpower that, when funneled into Crow Valley, could overrun the Confederate defenders there. At the beginning of the campaign, a Union victory here would force Johnston to retreat with a much-weakened army.[5]

Option 2

Another option appeared increasingly viable. Scouts indicated to Sherman that Johnston's line of defense did not extend past Dug Gap in Rocky Face Ridge. At the same time, it appeared to Sherman that Johnston was not guarding Snake Creek Gap, west of Resaca. As Maj. Gen. George Thomas had originally proposed in February, Sherman believed that if he could hold

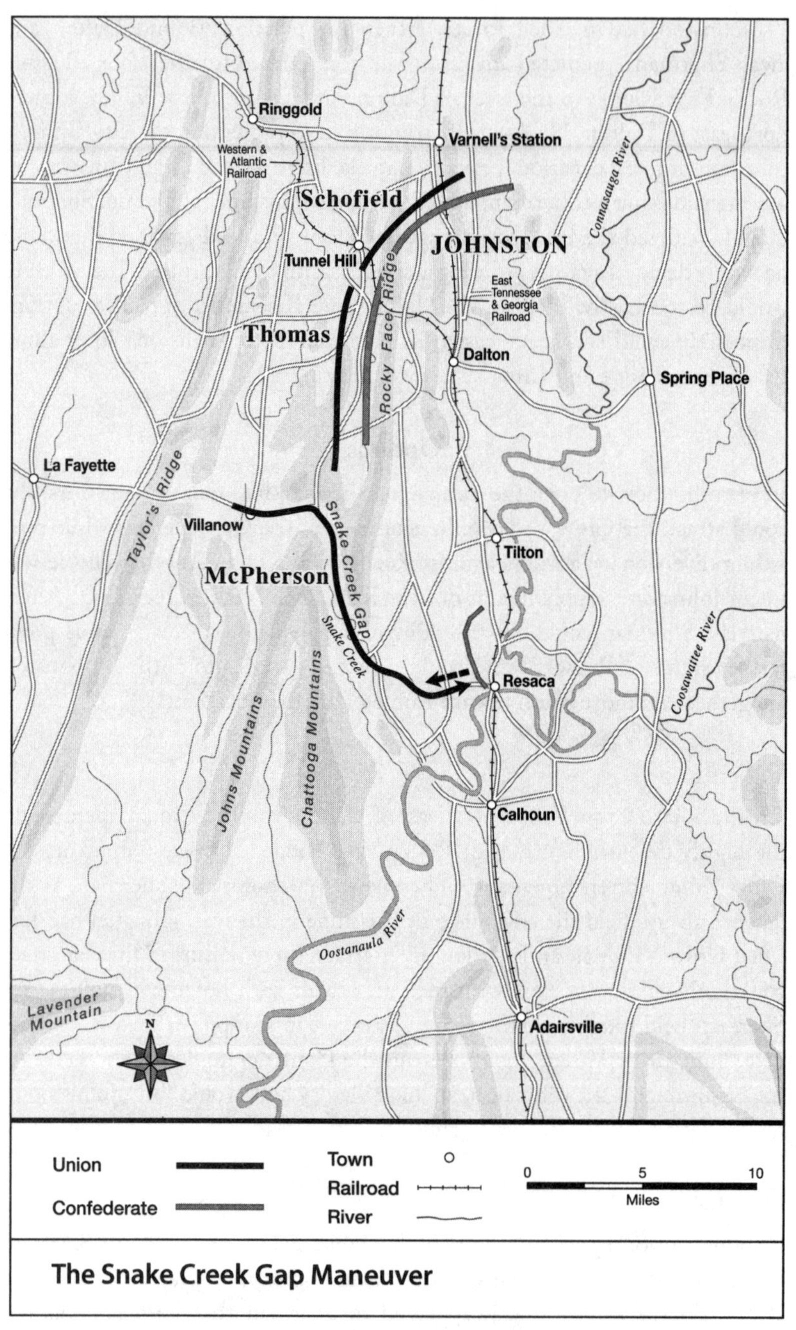

The Snake Creek Gap Maneuver

Johnston in place, he might be able to detach a significant force and send it south. The mountainous terrain west of Rocky Face Ridge would conceal the soldiers' movements. By conducting this turning movement via Snake Creek Gap, this force, if undetected, could move into Johnston's rear area, sever his supply line, and force him to attack an entrenched Union force to recover it, retreat, or surrender.[6]

Once Sherman's force cut the railroad supply line (and paralleling road), Johnston would be forced to react in one of three ways, none of which promised good results for his army. He could order an attack against this Union force at Resaca in order to reestablish his supply line. Alternatively, Johnston could simply remain in Dalton until surrounded and be forced to surrender. Finally, he could retreat from Dalton, marching around Resaca, probably to the east. However, in retreating, the Confederate Army of Tennessee would have reduced access to supplies and ammunition, rendering it at best temporarily ineffective for combat. Regardless, the Army of Tennessee would be constrained from significant further action.[7]

It would take whatever force Sherman ordered only a couple of days to gain the position at Resaca, possibly before Johnston even became aware of this action. If successful, this imaginative option would force Johnston to take action.[8]

Option 3

A third option was to attempt to cut Johnston's supply line, the Western and Atlantic Railroad, at some other point between his position at Dalton and Atlanta. If Sherman could successfully disable this railway, Johnston would have no choice but to attempt to regain it through a confrontation with Sherman. Without necessary supplies, Johnston's army would quickly become ineffective. Severing the Confederate supply line would require at least some of Sherman's men to depart his own railroad supply line, and this circumstance could become problematic. Sherman would have to constantly supply these men via wagons, which were not nearly as dependable as the railroad. However, a sizeable force could make the cut and force Johnston to move south to recover his supply line. Sherman could then march behind him, repairing and utilizing the same railroad Johnston had lost.[9]

Option 4

Sherman could target another Georgia or Alabama city of importance to the Rebels, with Rome, Georgia, being a prime consideration because of its foundries and manufacturing. Doing so would force Johnston out of Dalton to attempt to protect Rome or another similar military target. Sherman would then be compelled to leave his railroad supply line. Johnston might be able to retain at least part of his railroad, depending on which target Sherman designated. If Sherman ordered such a movement, it would force Johnston to react, giving Sherman the advantage of dictating the movements. However, at this time Sherman had to supply about twice as many men as Johnston, which severely limited his ability to leave the railroad.[10]

Decision

Sherman opted to conduct a turning movement through Snake Creek Gap to capture Resaca and sever Johnston's supply line. Sherman realized that if he could cut Johnston's supply line at Resaca, he had a good chance to eliminate the Army of Tennessee as an effective force. It would take Sherman's detached Army of the Tennessee only a couple of days to gain the position at Resaca, possibly before Johnston even became aware of this action.[11]

Sherman ordered Maj. Gen. James B. McPherson and his Army of the Tennessee (Sherman's former command) to march through Snake Creek Gap, veer east, capture Resaca, and disable the railroad there. This decision would avoid a large-scale frontal assault on Johnston. Most of Sherman's men would be spared from costly assaults, and Johnston would be forced to attack Sherman to regain his supply line. If successful, the virtual elimination of the Army of Tennessee as a fighting force would help achieve Union victory sooner.[12]

Results/Impact

Unfortunately, this well-conceived plan was not carried to fruition. Discussion of the next two critical decisions will address this turn of events. As a result, the campaign continued for several more months, causing thousands of additional casualties on both sides. It might also have cost Lincoln the presidential election of 1864.[13]

Alternative Decisions and Scenarios

If Sherman had been able to cut Johnston's supply line at a point farther south, he would have placed Johnston in an unenviable situation. To reestablish his line of supply, the Confederate general would have had to either attack a prepared and entrenched Union force on the railroad or lead his army away from Sherman. The second choice would have exposed Johnston to new danger of attack and left him with a lack of necessary supplies and ammunition. These alternatives will be discussed in more detail in analysis of the next two critical decisions.

The option of directing an advance on Rome would have forced Johnston to protect the city, thus requiring him to give up Dalton. Consequently, both

Union and Confederate armies would have at least temporarily shifted their respective railroad supply lines. This action would also be to Johnston's detriment. He would be forced to move south, giving up more Rebel territory to Sherman and the Union.[14]

Sherman Fails to Support McPherson's Turning Movement

Situation

Sherman's critical decision to attempt to cut Johnston's railroad line of supply at or near Resaca is defined in military terms as a turning movement. Sherman then needed to assign a force to conduct this designated operation via Snake Creek Gap, while also ordering his other troops to conduct probing attacks to keep Johnston in position at Dalton. Maj. Gen. William S. Rosecrans used a turning movement to force Gen. Braxton Bragg out of Chattanooga prior to the Battle of Chickamauga, and Sherman was now in a similar situation.[15]

Sherman needed to designate which of his commands and commanders would carry out his assignments for the turning movement. He had to provide enough force to give the maneuver a reasonable chance of success, and to keep Johnston occupied so that he would not discover the Union movements.[16]

Options

Sherman had four options to conduct the turning movement. He could assign the task to McPherson's Army of the Tennessee, or he could give the same orders to Thomas's Army of the Cumberland. A third option involved ordering McPherson's army to complete the movement and augmenting those troops with additional manpower. Finally, Sherman, as overall commander, could accompany whomever he assigned to the turning movement and utilize his extensive experience to oversee the maneuver's successful completion.[17]

<u>Option 1</u>

One option was for Sherman to order McPherson's army to conduct the maneuver. McPherson's twenty-five thousand men were presumably more than enough to overcome whatever Rebel force was located at or near Resaca. This command could then sever the railroad and entrench while awaiting reinforcements. If successful, this option would heap laurels on McPherson, a favorite of both Grant and Sherman. Moreover, Sherman trusted McPherson.[18]

The drawback to placing McPherson in command was his lack of experience. He had risen from first lieutenant of engineers to major general of volunteers in only fourteen months. He lacked the seasoning needed by an army commander. While McPherson's army was substantial, a turning movement would demand a significantly larger force to guarantee its successful completion. Sherman had another much larger army available, Thomas's Army of the Cumberland.[19]

Option 2

Another option would be for Sherman to choose a larger command to guarantee the maneuver's success. Thomas's army was the obvious choice because of its size and his greater experience as an army commander. Alone, the army's 72,938 men easily outnumbered Johnston's army; it could force its way to Resaca and the railroad, regardless of the size of any Rebel force stationed there. Comparatively few men were needed to maintain the probing attacks against Johnston at Dalton. Thomas was an expert at moving troops, and he had the experience, courage, and combat power to sever Johnston's supply line at Resaca. As noted above, Thomas had displayed great combat leadership ability at the Battle of Chickamauga, earning the sobriquet "the Rock of Chickamauga." However, he was also known to be very methodical at times. Both Grant and Sherman questioned Thomas's ability to independently initiate and sustain a movement, and Sherman had to consider these doubts while making his decision.[20]

Option 3

Sherman could give McPherson the assignment but reinforce his army with another division or two, or another corps placed under his command. This choice should give McPherson enough men and the confidence to fight his way into Resaca if necessary. If successful, McPherson would receive credit for the maneuver as Sherman apparently desired. Sherman and Grant admired McPherson and considered him a friend and supporter. If the augmented force came from Thomas's army, Thomas would still have most of his force available to hold Johnston in position at Dalton, with Maj. Gen. John Schofield's 12,805-man Army of the Ohio positioned nearby.[21]

Option 4

A final option was for Sherman to accompany whichever commander and army he ordered to perform the turning movement and see for himself that it was carried out to his satisfaction. Sherman's leadership experience would be of value to either McPherson or Thomas. He could override any of the designated commander's deleterious decisions to ensure that the movement was not compromised. This option, when added to any of the others, would significantly increase Sherman's chance of success with this turning movement. The disadvantage of this plan was that Sherman would not be present to direct his remaining forces at Dalton. However, compared to Gen. Robert E. Lee's situation at Chancellorsville, where he had to contend with a significant Federal army while Lieut. Gen. Thomas "Stonewall" Jackson performed the tighter flanking maneuver, only minor diversionary attacks were necessary at Dalton to keep Johnston's army pinned down in their trenches. So far Johnston had not given any indication of going on the offensive. Additionally, Sherman still had enough troops at Dalton to confront Johnston should he advance. Sherman's presence was not necessary at Dalton, and he could reasonably rely on whatever commander he left in charge to defend in the unlikely event of an attack by Johnston.[22]

Decision

Sherman ordered Maj. Gen. James B. McPherson to conduct this turning movement with his Army of the Tennessee, consisting of some twenty-five thousand men organized into three corps. He determined not to accompany McPherson but to remain at Dalton. There, Sherman would oversee his remaining troops and counter any movements Johnston might make.[23]

Results/Impact

As a result of Sherman's critical decision, McPherson and his army were the only forces ordered to carry out this turning movement. It was a potentially brilliant maneuver, and its success would have had some very positive ramifications for the Union and chilling prospects for the Confederacy. Yet Sherman placed all the responsibility on the shoulders of a very inexperienced army commander with a relatively small force. Even so, as will be discussed in regard to the next critical decision, McPherson had under his command more than enough soldiers to easily capture Resaca and disable the railroad.[24]

Alternate Decisions and Scenarios

As important as this turning movement was to Sherman, he could have better supported it, as Lee did with Stonewall Jackson at the Battle of Chancellorsville. Had Sherman been more aggressive in this situation, any one of the last three options would have given him a much better chance of success. Because of the maneuver's importance, it is difficult to explain why Sherman did not personally accompany whatever force he ordered to perform it. With little chance of Johnston going on the offensive, Sherman's presence near Dalton was unnecessary.[25]

Had he accompanied McPherson, Sherman could have drawn on his more extensive command experience to steady McPherson's nerves and order and support an advance into Resaca. The comparatively large attacking Union force should have easily overrun the small Confederate force there, captured Resaca, and severed the railroad. Sherman then could have ordered in reinforcements while preparing for a counterattack by Johnston.[26]

A better plan would have been for Sherman to assign the turning movement to Thomas's army and to accompany that army on the operation. If necessary, Sherman could have motivated Thomas to conduct the movement in a timely manner, reasonably guaranteeing success. Cut off from his supply line, Johnston would have had no choice but to fight, disperse, or surrender.[27]

McPherson Fails to Capture Resaca

Situation

Sherman ordered McPherson and his Army of the Tennessee to advance through Snak Creek Gap and then turn east and disable the railroad at or near Resaca. McPherson was an extremely likeable officer who had graduated first in his class from the United States Military Academy in 1853 (John Bell Hood was a classmate). Grant and Sherman protected him when possible and, in return, considered him a true supporter. As mentioned, Sherman desired that McPherson receive credit for this movement.[28]

McPherson was ordered to proceed south from Lee and Gordon's Mill and then southeast through Ship's Gap, via the small town of Villanow. Subsequently, he was to travel through Snake Creek Gap and turn east to the town of Resaca, on the railroad in Johnston's rear. McPherson marched as ordered and encamped at Snake Creek Gap on the evening of May 8. The next day, he and his army moved through Snake Creek Gap and approached Resaca. Just after noon, McPherson sent a dispatch to Sherman from Rome Crossing, about five miles west of Resaca, stating that his lead corps was fewer than two miles from the town. When he received this dispatch, Sherman said, "I've got Joe Johnston dead!" McPherson ordered the advance to continue.[29]

As McPherson and his men approached Resaca from the west, he was quite aware of how vulnerable the Army of Tennessee would be if he could sever its supply line. Discovering that the Confederates had not guarded Snake Creek Gap seemed to make the seizure of Resaca an easy and potentially successful assignment.[30]

Johnston's chief of cavalry, Maj. Gen. Joseph Wheeler, was more interested in fighting Federal cavalry than performing reconnaissance. He had not provided Johnston with enough information about the Federal movements.

Major General James B. McPherson, USA.
Library of Congress.

Eerily ignorant of the unguarded Snake Creek Gap, Johnston had finally become aware of a possible threat to his left flank and rear. On the morning of May 9, Johnston ordered Wheeler to reconnoiter the Snake Creek Gap area. Col. Warren Grigsby's brigade of Wheeler's Cavalry arrived there just ahead of McPherson's advance units.[31]

Johnston at last received some of the reinforcements he had been requesting (see Critical Decision 7—Davis Orders Reinforcements to Johnston). President Davis had ordered Lieut. Gen. Leonidas Polk to send any available units he could spare to Johnston's aid. Brig. Gen. James Cantey's brigade was the first unit of Polk's army to arrive in northern Georgia. He reached Rome on April 24, and Johnston ordered him to remain there to guard the city. On May 6 Johnston ordered Cantey to proceed to Resaca and guard it. On May 9 Cantey signaled to Johnston that Union troops were appearing west of Resaca.[32]

About 2 p.m. on May 9, Maj. Gen. Grenville Dodge's Sixteenth Corps drove the Confederates back to Resaca from the Bald Hill area just west of the town. Around 4 p.m. McPherson ordered Brig. Gen. James Veatch's division of Dodge's Sixteenth Corps forward to Resaca. A volley was fired at Veatch's troops by the small detachment of Georgia Military Institute cadets and State Line troops Johnston had stationed there in February. This small fight precipitated the next critical decision of the campaign.[33]

Options

McPherson's orders gave him two options. He could advance to the Western and Atlantic Railroad and sever it, virtually cutting off Johnston's army from its Atlanta supply depot. McPherson could also retreat at his discretion if he felt sufficiently threatened by any of Johnston's forces.[34]

Option 1

For Sherman to catch Johnston off guard by severing his main supply line, McPherson or someone else would have to cut the railroad near the town of Resaca. Sherman made this fact quite clear to McPherson and later described this movement as "the opportunity of a lifetime." By capturing Resaca and the nearby railroad, McPherson, and then Sherman and his other armies, had a good chance to force Johnston to fight for his survival to regain the line. This option was McPherson's primary objective, which was to disable the railroad and dig in while awaiting reinforcements. By fortifying Dalton and not insisting on cavalry reconnaissance, Johnston had set himself up for this maneuver.[35]

Option 2

McPherson's orders gave him the option of retreating toward Snake Creek Gap if necessary. This course of action would obviously compromise the whole objective of the turning maneuver through Snake Creek Gap, potentially allowing Johnston to fortify Resaca to protect his supply line. However, the Union command was unsure of the current Rebel presence at and near Resaca.[36]

Decision

McPherson encountered Confederate troops west of Resaca. After the Rebels fired on his advanced units, McPherson decided that the enemy force at Resaca appeared to be too strong for him to overrun. Although some of his men cut the railroad north of the town, the Confederates quickly repaired it. McPherson made the ninth critical decision of the campaign to retreat all the way to Snake Creek Gap. He was very concerned by the approaching darkness, and by some of his men's lack of provisions. McPherson also worried that Johnston, who was nearer to him than to Sherman, could rapidly move down and assault him.[37]

Results/Impact

The Battle of Resaca resulted from McPherson's critical decision to retreat. This battle did not, in itself, involve a critical decision on either side. Sherman chose to attack Johnston, but to do so as a diversionary action while he contemplated a different movement discussed next. Johnston had no choice but to defend his supply line. McPherson's retreat spared the Confederacy and Joseph Johnston from a potentially spectacular defeat. Johnston quickly ordered reinforcements joining his army to halt at Resaca. At the same time, he began sending troops south to that location. His men got there ahead of Sherman's, and they quickly fortified the Resaca area, protecting the critical railroad and road bridges crossing the Oostanaula River at the south end of the town.[38]

The Union forces entrenched west of Camp Creek while the Rebels entrenched east of it. After capturing Bald Hill, Federal troops placed artillery at its summit. From this location, artillery could fire directly on the road and railroad bridges over the Oostanaula River, as well as on the Confederate earthworks. A series of attacks and counterattacks marked the fighting on May 14 and 15 with little gain on either side.[39]

In hindsight, it is obvious that McPherson had more than enough combat power not only to follow his orders to sever the railroad at Resaca or just north of it, but also to occupy Resaca itself. He had some twenty-five thousand men while opposed by no more than a quarter as many Confederates defending the town and the railroad. However, McPherson's orders gave him the leeway to disable the railroad, if possible, and then retreat to Snake Creek Gap. Both verbally and in writing, Sherman clearly informed McPherson that he was facing the "opportunity of a lifetime." McPherson was cautious enough to not risk losing part or all of his army, but his inexperience made him overcautious. A more experienced commander would have determined the enemy's strength before committing to attack or retreat, then attacked and held the position by his overwhelming numbers. Having briefly challenged the Confederates at Resaca, McPherson retreated to the safety of the Snake Creek Gap area.[40]

Alternate Decisions and Scenarios

If McPherson had successfully cut Johnston's line of supply at Resaca, Johnston, like any commander, would have had three possible options: attack, retreat, or surrender.

Johnston could have planned and executed a direct attack on McPherson in an attempt to break through and regain the railroad supply line. However, by the time Johnston would have been able to carry out this attack, Sherman would have seen that Thomas, and perhaps Schofield, were reinforcing McPherson. This support would have further reduced Johnston's likelihood of success, tasking him with attacking a much larger, well-entrenched enemy. It is important for the reader to note that this alternate scenario at Resaca would

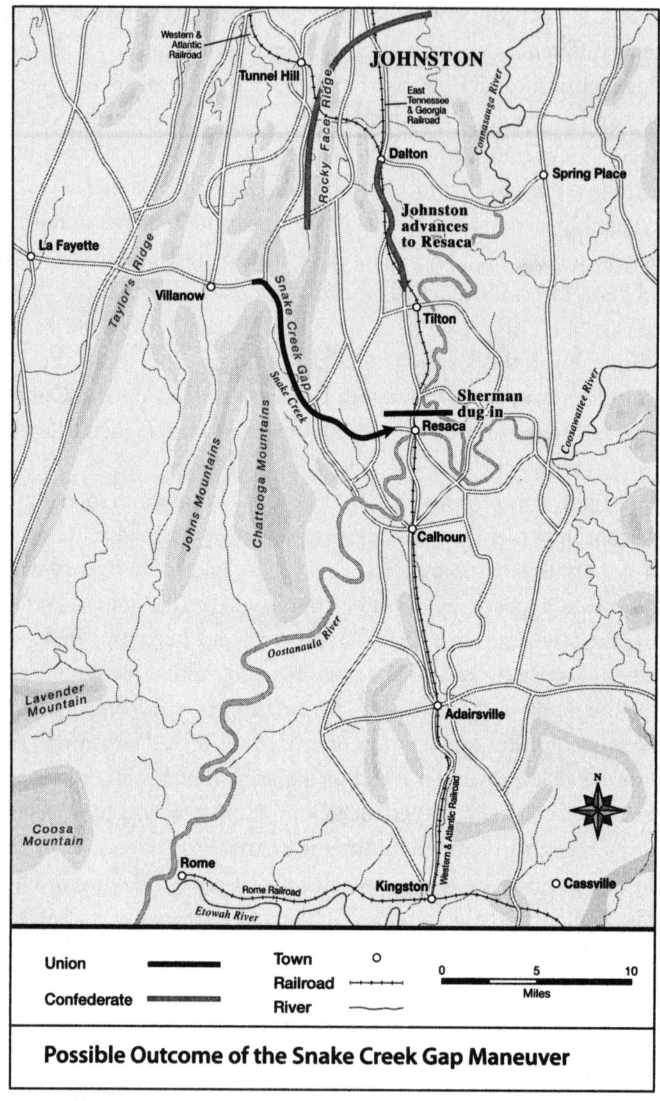

Possible Outcome of the Snake Creek Gap Maneuver

have forced Johnston to go on the offensive. In the actual Battle of Resaca, he remained largely on the defensive, protecting his supply line—a situation more to his liking.[41]

Another option would have been to retreat, bypassing Resaca. Johnston would continue to demonstrate his excellent ability to withdraw from action with minimal cost to his army. He was able to retreat from Resaca, initially undetected and literally in the face of his enemy. Learning of the Union's capturing and entrenching at Resaca, Johnston might have conducted the same

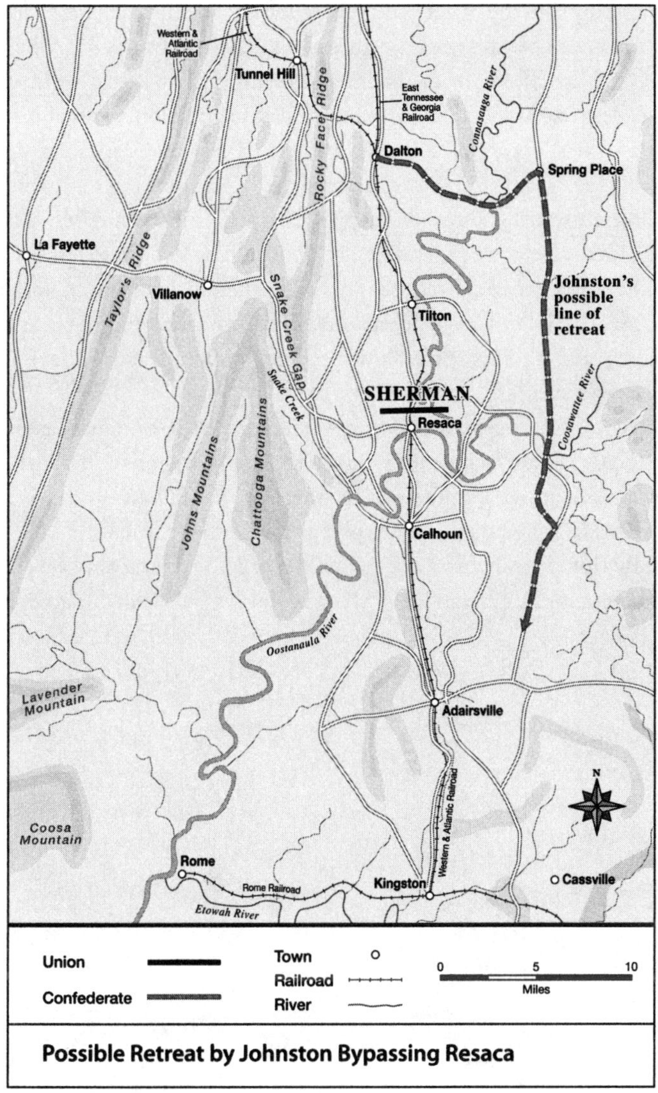

Possible Retreat by Johnston Bypassing Resaca

kind of retreat from Dalton, marching east all night to a location such as Spring Place and then turning south. If his luck held, he might have evaded Schofield, northeast of Dalton, and Thomas, northwest of Rocky Face Ridge. Johnston could then have marched south on the Spring Place Road, bypassing McPherson's entrenched army at Resaca. Had McPherson captured Resaca, he would have immediately ordered the construction of fortifications to withstand Johnston's likely assault to regain his supply line. Sherman and McPherson would not be expecting Johnston to retreat.[42]

Depending on the reaction time of Sherman and his men, Johnston might have been able to retreat south and rejoin the railroad somewhere prior to or at Cassville. There, he could have entrenched as he actually did after the Battle of Resaca. Possibly, he would have had to abandon some of his supply wagons and artillery to enhance his army's chances of escaping to fight another day. Sherman would likely have ordered a pursuit. The road south from Spring Place toward Canton did support Brig. Gen. Edward M. McCook's and Maj. Gen. George Stoneman's divisions of cavalry. These approximately fifteen thousand troopers moved relatively quickly on May 19 to surprise Hood near Cassville. Could Johnston's forty-five thousand men, as well as his artillery and at least some slower-moving supply wagons, have utilized this same road successfully?[43]

A variation of this escape option would have been to move east into the more difficult terrain and rendezvous with supply wagons. This plan would have been more unlikely to succeed, as Sherman would have aggressively pursued, rendering Johnston's army impotent for further combat.[44]

Finally, Johnston could have surrendered. However, it was very early in the campaign, and Johnston knew this choice was politically unacceptable.[45]

CHAPTER 3

RETREAT, RETREAT! MAY 14–JUNE 7, 1864

After the Battle of Resaca, Johnston continued to retreat rather than fight Sherman's armies. Johnston professed he would attack Sherman when the correct situation appeared, and he came close to doing so at Cassville, but no attack was ever carried out. This inaction upset many of his men and many others within the Confederacy. In the meantime, Sherman continued to maneuver farther southeast into Georgia. During this time frame, Johnston made one critical decision and Sherman two.

Sherman Outflanks Johnston at Resaca

Situation

Sherman joined McPherson at Snake Creek Gap the next day and prepared once again to capture Resaca. The reports of McPherson's appearance west of Resaca made Johnston realize that he was outflanked and in serious danger of being cut off from his supply base. Consequently, he retreated from Dalton. By May 12 the Confederates had entrenched in a fishhook-like pattern around the town of Resaca, with the bottom of the shank anchored at the Oostanaula River just above the mouth of Camp Creek. The Rebel line continued north about three and three-quarters of a mile before it bent sharply back to the east, anchoring the other end of the hook on the Conasauga River, a

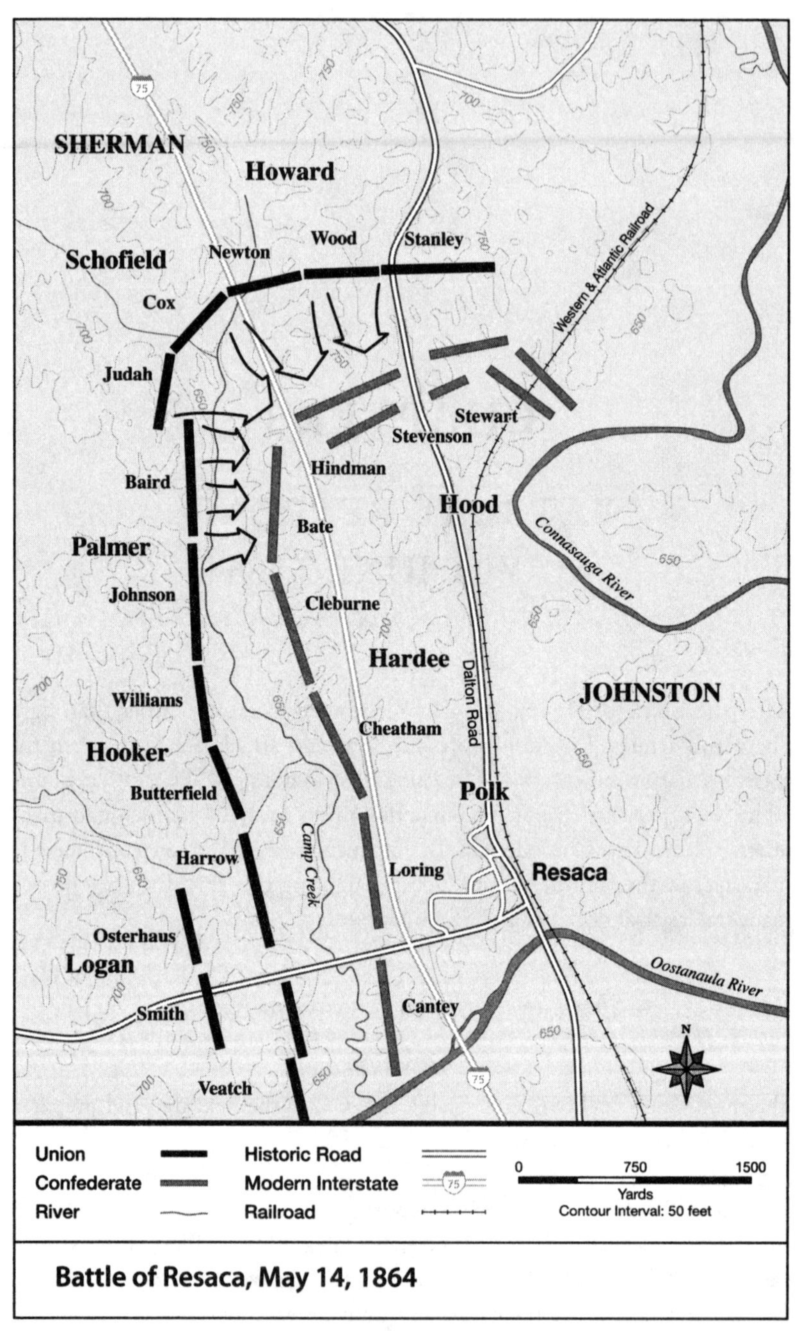

Battle of Resaca, May 14, 1864

tributary of the Oostanaula. Sherman marched his combined forces down through Snake Creek Gap and the Dalton–Resaca Road, and on the morning of May 13 he directed them into position opposite the already well-entrenched Confederate line.[1]

Options

As Sherman faced the Confederate Army of Tennessee at Resaca, he had three options: assault Johnston, attempt to hold the Army of Tennessee in place while determining a plan of action, or try and outflank Johnston.[2]

Option 1

A successful assault on Johnston's army here at Resaca could render the Confederates largely ineffective. Although his troops outnumbered Johnston's, Sherman knew that a frontal assault would succeed only at the cost of significant casualties. While he could sacrifice many of his men in an effort to overcome Johnston, he was not an aggressive commander who would unnecessarily order an assault. Sherman preferred maneuver as opposed to assault.[3]

Option 2

Holding Johnston in place would be a short-term solution, but it would not defeat Johnston's army. However, this option would spare a large number of casualties while Sherman devised a new plan of attack.[4]

Option 3

Outflanking Johnston would allow Sherman to continue to advance southward, compelling Johnston to do the same, while sparing the effusion of blood of many Union soldiers. This option would place Sherman in control of the offense, forcing Johnston to react to Sherman's movements.[5]

Decision

On May 14, Sherman tried to outflank Johnston by ordering Brig. Gen. Thomas Sweeny's Second Division of Maj. Gen. Grenville Dodge's Sixteenth Corps to cross the Oostanaula River at Lay's Ferry, located a few miles downstream from Resaca. After crossing the Oostanaula, Sweeny discovered he was being watched by Maj. Gen. W. H. T. Walker's Confederate division, which Johnston had posted south of Resaca, near Calhoun. Sweeny then retreated across the river. However, on May 15 Sherman ordered Sweeny to try again, and this time Sweeny gained a lodgment south of the Oostanaula.[6]

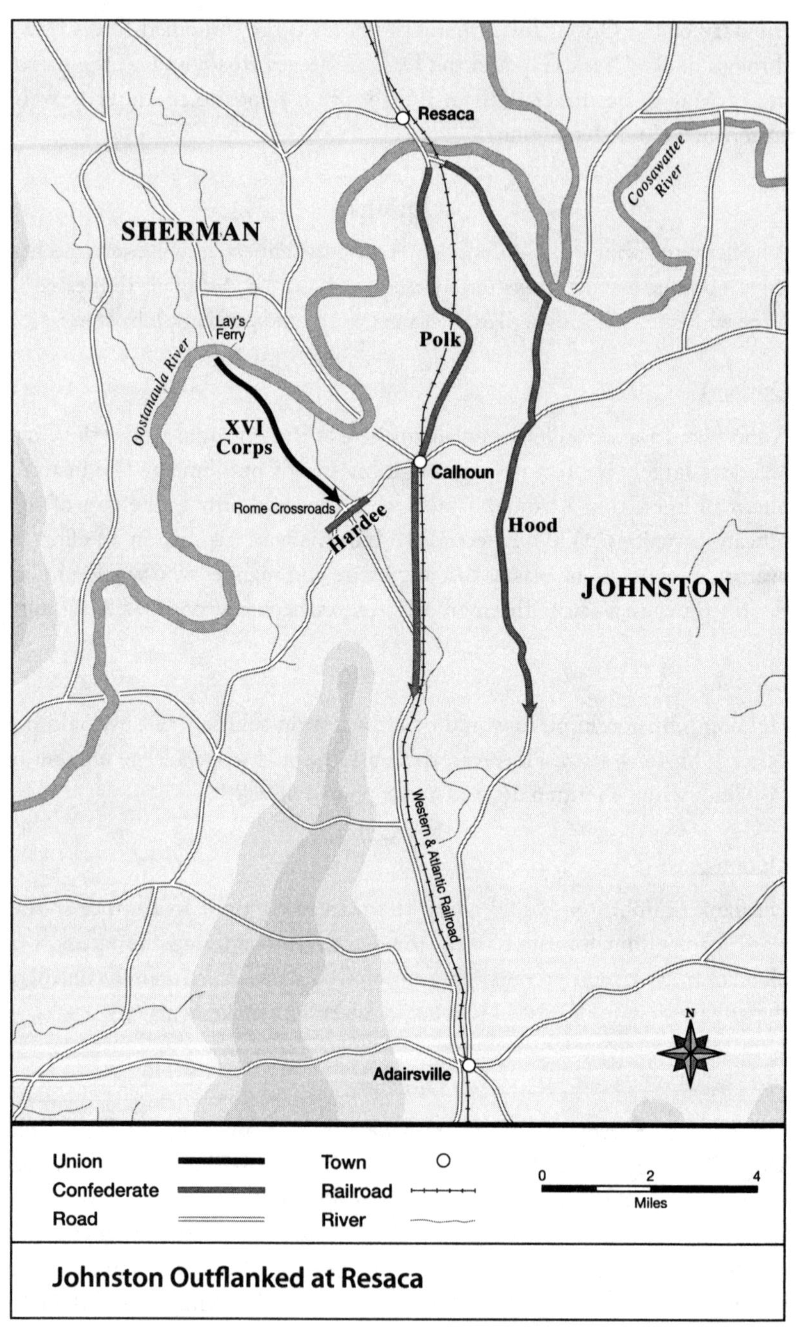

Johnston Outflanked at Resaca

This critical decision is interesting because Sherman actually utilized all three of his options! By ordering several assaults, Sherman kept Johnston from retreating from the battlefield until Union troops had outflanked him. This measure was also the equivalent of pinning Johnston in place until Sweeny's division successfully outflanked Johnston via Lay's Ferry. While Sherman's choice to outflank the enemy ultimately succeeded, his brief utilization of the other two options played a distinct role in the outcome—certainly an interesting management of the possibilities.[7]

Results/Impact

Once Walker informed him that Sweeny was south of the Oostanaula, Johnston realized that he had no choice but to retreat before he was outflanked. When darkness ended the fighting on May 15, Johnston conducted an exceptionally orderly withdrawal. The next morning, surprised Federal soldiers found that the Confederate army had stolen away.[8]

In fairness to Johnston, his position at Resaca was forced upon him by the maneuvering Union armies. He had to defend the railroad at the town. While Johnston's entrenchments were quickly built, the terrain at the southern end of the battlefield, directly west of Resaca, favored the Union. The terrain grew even more favorable for the Union when Sherman's men captured

Resaca Battlefield. *Photographic History*, Vol. III, 109.

Bald Hill, just west of the town. Federal artillery was now within range of Johnston's primary escape route over the bridges at Resaca. The Confederates' failure to retake this hill doomed Johnston's ability to keep his army at Resaca for any significant amount of time. Sweeny's successful crossing at Lay's Ferry forced Johnston to immediately retreat.[9]

Alternate Decision and Scenario

Had Sherman remained on the battlefield without intending to outflank Johnston, his superior numbers might have allowed him to successfully assault Johnston, who would have remained entrenched to protect his supply line. Were Sherman successful with an overwhelming assault, he could have defeated or destroyed Johnston at Resaca. Much of the Confederacy would then have been helpless to stop him from capturing such target cities as Atlanta and Mobile. The entire war could have been shortened as a result, especially if Grant had ordered Sherman to bring at least some of his armies to reinforce the Army of the Potomac against Lee in Virginia.[10]

Johnston knew that he could not retreat indefinitely without giving battle—he would lose the confidence of the Confederate government. While this circumstance was not totally Johnston's fault, he should have been more aware of the vulnerability of his position at Dalton. He certainly was aware of how crucial the Western and Atlantic Railroad was to supplying his army, and he could not allow a surprise Union attack to compromise it. While Johnston believed that he was so outnumbered as to make directly attacking the enemy futile, he should have been more perceptive as to Sherman's possible movements. Johnston apparently believed that Sherman would maneuver where Johnston expected him to. Unfortunately for his soldiers and the Confederacy, Johnston was now forced to react to Sherman at Resaca, rather than become the aggressor. With his left flank threatened, Johnston ordered a retreat.[11]

Johnston Plans to Attack near Cassville

Situation

On the sixteenth, Lieut. Gen. William J. Hardee's corps conducted a brief delaying fight against Maj. Gen. Thomas W. Sweeny's division at Rome Crossroads, northwest of Calhoun, covering Johnston's retreat. As Johnston retreated, he began searching for a place to confront Sherman.[12]

Maj. Gen. William T. Sherman quickly moved his three armies across the Oostanaula River. The Twentieth and Twenty-Third Corps made a wide arc to the east, first crossing the Conasauga River and then the Coosawattee

River, both tributaries of the Oostanaula. Thomas marched his Fourth and Fourteenth Corps through Resaca and across the Oostanaula on the rebuilt bridges. McPherson's army crossed the Oostanaula at Lay's Ferry. All of the armies marched south.[13]

Options

Johnston had three options: He could continue to retreat in the face of, from his perspective, overwhelming odds. Alternatively, he could attempt to attack any exposed units of Sherman's armies, or he could pick a defensive position and entrench, waiting for Sherman to assault him again.[14]

Option 1

One option was for Johnston to continue to retreat. However, he had already withdrawn far enough to raise the suspicion that he was not going to fight. He did not desire to sacrifice his men needlessly, but he realized that he could not retreat indefinitely without making a stand.[15]

Option 2

Another option was to attack a part of Sherman's forces that were isolated from the rest. This plan would somewhat equalize the disparity of manpower and grant Johnston a better chance of success. He could try to take advantage of the terrain and the independent marching orders Sherman would likely issue.[16]

Option 3

A final option was to retreat to a strong defensive position and wait for Sherman to attack there. Johnston would have to hope that Sherman would attack him and not outflank him once again.[17]

Decision

Johnston made the critical decision to attempt an ambush. He devised a plan based on the assumption that Sherman would divide his armies to ensure ease of movement and march on multiple routes while in pursuit. Johnston believed this course of action would provide him the opportunity to attack the enemy armies piecemeal.[18]

Lest his retreating be questioned, Johnston knew he needed to catch Sherman off guard before he yielded too much territory. Johnston had already retreated some fifteen miles, and he sought a proper location for an offensive maneuver.[19]

South of Adairsville two primary roads headed south. The first paralleled the Western and Atlantic Railroad straight south to the small town of Kingston, before turning east toward Cassville. The second ran southeast directly toward Cassville. It was logical for Sherman to use both roads to more efficiently march his men to the Cassville area. To bait Sherman, Johnston ordered Hardee's Corps to move to Kingston, while he ordered Leonidas Polk's and John B. Hood's corps to proceed directly to Cassville. Sherman took the bait by sending two corps of Maj. Gen. George Thomas's large Army of the Cumberland after Johnston at Kingston. At the same time, Maj. Gen. James B. McPherson's Army of the Tennessee headed slightly west and parallel to Thomas. Sherman ordered Maj. Gen. John M. Schofield's Army of the Ohio to march directly toward Cassville, with Maj. Gen. Joseph Hooker's Twentieth Corps (Army of the Cumberland) behind and on Schofield's right flank for protection.[20]

In order to protect his baggage train, which was still moving through Adairsville, Johnston placed Maj. Gen. Benjamin F. Cheatham's division about three miles north of Adairsville as a rear guard. Late on May 18, elements of Brig. Gens. George Maney's, John Carter's, and Alfred Vaughan's brigades fought a sharp delaying action at and around Robert C. Saxon's Octagon House.[21]

Johnston placed Hardee's Corps astride the road and railroad just east of Kingston. On the morning of May 19, he deployed Polk to cover the Adairsville–Cassville Road. Johnston also positioned Hood out on the Spring Place Road, which was just east of, and somewhat parallel to, the Adairsville–Cassville Road. Hood was then in position to ambush Schofield by striking Schofield's left flank while Polk blocked frontally. This tactic might result in the defeat and perhaps the destruction of Schofield's relatively small force. Johnston issued a stirring order to his men, concluding, "I will lead you in battle!" Quite possibly, this was Johnston's best opportunity of the entire campaign to defeat a portion of Sherman's combined armies.[22]

Results/Impact

Instead of carrying out his part of the plan, Hood suddenly began to fall back. He later reported that he had observed Federal cavalry on his right, causing him to retreat and redeploy his corps. This was Brig. Gen. Edward McCook's Union cavalry division, which Sherman had sent to threaten the railroad south of Cassville. These troops effectively ruined the opportunity to catch Schofield in the flank. Ironically, Hood, who had complained to Richmond about Johnston's previous failures to attack Sherman, was the first to back away from the planned attack at Cassville. Johnston canceled his planned attack and ordered a retreat approximately a mile south to a ridge east of Cassville.[23]

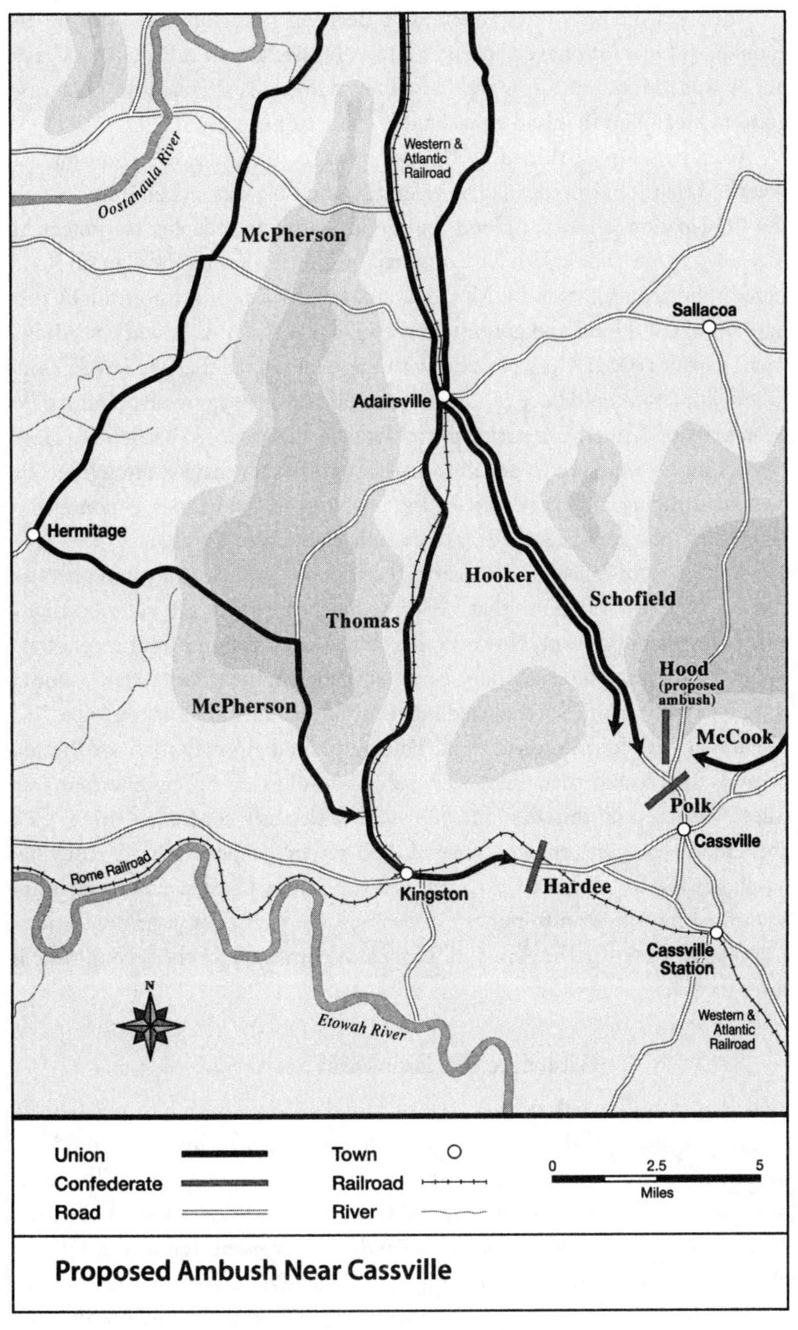

Proposed Ambush Near Cassville

This was the only critical offensive decision Johnston made during the campaign. He might have planned a later offensive attack at Peachtree Creek, but he was relieved of command before he could order this assault. This was a good tactical plan that had a reasonable chance of success.[24]

To have the plan ruined by the one corps commander who continuously preached that Johnston needed to go on the offensive was indeed ironic. Given the information available, Hood had good reason to redeploy to protect his divisions, but he should also have scouted the Union force on the Canton Road. Hood rebuffed an attack by McCook and his division. Johnston might then have realigned Hood and continued with his planned attack, while sending a small part of Hood's Corps to deal with the Union force that appeared behind Hood. Johnston could have conducted himself as a more aggressive commander here, perhaps directly conferring with Hood on the proposed battlefield. However, doing so would have been inconsistent with his behavior throughout the war. By utilizing his knowledge of the positions of the various Union armies and corps, Johnston might have successfully carried out his plan.[25]

As a result of canceling the planned attack at Cassville, Johnston retreated about a mile to a ridgeline that he immediately fortified. He believed that it was an excellent position. However, his chief of artillery and an army engineer pointed out that Union artillery could enfilade the line. Later that evening, after Sherman's armies had moved into position parallel to Johnston's new line, Hood met with Johnston and Polk. Polk and Hood strongly advocated retreat because they feared their lines were subject to enfilade fire by Sherman's artillery. Stunned by this thought, Johnston reluctantly concluded that if Polk and Hood were concerned because of their respective positions, he really had no choice but to fall back across the Etowah River. Hardee arrived later and advocated for Johnston to remain in position. Nevertheless, Johnston ordered a retreat on May 20. The Army of Tennessee withdrew for the second time in three days.[26]

Alternate Decisions and Scenarios

Had Johnston directed at least part of Hood's Corps back into position, he might have successfully salvaged an attack on Schofield. Johnston could reasonably have defeated at least a part of the Union units in ambush. This decision would then have resulted in a small victory providing several benefits. It would have boosted the morale of not only the Army of Tennessee, but also the entire Confederacy, if only for a short time. President Davis would have felt renewed confidence in Johnston, believing that he could hold off Sherman at least until the Northern presidential election. Sherman would likely have become more cautious in his movements, allowing some respite for Johnston.[27]

Johnston ordered a retreat south to the rugged Allatoona Mountains, approximately eleven miles south of the Etowah River. Here the Western and Atlantic Railroad passed through Allatoona Pass, a deep cut into the mountains, where he placed his army to defend the pass. Sherman was quite familiar with this part of Georgia, as he had traveled here many years earlier, taking dispositions from veterans of the Seminole War. He knew that it would be extremely costly, if not virtually impossible, to attack and defeat Johnston's well-entrenched army at Allatoona Pass. Therefore, he made the next critical decision of the campaign.[28]

Sherman Decides to Leave the Railroad

Situation

Aware of the cost of a direct assault on Johnston's entrenchments at Allatoona, and building on his previous success, Sherman believed that careful maneuvering would again force a Confederate retreat, eliminating a costly battle and placing the Federals yet closer to Atlanta. At the same time, such a movement denied that much more territory to the Confederacy. But a Federal maneuver away from the railhead would require the accumulation of supplies and the use of many wagons to provision the men and animals.[29]

Allatoona Pass. United States Military Academy Library.

Options

Sherman had two options: he could continue to march down the Western and Atlantic Railroad, facing a confrontation at Allatoona Pass, or he could maneuver away from the railroad, circumventing Allatoona Pass.[30]

Option 1

Sherman knew from previous experience that attacking Johnston's entrenched army at Allatoona Pass would cost his own armies significant casualties. There was no guarantee of success, and he was always reluctant to sacrifice his men needlessly. However, Sherman was almost entirely dependent on the railroad for material of war. He knew his ability to supply his armies would be compromised if he resorted to the extensive use of wagons for supplies away from the railroad.[31]

Option 2

To avoid a destructive frontal assault, Sherman's other option was attempting to outflank Johnston by leaving the railroad. This would make Sherman totally dependent on quartermaster wagons to haul supplies from the railroad north of Allatoona Pass to his armies. Also, Wheeler's Cavalry had given Johnston the ability to detect flanking movements and block them.[32]

Decision

While his men rested and were resupplied from May 20 until May 23, Sherman, residing in his headquarters in Kingston, made the critical decision to leave the railroad. His eventual destination was Marietta, Georgia, where he planned to rejoin the Western and Atlantic Railroad, the last major station north of the Chattahoochee River. Sherman's initial orders called for a concentration at Dallas, Georgia, a small town approximately fifteen miles south of Cartersville and the railroad. Dallas would be the center of deployment for the Federal armies. The large Army of the Cumberland, commanded by Thomas, was ordered to cross the Etowah River a little southeast of Kingston, and to march southeast through Euharlee and Stilesboro to Burnt Hickory, which was seven miles north of Dallas. The much smaller (one-corps) Army of the Ohio, commanded by Schofield, was to follow on Thomas's left flank. After crossing the Etowah, the Army of the Tennessee, commanded by McPherson, was ordered to proceed in a more westerly direction through the small town of Van Wert (today's Rockmart), and then to move against Dallas from the west. All of these movements were successful.[33]

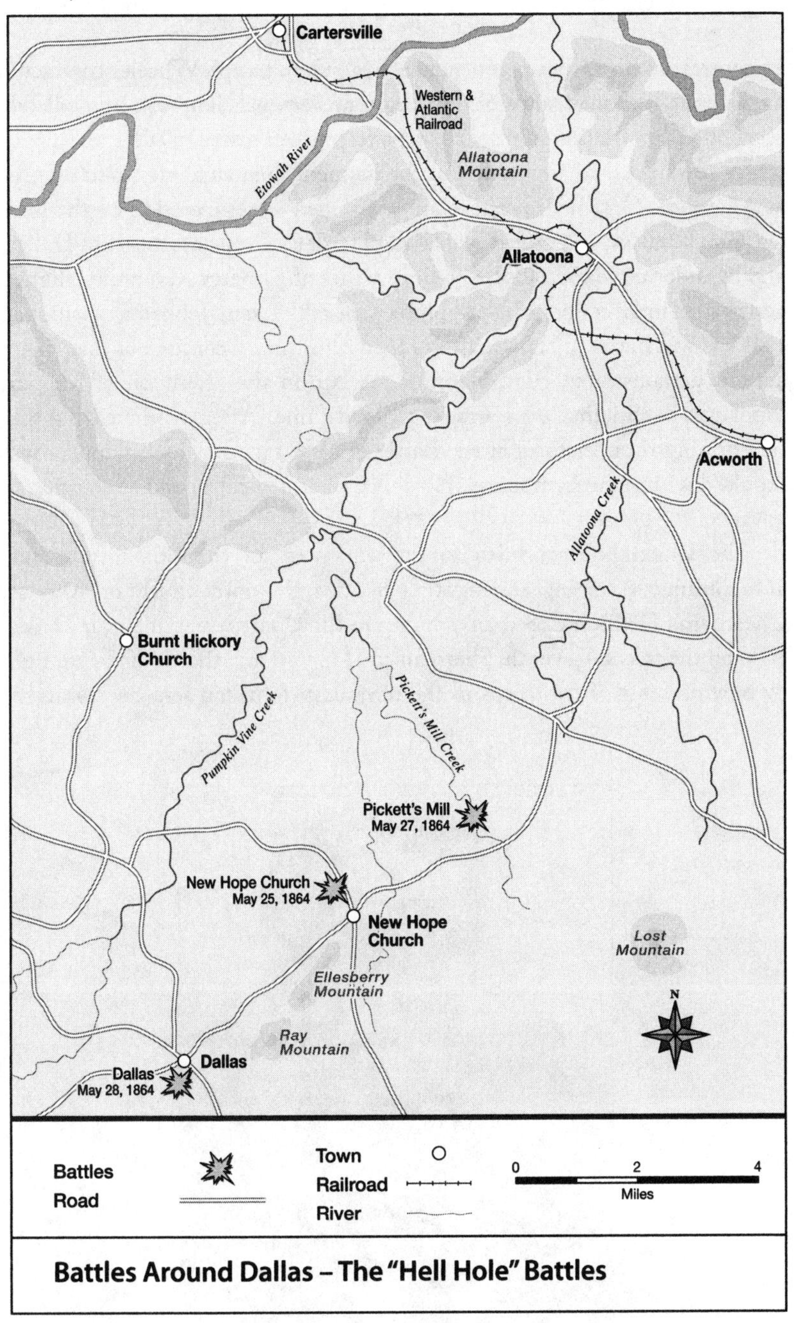

Battles Around Dallas – The "Hell Hole" Battles

Results/Impact

In contrast to his earlier performance, Maj. Gen. Joseph Wheeler conducted an accurate reconnaissance of the Union movements. Johnston immediately responded by ordering Hardee's Corps to proceed toward Dallas and Polk's Corps toward Lost Mountain. For the moment, Johnston left Hood's Corps at Allatoona. On May 24, Sherman's combined forces closed in on the Dallas area. Johnston responded by placing Hardee's Corps northeast of Dallas, and by ordering Hood's Corps to deploy east of Elsberry Mountain, aligned across the intersection at New Hope Church. Later, Johnston positioned Polk's Corps between Hardee's and Hood's, forming a continuous line. These actions demonstrated good planning, as late in the afternoon of May 25, Hooker's Twentieth Corps attacked Hood's line. After continued fighting in a driving thunderstorm at the Battle of New Hope Church, Hooker was repulsed with significant losses. However, Sherman continued attempting to advance.[34]

The Union line solidified to the northwest of the Confederate line, and continuous sniping and fighting became the norm. Early on May 27, Cheatham's Division closed an opening in the Confederate line near Dallas. Also on the twenty-seventh, Sherman tried to outflank the Confederate right by moving most of two corps to the northeast. Johnston sent division com-

Major General Patrick R. Cleburne, CSA.
The Military Annals of Tennessee, 153.

The "Hell-Hole." United States Military Academy Library.

mander Maj. Gen. Patrick Cleburne, one of the Confederacy's best combat generals, to counter any movement against the right flank. Cleburne marched his brigades to an area around Pickett's Mill and quickly prepared for a Union assault. Commanded by Maj. Gen. Oliver O. Howard, the Union forces moved through dense and hilly woods and attacked what they thought were disorganized and unprepared troops. Surprised by the strength of Cleburne's position, the Federals suffered significant casualities.[35]

Soldiers quickly labeled this area of the Atlanta Campaign the "Hell Hole." There was no end to the fighting; the front lines were constantly shifting as Sherman tried to maneuver to outflank Johnston. Moreover, Johnston continuously sent troops to forestall Sherman's men from outflanking his own. This fighting and maneuvering was conducted both day and night, in rain, heat, and humidity, and with little rest for both sides. These field conditions put severe pressure on the soldiers of both sides to complete their maneuvers. The conditions also reduced quartermasters' ability to maintain an adequate supply of food, feed, and ammunition.[36]

Sherman believed that by hard marching he could stretch Johnston's lines until the Confederate general did not have troops to extend his line. Johnston's swift response to the situation resulted in his keeping pace with Sherman's maneuvering. Sherman had not expected Johnston to react so quickly, and his failure to outflank Johnston surprised him. The effort to outmaneuver

Johnston by the northeast resulted in the debacle at Pickett's Mill, which ruined Sherman's long-term plans for outflanking the Confederate officer.[37]

After the Battle of Pickett's Mill, Sherman realized that he was unlikely to outflank Johnston to either the southwest or northeast. With supplies running low, Sherman had no choice but to abandon this effort and return to his dependable supply line, the Western and Atlantic Railroad. The one significant benefit to Sherman's movement off of the railroad was that he had successfully drawn Johnston away from Allatoona Pass and outflanked him. On May 28 Sherman ordered a movement toward the railroad, sending two cavalry divisions commanded by Maj. Gen. George Stoneman and Brig. Gen. Kenner Garrard to regain the line south of Allatoona Pass. Johnston had suspected Sherman's plans. He thus ordered Hardee to conduct a reconnaissance in force to determine if the Union forces at Dallas were withdrawing. Hardee designated Maj. Gen. William Bate's division to ascertain the presence of any Northern soldiers. Although McPherson had already ordered the Union troops' withdrawal from Dallas, they had not yet departed. Bate realized the Union forces were still in place, and he canceled the attack. However, the men of the Orphan Brigade (so called because they were from Union-controlled Kentucky and could not return home) did not receive word of the cancelation. They attacked anyway, suffered heavy casualties, and ended the Battle of Dallas. The three small battles at New Hope Church, Pickett's Mill, and Dallas, as well as the continuous skirmishing, all resulted in numerous casualties on both sides. But these engagements did not deter Sherman's continued maneuvering farther south into Georgia.[38]

The extended use of wagons on the muddy Georgia roads was too much to ask of Sherman's quartermaster department. In the wet weather the wagons bogged down in the mud, requiring extra manpower and animal power to keep them moving. Additional manpower was required to maintain a fighting presence. Given the sheer number of Sherman's soldiers, dependence on the Western and Atlantic Railroad was the only reasonable way to sustain them.[39]

Alternative Decisions and Scenarios

If Sherman had continued trying to outflank Johnston to the southwest, he would have moved farther and farther away from the railroad, magnifying his supply problems. One option would have been to move directly south and cross the Chattahoochee River west of Atlanta before Johnston could confront him. Alternatively, Sherman could have gone south, then east, bypassing the Kennesaw Mountain Line and rejoining the railroad near Marietta. Johnston would have tried to block these moves. But Sherman, by means of further flanking movements, would presumably have continued toward Atlanta. The extended overland supply line Sherman would have maintained would have precluded these movements. Wagons would have delivered required supplies and ammunition from the railhead somewhere around Acworth, and this route would have been heavily guarded. Johnston might well have tried to sever it. At some point, Sherman would have had no choice but to return his force to the vicinity of the railroad.[40]

Most students of the Civil War tend to concentrate on the battles, the skirmishes, and the strategy and tactics used by both sides. What is often overlooked is the importance of supplying each army with enough ammunition, food, forage for the animals, and other necessities required by the soldiers. Somehow, it is taken for granted that the supply line is always operable, maintained by "somebody" in the background. Without a continuously operating supply line, an army quickly loses its status as an effective fighting force. Sherman supplied his armies much more efficiently than many other generals.[41]

Supplying armies during the Civil War was a huge operation. For instance, a six-gun Union artillery battery theoretically needed approximately one horse per artilleryman, or about 150 horses per battery. In addition to the demand placed on the commissary department to feed the men, each horse also required forage (oats, grain, and hay). Feed was often unavailable from local resources and had to be brought forward from supply depots. Forage dispatched to the field was hauled by more horses, which also required forage. If the railroad were unavailable, Sherman required five thousand or more wagons, each pulled by four to six horses or mules, all requiring several pounds of forage per day per horse.[42]

In contrast, the Confederates often had to survive with lesser proportional numbers of wagons, as they simply did not have the resources that were available to the Union.[43]

Rain further complicated supply operations, becoming the bane of wagon drivers during the Atlanta Campaign. The roads quickly became quagmires after even a little precipitation, resulting in mud up to the carts' axels.[44]

CHAPTER 4

ATTACK! JUNE 8–JUNE 27, 1864

Sherman grew tired of the constant flanking movements and decided to try a different approach. Meantime, to help him defeat Sherman, Johnston requested that Forrest's Cavalry cut the enemy supply line. Yet Johnston refused to utilize his own cavalry for the same function. Two critical decisions, one each by Johnston and Sherman, were made during this time period.

Johnston Decides Not to Order His Cavalry to Sever Sherman's Supply Line

Situation

After Maj. Gen. William T. Sherman regained his railroad supply line at Acworth, he prepared to resume the offense. Gen. Joseph E. Johnston characteristically waited for Sherman's next move. The Confederates responded to the Union probes with a series of defensive positions, beginning with the Lost Mountain–Brushy Mountain Line. Sherman was not going to give up his railroad supply line again, and he maintained a large force spread out along it to protect it from Confederate raiding. Johnston had repeatedly asked Richmond for the help of Confederate cavalry, specifically that commanded by Maj. Gen. Nathan Bedford Forrest, presently in Mississippi. Starting back in May, Johnston had requested that President Davis order Forrest's Cavalry to Tennessee or Georgia. There, Johnston wanted Forrest's men to destroy enough of the railroad behind Sherman to force the Federals to retreat.[1]

Railroad bridge on Sherman's supply line. Library of Congress.

Why did Johnston desire help from Forrest? Born in 1821, Forrest had received virtually no formal education but had become wealthy as a planter and slave trader. When the war had broken out, he had raised a battalion of mounted troops and been elected its lieutenant colonel. Forrest had refused to surrender his men at Fort Donelson, safely leading them to freedom instead. He was a natural leader of men who quickly became notorious as the leader of a most effective cavalry. In fact, Forrest's raiding ability remained virtually unchallenged. His success at the Battle of Brice's Crossroads had Sherman conclude, "Forrest is the very devil. . . . There will be no peace in Tennessee till Forrest is dead."[2]

The problem with ordering Forrest east was that he and his men were needed to defend the parts of Tennessee and Mississippi still under Confederate control. Davis's policy of attempting to defend almost all Confederate territory by his departmental system had not always worked. The dispersion of forces had reduced the Confederates' ability to resist specific Union advances. Nonetheless, if Forrest was ordered to assist Johnston, much of the area Forrest was protecting might be lost to local Union forces. Earlier, the Union command had sent Brig. Gen. Samuel D. Sturgis's cavalry into Mississippi on a diversionary raid to keep Forrest's men there. The result was the rout of Sturgis by Forrest at the Battle of Brice's Crossroads.[3]

However, Davis needed to consider that the loss of territory in Mississippi and Tennessee would be of little consequence to the Confederacy if Atlanta was captured, or, perhaps more importantly, if Johnston's Army of Tennessee was destroyed or rendered ineffective. Davis had to observe the big picture. His fear of the political ramifications of losing territory would become secondary to his fear of losing key cities or one or more Confederate armies. Nonetheless, Johnston desired that President Davis order Forrest's Cavalry east to sever Sherman's railroad supply line.[4]

Options

Johnston had three options: He could send most of his cavalry to attack and destroy parts of the Western and Atlantic Railroad, keeping some cavalry for reconnaissance. He could also send part of his cavalry, possibly augmented by infantry, to complete the task. Or he could altogether ignore the prospect

Major General Nathan B. Forrest. CSA. Library of Congress.

of cutting Sherman's line of supply. Even a brief disruption of supplies would somewhat hinder Sherman's movements while he dealt with the resulting disruptions of service.[5]

Option 1

What seemed very logical was for Johnston himself to sever Sherman's railroad supply line. While refusing to attack Sherman, Johnston could reasonably spare much of his cavalry in an attempt to disable the railroad. He would not have to rely on assistance from others. Sherman was almost totally dependent on the railroad, and any disruption by destroying even a small part of it would seriously affect his ability to supply his armies. A major interdiction of the railroad in northern Georgia would force Sherman to pull his force back toward Chattanooga until he could rebuild the line. Since Johnston apparently had no desire to confront Sherman directly, while awaiting the enemy's next moves, he could utilize his own cavalry to inflict damage on Sherman's supply line.[6]

Option 2

Johnston could also utilize some of his cavalry and infantry units in a joint effort to cut the railroad providing Sherman with supplies. Infantry was notoriously better at destroying railroads than cavalry. As noted in Option 1, the reward would be great if this mission could be accomplished even temporarily.[7]

Option 3

Johnston's final option was to simply ignore Sherman's supply line and prepare to attack a part of Sherman's armies as the opportunity arose. This course of action would allow Sherman to be continuously supplied with all that was necessary to keep his armies in the field. At the same time, this option would allow Johnston to utilize the maximum number of his available men to confront Sherman.[8]

Decision

Johnston made the critical decision not to assign any of his cavalry or infantry to interdict Sherman's supply line. He apparently refused to use these soldiers because he presumed that he needed every man he could retain to retard the Union advance.[9]

Results/Impact

Severing Sherman's supply line, the Western and Atlantic Railroad, would have been an obvious advantage for Johnston. But he apparently didn't believe it was worth reducing his available manpower to accomplish the task. Cutting Sherman's line would have slowed the Federals' southern movement, if only for a short time. Johnston could only have benefited from this circumstance, and from the fact that his own cavalry was much closer to the railroad than Forrest's or any other Confederate cavalry. Johnston needed some cavalry for reconnaissance. If the rest of his cavalry could destroy only a short section of the railroad, Sherman would have assigned more troops to protect the tracks. With the flexibility of cavalry, Johnston might have benefited more from repeated attempts to cut the railroad than from keeping these cavalrymen as a source of manpower. As Sherman would have been forced to assign additional troops to protect his railroad, the opposing sides would have become more equal in manpower, another advantage for Johnston.[10]

Alternative Decisions and Scenarios

A more aggressive commander might have ordered an attack on the railroad. Since Johnston stuck to his decision not to send Maj. Gen. Joseph Wheeler's cavalry to cut the railroad, Sherman kept advancing, and Johnston kept retreating. The farther Johnston retreated south, the farther Wheeler had to advance to reach a suitable location to disable the railroad.[11]

Wheeler would have been receptive to attacking Sherman's supply line and gaining glory for himself and his cavalry. However, after the Battle of Resaca he became the eyes and ears of Johnston's army and performed continuous reconnaissance. Wheeler and his subordinates, such as Brig. Gen. William H. "Red" Jackson, were utilized in this dedicated role.[12]

However, later in the campaign after Hood was appointed army commander, he sent Wheeler to raid the Western and Atlantic Railroad. This raid caused minimal damage, and the line was quickly repaired. Cavalry was typically less effective at destroying railroads than infantry.[13]

Sherman Orders a Direct Attack on the Kennesaw Mountain Line

Situation

As a result of Johnston's decision not to interdict it, Sherman's supply line it remained intact, and he continued to maneuver south toward Atlanta. In response, Johnston established the Confederate Mountain Line, anchored by Lost Mountain on the west and Brushy Mountain on the east, across the Western and Atlantic Railroad. Maj. Gen. William B. Bate's division of Lieut. Gen. William J. Hardee's corps held a salient of this line located on the small eminence of Pine Mountain. Here, on June 14, Union artillery

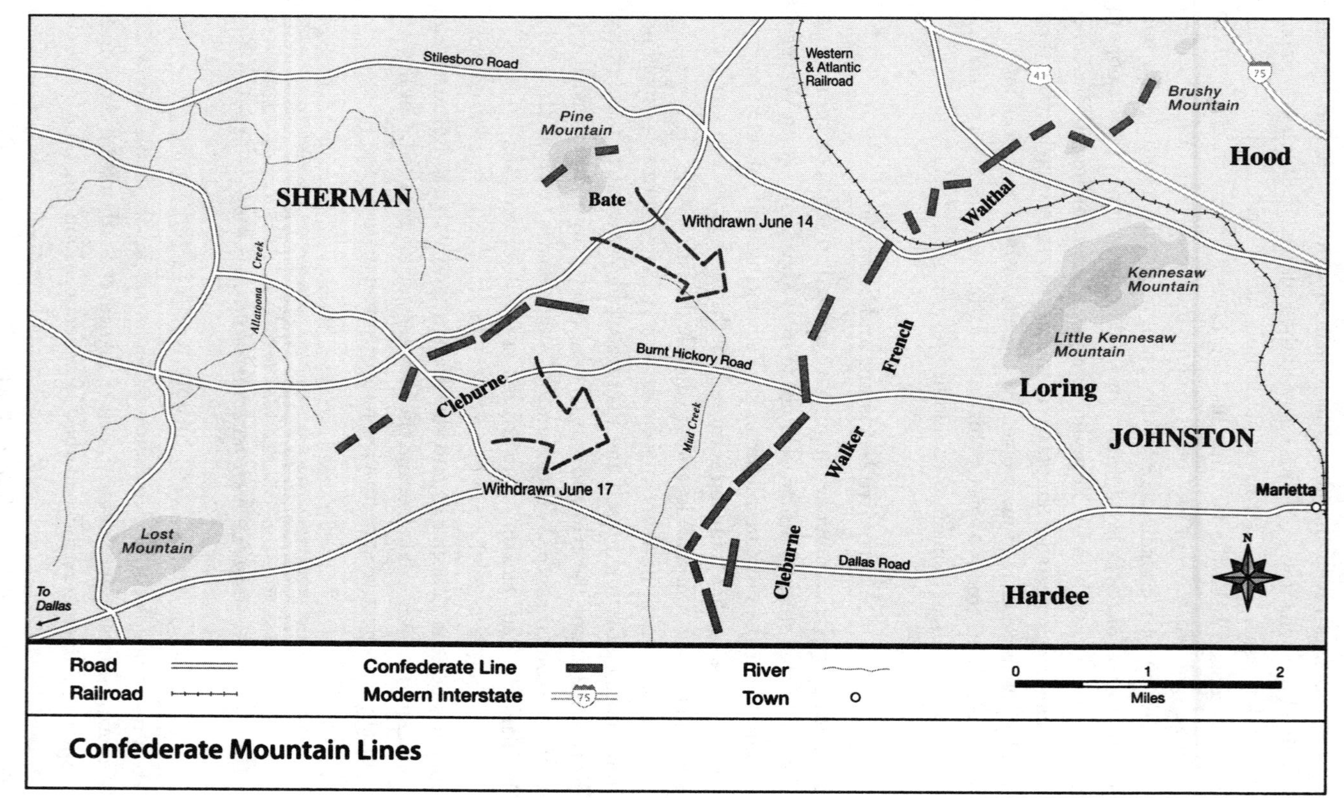

Confederate Mountain Lines

killed Lieut. Gen. Leonidas Polk. The next day, Maj. Gen. Joseph Hooker's Twentieth Corps charged Maj. Gen. Patrick Cleburne's division of Hardee's Corps at the Gilgal Church and was repulsed. As Sherman's troops gradually threatened to overlap Johnston's position, Johnston withdrew his left back to Mud Creek, where Cleburne withstood another attack on June 19. This withdrawal created another salient that made the new Mud Line untenable. Johnston retreated once more to what would become the very strong Kennesaw Mountain Line.[14]

The terrain along the Kennesaw Mountain Line provided a naturally strong defensive position for the Confederates. From the Confederate far right near Brushy Mountain, the line ran southwest across the Western and Atlantic Railroad between Big Shanty (today's Kennesaw) and Marietta, then southwest in front of Kennesaw Mountain and south by Pigeon Hill, then on to what became Cheatham Hill, finally terminating to the east of Kolb's Farm. Wheeler's Cavalry protected the Confederate far right, while Lieut. Gen. John B. Hood's corps initially occupied the line west from Wheeler. Fearing that Sherman might try to outflank him to the south, Johnston sent Hood's Corps to fortify the south end of his line on the night of June 21. Maj. Gen. William W. Loring's corps (Polk's former corps) occupied the line from east of the railroad around Kennesaw and Little Kennesaw Mountains

Union trenches in front of Kennesaw Mountain. *Photographic History of the Civil War*, Vol. III, 127

to Pigeon Hill. Hardee's Corps continued the position south past what would become Cheatham Hill, and then south almost to Kolb's Farm. Upon the line's occupation on June 18, it was even more strongly fortified with entrenchments and abatis.[15]

As Sherman approached the Kennesaw Mountain Line, he placed Maj. Gen. James B. McPherson's Army of the Tennessee on his left opposite Kennesaw and Little Kennesaw Mountains. Maj. Gen. George Thomas's Army of the Cumberland manned the center opposite the Confederate line, facing a salient soon to be named Cheatham Hill. The Army of the Ohio (the Twenty-Third Corps), commanded by Maj. Gen. John Schofield, formed the Union right near Kolb's Farm. As noted, on the night of June 21, Johnston, fearing a flanking maneuver to his left, moved Hood's corps from its position on the Confederate right. He sent it through Marietta to reinforce his left and defend the Powder Springs Road. The next day, Hood independently decided to attack the probing forces of Schofield and Maj. Gen. Joseph Hooker's Twentieth Corps as they extended the Union line southward. Discovering the pending offensive, the Union forces quickly dug in and repulsed Hood's unauthorized attack at Kolb's Farm. Hood suffered significant casualties. His unsuccessful attack, later dubbed the Battle of Kolb's Farm, involved almost one-third of Johnston's army without his knowledge, a violation of protocol.[16]

By this time, Sherman had grown impatient of flanking maneuvers, even though they had been successful. He began to believe that there might be a different solution to these almost continuous movements. Sherman also knew that Lieut. Gen. Ulysses S. Grant was now stymied at Petersburg and believed that the Northern populace needed to hear of a victory.[17]

Options

Sherman was faced with three options. One was to try to outflank Johnston to the south, as this would be the shortest distance to Atlanta. Alternatively, he could try to outflank Johnston to the north and east. Finally, believing that Johnston had been stretched to the limit, Sherman could assault his center, hoping for a breakthrough.[18]

Option 1

Sherman had tired of outflanking Johnston, but this method had certainly worked up to this point, and there was little reason not to expect it to continue to work. However, outflanking made supplying some of Sherman's men more difficult as they moved farther away from the railroad.[19]

Option 2

To date, Sherman had always outflanked Johnston to his left. Perhaps an attempt to outflank him to his right might catch him off guard. A movement in this direction would allow Sherman to remain close to the railroad.[20]

Option 3

With Johnston's army stretched out over some seven miles, Sherman wondered if Johnston might have weakened his center in order to extend his right and left flanks. Thus an assault against the Rebels' center might provide the breakthrough Sherman had been seeking. Perhaps tied into this option was the notion that the Yankees were tired of constantly conducting flanking maneuvers.[21]

Decision

Sherman made the critical decision to order a direct assault on the center of the Kennesaw Mountain Line. While their line was solid, the Confederates once again faced a situation whereby the terrain created a salient just south of the Dallas–Marietta Road, at what would eventually be named Cheatham Hill. Maj. Gen. Benjamin F. Cheatham, whose division was entrenched along this part of the line, was quite aware of the problem. His preparations for defending the area included the extensive use of entrenchments and abatis, as well as the concealment of cannon. To Sherman, this salient was the logical point to be assaulted, as its exposure enabled it to be attacked from front and flanks. The salient was also an easy target for the Union artillery. Therefore, he ordered an assault for the morning of June 27. Sherman's orders called for some diversionary fire from the left and a supporting attack against Pigeon Hill, located south of Little Kennesaw Mountain, several miles north of Cheatham Hill. The main attack was to be against Cheatham's salient. Sherman hoped the this assault would develop into a breakthrough that would disrupt Johnston's defenses.[22]

Results/Impact

On the morning of June 27, after an artillery barrage, the assaults commenced. Maj. Gen. John Logan's Fifteenth Corps charged toward Little Kennesaw Mountain and Pigeon Hill. The troops were repulsed by Maj. Gen. Samuel French's division of Polk's Corps (now commanded by Maj. Gen. William Loring), which suffered few casualties. Elements of the Fourth and Fourteenth Corps of Thomas's army made the assault against Cheatham's and

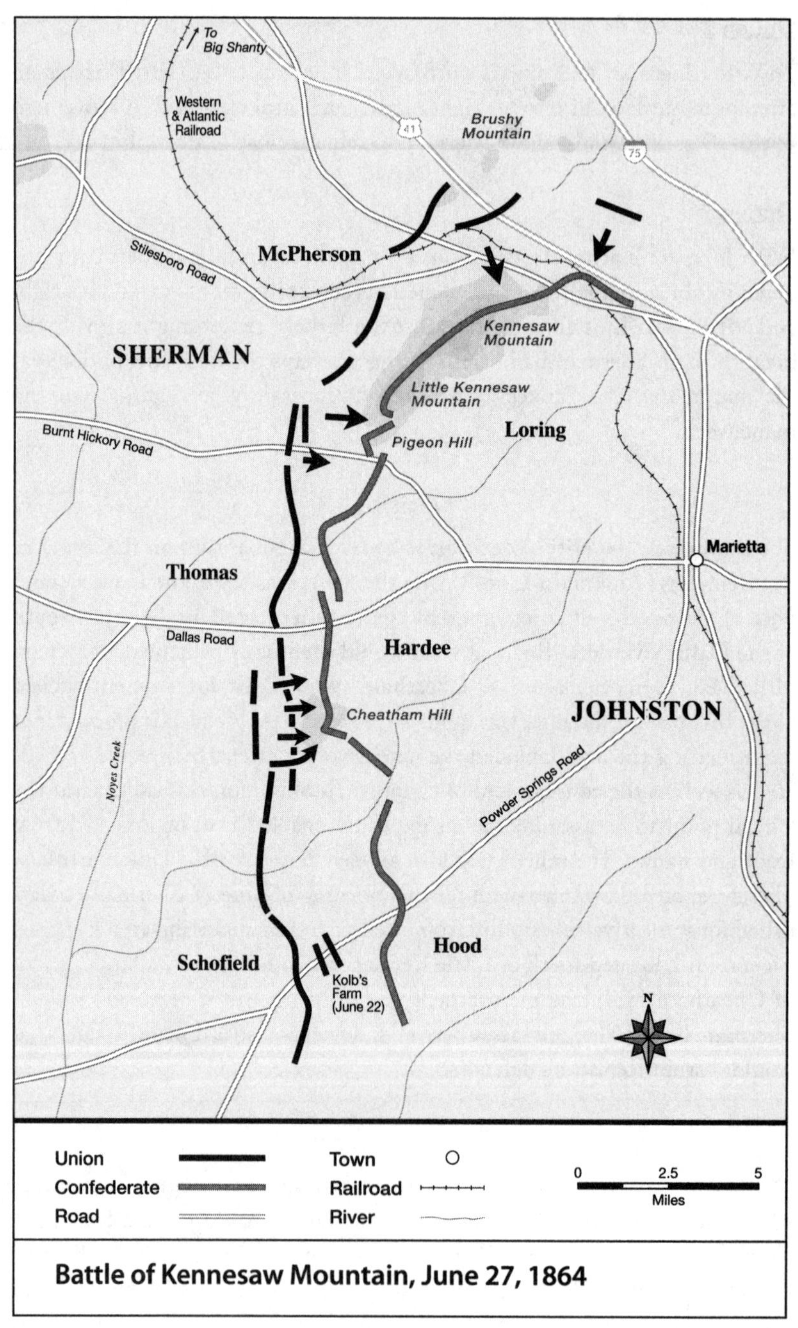

Battle of Kennesaw Mountain, June 27, 1864

Maj. Gen. Patrick Cleburne's divisions (Cleburne was to the right or north of Cheatham). Five brigades attacked on very narrow fronts but were decisively thrown back. Cheatham's hidden artillery wreaked havoc on the attackers, and then it became a matter of the well-entrenched Confederates' shooting down the exposed Yankees. Some hand-to-hand combat occurred when the Federals reached the Confederate line, but Thomas's troops never really had a chance.[23]

The fighting ended after about an hour, at which point some one thousand dead Union soldiers were lying in front of Maney's and Vaughan's Brigades. Maney's and Vaughan's men had defended the salient, soon to be labeled the Dead Angle. These Confederate brigades suffered light casualties, while Sherman's losses totaled at least three thousand men.[24]

This was a critical decision, as Sherman temporarily forsook flanking movements and attacked Johnston head on. While Sherman could afford the casualties, his choice proved once again that, by this time in the war, it was nearly impossible to charge an entrenched position with any real expectation of success. Sherman relearned from this unsuccessful attack that what had worked in the past (outflanking Johnston) would be the better way to achieve victory. After the battles for Pigeon Hill and the Dead Angle, when Sherman asked Thomas if he might successfully conduct another assault, Thomas famously replied, "We have already lost heavily today without gaining any material advantage. One or two more such assaults would use up this army!" The only other maneuvers Sherman could likely have conducted here were turning either of Johnston's flanks. This became Sherman's next effort.[25]

Sherman's critical decision affected Johnston as well. The Confederate general had been continually requesting more troops from the government at Richmond. He maintained that Gen. Robert E. Lee had proportionately more soldiers to fight Grant than he (Johnston) had to fight Sherman. Seemingly unable to visualize the big picture—that there was a shortage of manpower throughout the Confederacy—Johnston wanted to wait until he had some semblance of equality in numbers before going on the offensive. Refusing to accept the fact that no great numbers of reinforcements were available, he continued to maintain that he could only attack Sherman piecemeal should the opportunity arise. Alternatively, Johnston could hope that Sherman would attack his army while it was securely entrenched. Sherman's attack on the Kennesaw Mountain Line and especially at the Dead Angle only reinforced Johnston's concept of managing the campaign. Indeed, he hoped for more attacks on the formidable Kennesaw Mountain Line. Sherman's critical decision to order a frontal assault made Johnston's reaction very easy; all he had to do was repel this and any other frontal maneuvers against his

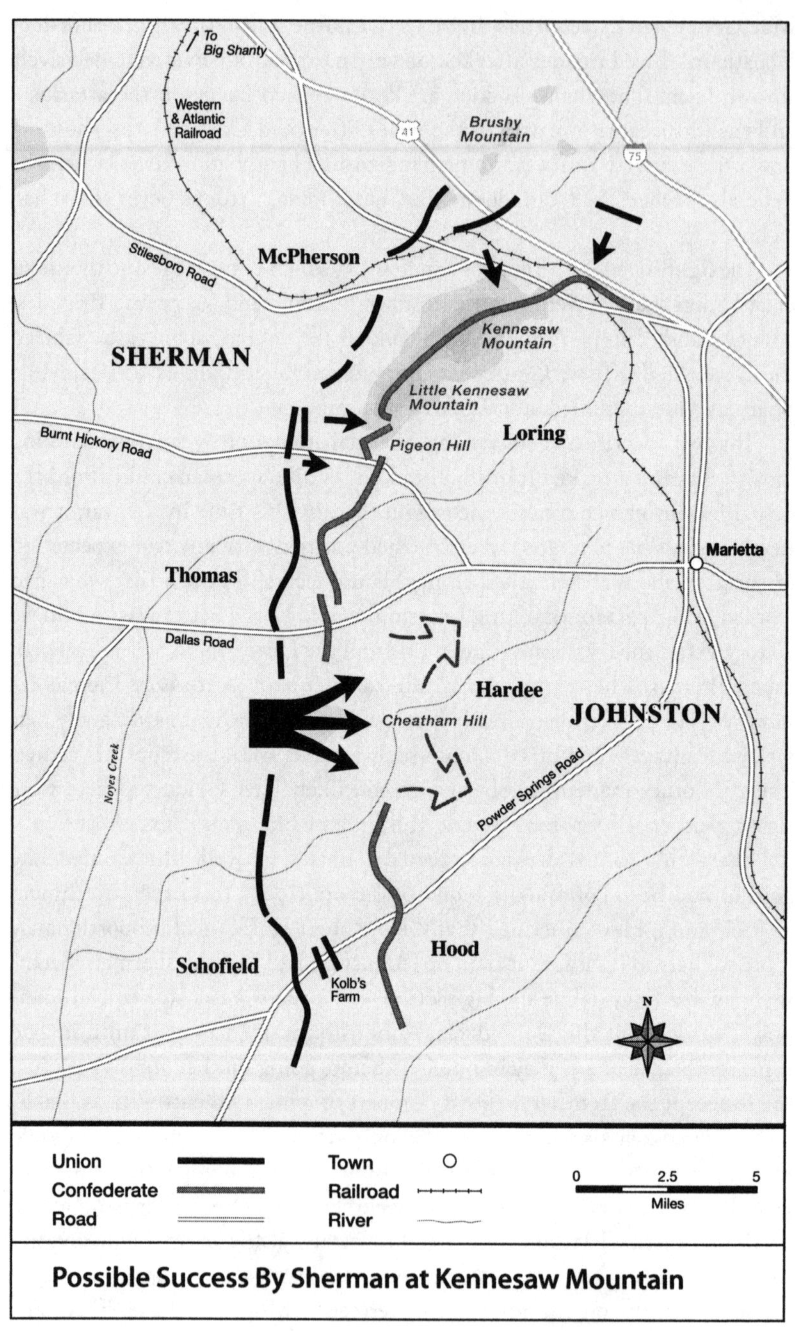

Possible Success By Sherman at Kennesaw Mountain

well-fortified line. Sherman played right into Johnston's plan to remain on the defensive and score a victory. However, Johnston merely responded to Sherman's movements. While it was easy to react to assaults while manning well-entrenched lines, the initiative remained with Sherman.[26]

Alternate Decisions and Scenarios

Sherman's next movement was essentially Option 1 above, as he once again outflanked Johnston to the south. Chances were that if he had tried to outflank Johnston to the north, Sherman would have been equally successful.[27]

After the assault on June 27, Sherman prepared again to outflank Johnston as the method of maneuver. Even as he attacked the Kennesaw Mountain Line, he realized that Johnston's left was vulnerable to such an attack. As the local roads become drier, Sherman ordered McPherson's Army of the Tennessee to pass behind the other armies and proceed southeast along the Sandtown Road toward the Chattahoochee River. Schofield's Army of the Ohio was to follow McPherson. This movement commenced on July 2 and was quickly reported to Johnston, placing him in the position of having no choice but to fall back—but to where? The Confederates had prepared a temporary defensive line. The Smyrna Line, so named because it ran through the Smyrna Campground, was a whistle-stop on the Western and Atlantic Railroad located just a few miles north of Vining's Station. This defensive position ran west roughly three miles from Rottenwood Creek along today's Windy Hill Road to the Smyrna Station/Campground. It then continued along today's Concord Road about two miles to Ruff's Mill, where it bent south along Nickajack Creek. During the night of July 2–3, Johnston conducted an orderly withdrawal from the Kennesaw Mountain Line to the Smyrna Line. Hood's Corps manned the Confederate left around Ruff's Mill, while Hardee's Corps covered the center, including the railroad. Loring's Corps held the far right to Rottenwood Creek. Johnston assigned most of Wheeler's Cavalry to guard the right flank and Brig. Gen. William H. "Red" Jackson's cavalry division to guard the left flank.[28]

Ever the optimist, Sherman concluded that Johnston would retreat across the Chattahoochee River to avoid having it as an obstacle behind him. When the Union armies arrived opposite the Smyrna Line, Sherman initially refused to believe that the Confederates were entrenched. Brig. Gen. William Grose's brigade attacked and was repulsed at or near the Smyrna Campground, just east of the Western and Atlantic Railroad. Another attack on the Confederate far left at Ruff's Mill was likewise repulsed. However, the Seventeenth Corps was now closer to Atlanta than the Confederate Army of Tennessee. Johnston consequently ordered another retreat. The Rebels' departure commenced late on July 4 and lasted into July 5. Once again, Sherman expected Johnston to cross the Chattahoochee River to avoid being entrapped with the river directly behind him. He was again surprised to find the Army of Tennessee entrenched north of the river. This last line of defense was designated the (Chattahoochee) River Line. However, it took a different form than all previous lines had, consisting of some thirty-six Shoupades, structures named for the officer who conceived and supervised the entrenchment's construction. Knowing that at some point the Army of Tennessee would need to entrench north of the Chattahoochee River, Brig. Gen. Francis A. Shoup, chief of artillery for the Confederate army, had received permission on June 18 to construct the line. Using slave labor, he had largely finished it. A Shoupade was a small fort to be manned by some eighty men. Protected by walls ten to twelve feet thick and about twelve feet high, the structure could absorb most artillery fire without harm to its defenders. Each Shoupade was connected to the next one by a stockade of logs placed vertically and extending about eight feet above ground. Artillery redans, placed at key intervals between Shoupades protected the forts by allowing wide fields of fire. The Chattahoochee River Line was an ingenious defensive structure.[29]

Unfortunately, no matter how effective the River Line was, it could be outflanked. Sherman planned another flanking maneuver, and on July 7 he ordered Schofield to find a suitable river crossing beyond Johnston's right flank, or northeast of his position. Sherman took pains to make Johnston expect the crossing to the southwest. Johnston took the bait. Schofield found a decent crossing location the next day, and by midafternoon he had put most of a division across the river. Once again, Johnston had been outflanked.[30]

Sherman had previously ordered Brig. Gen. Kenner Garrard's cavalry division to destroy the mills at Roswell, about sixteen miles northeast up the Chattahoochee. Garrard's division crossed the river on July 9 at Roswell. When Johnston learned of these crossings, he realized that he was being outflanked once more. In response, he ordered a retreat across the Chattahoochee on the evening of July 9. General Shoup was astounded! On July 9 Shoup remarked, "I could not then, and I have never been able since, to see why the position should not have been held indefinitely." However, by being outflanked, the position was rendered useless.[31]

CHAPTER 5

NEW PLANS, JUNE 28–JULY 22, 1864

Maj. Gen. William T. Sherman revised his assignment to capture or destroy Johnston's elusive army and concluded that the capture of Atlanta was a more purposeful objective. To do so, Sherman decided to destroy the railroads supplying the city. Sherman believed that he would gain an advantage by Davis's temporary appointment of John B. Hood to the rank of general over the Army of Tennessee. Hood went on the offense and, after the Battle of Peachtree Creek, ordered a conceptually brilliant flanking maneuver against McPherson's army.

Sherman then began to contemplate another critical decision for which many have faulted him. However, a closer examination shows that his decision-making was precise and rational. This choice would have a major influence on the campaign from that point on.

Sherman Makes Atlanta His Objective

Situation

Lieut. Gen. Ulysses S. Grant originally intended for Sherman to attack and destroy Gen. Joseph E. Johnston's Army of Tennessee. Sherman was also to prevent Johnston from detaching units to reinforce Gen. Robert E. Lee's Army of Northern Virginia. In a private and confidential letter to Sherman, Grant wrote as follows: "I propose for you to move against [Gen. Joseph E.]

Johnston's army, to break it up and to get into the interior of the enemy's country as far as you can, inflicting all the damage you can against their war resources." Many historians note that Johnston's army, not the capture of Atlanta, was Sherman's primary objective. However, these historians may not be aware of a series of messages exchanged between Sherman, Grant, and Halleck after the assault on the Kennesaw Mountain Line. On the evening of June 27, not long after his aborted assaults at Kennesaw, Sherman gave Halleck a brief summary of the day's failures, stating, "I can press Johnston and keep him from re-enforcing [*sic*] Lee, but to assault him in position will cost us more lives than we can spare." The next day Grant sent Halleck the following orders: "Please telegraph General Sherman that he can move his army independent of the desire which he has expressed of detaining all of Johnston's army where it is. I think Lee now would only be weakened by re-enforcements [*sic*]. He has to act defensively behind his intrenchments [*sic*], and any addition would only consume supplies, which he must find it difficult to transport." Later the same day, obeying Grant's request, Halleck messaged Sherman: "Lieutenant-General Grant directs me to say that the movements of your army may be made entirely independent of any desire to retain Johnston's forces where they are. He does not think that Lee will bring any additional troops to Richmond, on account of the difficulty of feeding them."[1]

On July 5, Sherman arrived at Vining's Station and climbed a hill just north of the railroad tracks that was named either Vining's Hill or Mount Wilkinson. For the first time in the campaign he could see Atlanta, only nine miles away. Next to Richmond, Virginia, Atlanta was the most strategic city left to the Confederacy.[2]

Four railroads connected Atlanta to all parts of the remaining Confederacy, enabling the movement of supplies and troops anywhere within the Confederate borders. Bragg traveled from Mississippi through Atlanta when he moved his army to Chattanooga to begin the Kentucky Campaign of 1862. Longstreet's corps moved from Virginia through Atlanta to reinforce Bragg's army in 1863, again because Chattanooga was Union controlled. If Sherman captured Atlanta, the Confederacy's ability to supply its soldiers, reposition armies or parts of armies, and distribute supplies to civilians would be seriously compromised.[3]

In addition, Atlanta had become a major supply depot and manufacturing center. These features became increasingly important, as Union armies had captured other major Confederate cities. Whether Atlanta was captured or protected had enormous political and material consequences for both sides of the conflict.[4]

Options

Sherman now faced two options: he could continue to pursue Johnston and his Army of Tennessee, or he could maneuver to capture Atlanta.[5]

Option 1

Sherman could continue to pursue the Army of Tennessee as Grant had originally desired. However, Sherman had discovered several unpleasant truths he had previously ignored. He learned that, after the Battle of Resaca, Confederate morale in the Army of Tennessee was indeed good, and not poor as he had predicted. Further, it was apparent to Sherman that it would be difficult to actually trap Johnston and his men. Johnston had demonstrated that he was too tactically proficient to allow his army to be cornered somewhere. Sherman had begun to realize that chasing the Army of Tennessee would further lengthen his supply line. While he would be forced to leave the railroad, Johnston would remain in friendly territory.[6]

Option 2

Sherman could focus on capturing Atlanta and repelling any of Johnston's assaults on his armies. Though this change in focus was technically a violation of Sherman's original orders, Grant was not the commander on scene. He had since given Sherman leeway to maneuver as he felt most beneficial to the Union cause.[7]

Sherman realized that the Lincoln administration considered Atlanta itself a political objective. Because of its important railroad junctions, supply depots, and manufacturing capabilities, Jefferson Davis considered Atlanta next to Richmond in political importance. By selecting this option, Sherman would have to gamble that the capture of Atlanta, without the effective elimination of the Confederate Army of Tennessee, would be sufficient to get Lincoln reelected.[8]

Decision

While we don't know exactly when Sherman made this critical decision, he finally made Atlanta's capture his primary goal. He stated, "This was one, if not the chief, object of the campaign, viz, the advancement of our lines from the Tennessee to the Chattahoochee, but Atlanta lay before us, only eight miles distant, and was too important a place in the hands of the enemy to be left undisturbed, with its magazines, stores, arsenals, workshops, foundries, & etc., and more especially its railroads, which converged there from the four great cardinal points." Sherman further observed, "The capture of Atlanta . . .

[would] give us the fruits of victory, although the destruction of Hood's army was the real object to be desired. Yet Atlanta was known as the 'Gate-City of the South,' was full of founderies [*sic*], arsenals, and machine-shops, and I knew that its capture would be the death-knell of the Southern Confederacy."[9]

Results/Impact

Once he made capturing Atlanta his objective, Sherman changed the maneuvering of his armies in order to begin a semi-siege of the city and prevent supplies and ammunition from reaching the Confederate army located within.[10]

Sherman thought that once he had outflanked Johnston by crossing the Chattahoochee River, Johnston would withdraw his army into the prepared defenses surrounding Atlanta. Achieving this strategic objective eventually provided Lincoln with progress toward ending the war. His chances for reelection improved, which would ensure the war continued to eventual Union victory.[11]

Alternate Decisions and Scenarios

Sherman's only other option was to fight Johnston's Army of Tennessee and detain it or render it combat ineffective, thus postponing the capture of Atlanta. Had this army been eliminated or left unable to fight, Sherman could have moved on Atlanta, or any other major Confederate city. However, Johnston had never allowed his army to be placed in a position where it could be ineffective.[12]

Sherman knew that, even with his seven corps, he probably could not successfully assault the Atlanta defenses. Had victory been achieved, it likely would have come with too many casualties, something inadvisable after Grant's huge losses in the Overland Campaign. This situation led Sherman to the next critical decision.[13]

Sherman Decides to Destroy the Railroads Supplying Atlanta

Situation

As previously noted, Atlanta was the junction of four railroads that provided crucial transportation throughout the Confederacy. The Western and Atlantic Railroad (owned by the State of Georgia) ran northwest from Atlanta to Chattanooga, where it connected with four other railroads. The Georgia Railroad ran east from Atlanta through Decatur to Augusta, where it connected to points east. A third railroad, the Macon and Western, ran southeast to Macon, where a connection to Savannah and the East Coast was available. The fourth railroad, the Atlanta and West Point, ran south–southwest from Atlanta to West Point, where connections were available all the way to Vicksburg and points west. The Macon and Western and the Atlanta and West Point Railroads shared the same track from East Point, which was slightly south of Atlanta, into the city.[14]

Options

Sherman had three options: he could assault the city, he could besiege the city, or he could sever the railroads that brought most of the supplies into and out of the city.[15]

Option 1

Sherman could command a direct assault against Atlanta. This plan would be costly in terms of soldiers' lives, and it had no guarantee of success. The citizens of the Union were becoming increasingly intolerant of the mounting casualty lists from Grant's Overland Campaign, and a failure here producing significant casualties would be was politically unacceptable. Sherman's lack of success at the Kennesaw Mountain Line would cast doubt on this option, as would his innate dislike of direct assaults that would needlessly sacrifice his men.[16]

Option 2

Sherman could also besiege Atlanta. However, the city's large periphery would make this course of action very difficult. With some ten or more miles of Rebel entrenchments to guard, it would be nearly impossible to fully contain all movements to and from Atlanta.[17]

Option 3

Finally, Sherman could capture and destroy the railroads leading into and out of Atlanta. Cutting Atlanta's largest supply system would force the city's capitulation.[18]

Decision

Sherman quickly made the critical decision to destroy the railroads supplying Atlanta, knowing that the city could not hold out without its main source of supplies. However, while attempting to carry out his mandate to wreck the railroads, Sherman did maintain a semi-siege of Atlanta, including an extended artillery bombardment of the city.[19]

Results/Impact

The railroads allowed supplies and personnel to be effectively transported most anywhere within what remained of the Confederacy. The loss of this hub would have considerable negative ramifications for the Confederacy's supply system. The various railroads also supplied Atlanta with most of the necessary food, wood, clothing, and other necessities of life.[20]

Of the four railroads terminating in Atlanta, Sherman already possessed one, the Western and Atlantic Railroad, which was his supply line. The Union advance, after crossing the Chattahoochee River northeast of Atlanta, placed part of Sherman's forces near the town of Decatur, which lay astride the Georgia Railroad that ran from Atlanta to Augusta, Georgia. Sherman ordered Maj. Gen. James B. McPherson's Army of the Tennessee, along with Brig. Gen. Kenner Garrard's cavalry division, located the farthest east of all the units of Sherman's armies, to destroy a large segment of the Georgia Railroad extending eastward from Decatur. This destruction would eliminate a second railroad's ability to supply Atlanta. It also greatly reduced the possibility of Confederate reinforcements being sent to Atlanta from the east, as had been done during the Chickamauga Campaign with Longstreet's Corps in September 1863. When this devastation was completed, McPherson led his men west toward Atlanta.[21]

Two railroads remained to supply both the Army of Tennessee and Atlanta: the Macon and Western Railroad and the Atlanta and West Point Railroad. Beginning at East Point, both shared the same track for the last few miles into Atlanta. East Point was therefore an inviting target for Sherman. Union possession of East Point would sever the last two railroads into Atlanta, isolate the city, and force its surrender. In July, however, Maj. Gen. Lovell H. Rousseau had cut the western connecting railroad, the Montgomery and West Point, to the Atlanta and West Point Railroad at Opelika, Alabama, rendering it virtually useless. Sherman would make sure the line remained that way.[22]

Due to the proximity of Sherman's armies, some industries had relocated elsewhere. Much of Atlanta's civilian population had departed in anticipation of the eventual capture of their city. However, the remaining population needed provisions just as much as the Army of Tennessee did. To all who remained within the city, the railroads were the dominant sources of supply.[23]

Sherman's critical decision to destroy the railroads supplying Atlanta eventually forced Confederates to abandon the city. In turn, the Union achieved a significant victory and contributed to President Abraham Lincoln's reelection.[24]

Alternate Decisions and Scenarios

The outcome of this decision would have been somewhat countered had the Confederates prevented Atlanta's fall long enough to frustrate Lincoln's re-election. A successful Confederate attack on an exposed part of Sherman's forces also might have delayed the capture. However, another critical decision profoundly affected Sherman's choice to destroy the railroads and capture Atlanta. This decision was completely beyond his control, but it met with his approval.[25]

Davis Appoints Hood to Command the Army of Tennessee

Situation

Confederate president Jefferson Davis, along with many within the Confederacy, became increasingly dissatisfied with Johnston's continuous retreating without engaging Sherman, or at least slowing his advance. Davis had supplied what few reinforcements were available to Johnston. Yet the general continued to refrain from fighting because of the numerical disadvantage he faced. Other than the effort near Cassville to defeat an exposed part of Sherman's force, Johnston had attempted no offensive action. By July, Davis finally became convinced that Johnston would not defend Atlanta, or not defend it for long, and so began the search for a replacement. On July 12 Davis received a telegram from Johnston stating, "I strongly recommend the distribution of the U.S. prisoners, now at Andersonville, immediately." Davis interpreted this message as a further indication that Johnston would not defend Atlanta.[26]

Options

Three options were available to Davis: He could leave Johnston in command, or he could replace Johnston with another general. Davis's final option was to replace Johnston with someone of lesser rank.[27]

Option 1

Davis could continue to hope that Johnston would finally dig in and fight. With Sherman at the outskirts of Atlanta, a Confederate change of command would be inopportune. It would also take time to bring a new commander up to date on the positioning of his various units, and to familiarize him with his many subordinate commanders. The learning process would be especially lengthy for an appointee outside of this army.[28]

Option 2

If Davis decided to replace Johnston, he did not have a large pool of other general officers to choose from. Davis despised Gen. P. G. T. Beauregard and did not seriously consider him. Gen. Braxton Bragg had only recently been removed from this very command, and his reappointment would reignite the animosities previously created there.[29]

Option 3

Of the potential lieutenant generals, William J. Hardee seemed to be a good candidate. However, in December 1863 he had turned down the offer of command prior to Johnston's appointment. James Longstreet had demonstrated mediocrity in independent command during his stint in the West, but he was unavailable due to his wounding from friendly fire at the Battle of the Wilderness. Edmund Kirby Smith, a personal friend of Davis's, was located west of the Mississippi River and bogged down commanding forces in the Trans-Mississippi. Also, Smith had illegally promoted several of his colonels to the rank of brigadier general without Davis's approval. Richard O. Taylor had demonstrated competency during the Red River Campaign and was not foolhardy. Yet he had proven uncooperative with his commander, Kirby Smith. Lieut. Gen. Richard Ewell had performed poorly and was in poor health. A competent general officer, Alexander P. Stewart had been in corps command for only ten days and lacked sufficient experience at that level, much less at independent command. After his wounding at the Battle of Chickamauga and while convalescing in Richmond, John Bell Hood had spent much time with Davis and earned his favor. Serving under Johnston as a corps commander from February 1, 1864, Hood had occasionally written Davis, unbeknownst to Johnston. Hood's letters indicated doubt in Johnston's ability to attack Sherman, even as Hood had declined to attack at Cassville.[30]

Davis asked Gen. Robert E. Lee for his thoughts on a replacement. Lee agreed that Hood was probably the better choice but cautioned that, while he was a good fighter, Hood might lack the other qualities necessary for high command.[31]

Decision

Davis made the critical decision to replace Johnston, relieving him of command late on the evening of July 17. Hood was temporarily appointed to the rank of general and placed in command of the Army and Department of Tennessee. He knew that he was expected to fight, and fight he would. This critical decision was significant in that Hood's appointment would shift the

General John B. Hood, CSA.
Photographic History, Vol. III, 123.

Army of Tennessee from a defensive style of combat to offensive operations, undoubtedly with an increase in casualties.[32]

Results/Impact

The ramifications of Hood's assuming command of the Army of Tennessee were enormous. In fairness to Hood, he was thrust into a situation in which few, if any, generals at the time could have brought success to the Confederacy by defeating Sherman. The numerical and logistical odds decidedly favored the Union. Hood was to defend Atlanta, and he was limited in his choice of locations to do so or to bring on a fight. Upon learning of the change of command and foreseeing the future, some of his men simply deserted or went over to the enemy and surrendered. Hood's inability to manage an independent army would quickly become obvious to the members of the Confederate government. President Davis would come to regret the loss of Rebel soldiers in battle after Hood's appointment.[33]

Hood had only been in corps command since February, and he had no command experience at the army level. His method of leadership during battle was to emulate his former commander Robert E. Lee, issuing orders, revising them as necessary, and trusting to luck and his subordinate commanders to carry them out. While this plan worked for Lee, who had excellent subordinates such as Lieut. Gen. Thomas "Stonewall" Jackson, Hood had only one experienced corps commander in Lieut. Gen. William J. Hardee. Hardee would quickly come to despise Hood's inability to command an army. Hood's two other corps commanders, Lieut. Gen. Alexander P. Stewart, only recently appointed, and Maj. Gen. Benjamin Cheatham, temporarily appointed to command Hood's Corps, were inexperienced at the corps level and needed guidance. Hood's inclination was to attack head on with brave, determined soldiers who didn't need his battlefield supervision and could overrun the enemy with physical strength. This methodology was not likely to work against a cagey tactician such as Sherman. Sherman later wrote, "At this critical moment the Confederate Government rendered us most valuable service. Being dissatisfied with the Fabian policy of General Johnston, it relieved him, and General Hood was substituted to command the Confederate army. No officer who ever served under me will question the Generalship of Joseph E. Johnston. His retreats were timely, in good order, and he left nothing behind."[34]

Alternate Decisions and Scenarios

President Davis's two other options were to leave Johnston in command, especially since the Union forces were so near to Atlanta, or to place Hardee in command. Changing the army commander at this critical time was certainly inexpedient. However, leaving Johnston in command was almost unthinkable for President Davis, as Johnston had demonstrated no inclination to fight for Atlanta. The general's few communications to the president gave Davis no outward hope of a change in strategy or tactics. Johnston claimed to have a plan to attack the Union forces approaching Peachtree Creek, and had he remained in command, he might have succeeded in scoring a victory there. Obviously his plans for action beyond Peachtree Creek were unknown, if they even existed. He would have been largely helpless to prevent Sherman from eventually destroying the railroads supplying Atlanta. Still, Johnston might have preserved the Army of Tennessee to fight at another time and place more favorable for the Confederacy.[35]

Had President Davis communicated with Hardee, he might have ascertained that Hardee would now accept command of the Army of Tennessee, especially if Hardee was aware that Hood was a potential successor. Politically, Hardee was not considered for the position. Gen. Braxton Bragg, now military advisor to President Davis, disliked him and did not recommend him for the command. Had Hardee been selected, his ability to manage an independent army would have been quickly tested. However, it would have been surprising had he performed any better than Hood. Hardee would likely

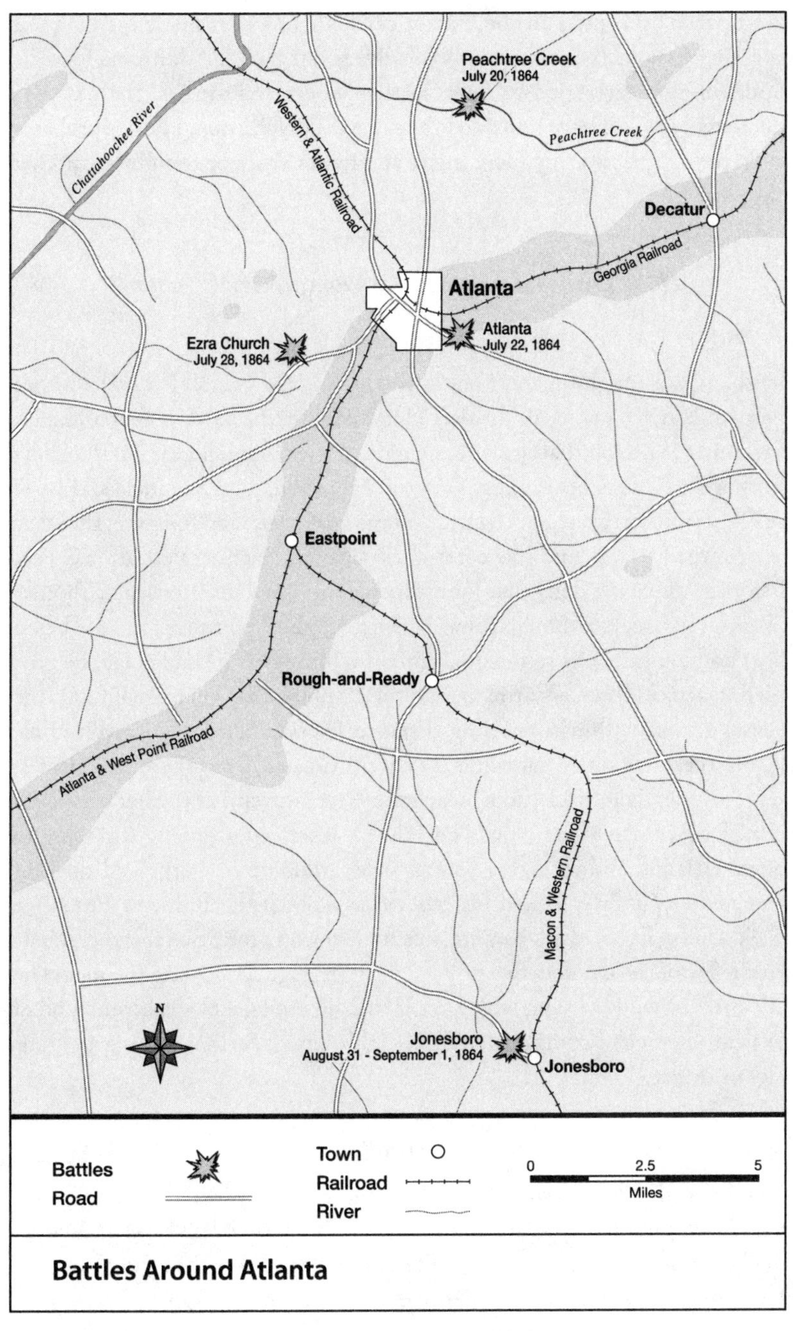

Battles Around Atlanta

have managed his men on the field of battle in a more realistic manner, not expecting too much from them physically, as did Hood. Additionally, while Hardee might have tried to fight parts of Sherman's armies, the outcome undoubtedly would have remained the same. Like Johnston, Hardee probably would have kept his army more intact and in better shape to fight at another time and place.[36]

Hood Orders a Flank Attack against McPherson

Situation

Hood knew, as did Johnston, that in conducting the overall Federal advance Sherman had separated his armies. Hood believed he stood a better chance of winning if he could attack these Union armies individually. McPherson's Army of the Tennessee was near Decatur. Maj. Gen. John Schofield'sArmy of the Ohio was northeast of Atlanta, and most of Maj. Gen. George Thomas's Army of the Cumberland was north of the city approaching Peachtree Creek. Historians generally deny that Johnston had an actual plan to attack Thomas at Peachtree Creek, although some evidence might support this theory. Upon Hood's appointment to command, similar to Johnston's possible plan, he proposed to attack Thomas's army before the combined advance brought all the Federal armies within supporting distance. Hood's battle plan involved attacking these Union corps while they were isolated from the other armies, then pushing them back from Peachtree Creek toward the Chattahoochee River. Unfortunately for Hood, on July 20, after repositioning his army to protect Atlanta, and incurring serious delay in doing so, corps and division commanders poorly executed his ordered assaults at the Battle of Peachtree Creek. Union forces involved were able to throw up protective entrenchments while a few of the Confederate units failed to engage. Following the model he had observed while serving with Lee, Hood did not take tactical command of the field. Inefficient command and control resulted, further leading to Confederate defeat.[37]

Options

Hood knew that he was expected to halt Sherman's approach to Atlanta, and he had two options for achieving this goal. The Confederate general could fall back into the entrenchments protecting Atlanta. Another choice was for Hood to again undertake an offensive maneuver in an effort to battle with only a part of Sherman's entire command.[38]

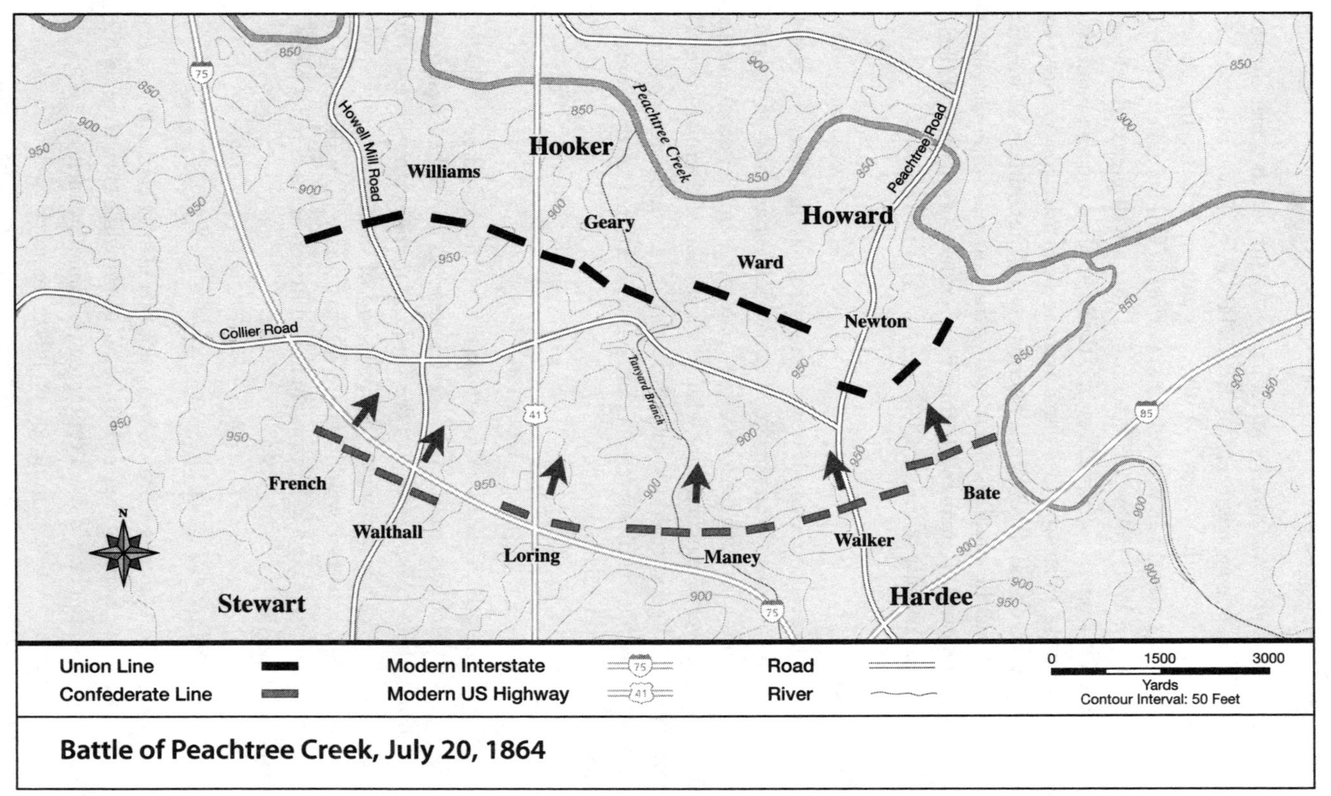

Battle of Peachtree Creek, July 20, 1864

Option 1

With a strong line of earthworks surrounding Atlanta, built under the supervision of Confederate engineer Col. Lemuel P. Grant, Hood believed that Sherman probably would not order a direct assault on Atlanta. This choice would simply be too costly in with regard to the loss of Union soldiers. At this stage of the Civil War, troops had determined that a well-prepared defense would most likely repulse an attack, even if the enemy had superior numbers. The entrenchment lines around Atlanta were too extensive for Sherman to effectively lay an official siege. While Sherman would not initially secure the capture of Atlanta, he could go about cutting the railroads while remaining virtually unmolested. Remaining within these entrenchments would likely delay Sherman's capture of the city.[39]

Option 2

Hood did not expect to retreat; it was not his nature as an officer. He could again go on the offensive and engage Sherman if he could find an isolated part of the enemy's command. With a good part of his smaller army and his men in a more evenly matched fight with only a portion of Sherman's overall force, Hood had good reason to anticipate victory. In turn, victory would potentially slow Sherman's movements and preserve Atlanta for the Confederacy for at least a while longer.[40]

Decision

Hood made the critical decision to attack the left flank and rear of Maj. Gen. James B. McPherson's Army of the Tennessee as it marched west from Decatur to Atlanta. McPherson had been ordered to thoroughly destroy the railroad east of Atlanta to reduce the likelihood of the Confederacy sending more troops. This task would require soldiers weary from the Battle of Peachtree Creek to make a long, tiring march of fifteen or more miles before commencing battle.[41]

Results/Impact

Hood designated Hardee's Corps to carry out this plan of battle. If successful, Hood would catch McPherson's corps off guard while they were on the march and unentrenched: it was a conceptually brilliant maneuver.[42]

The march began around midnight on July 21, required twelve hours, and was performed by men already worn out from the July 20 Battle of Peachtree Creek. While this was a masterful plan on paper, unsurprisingly, Hardee's units were not in position by the time Hood had proposed. By the time these

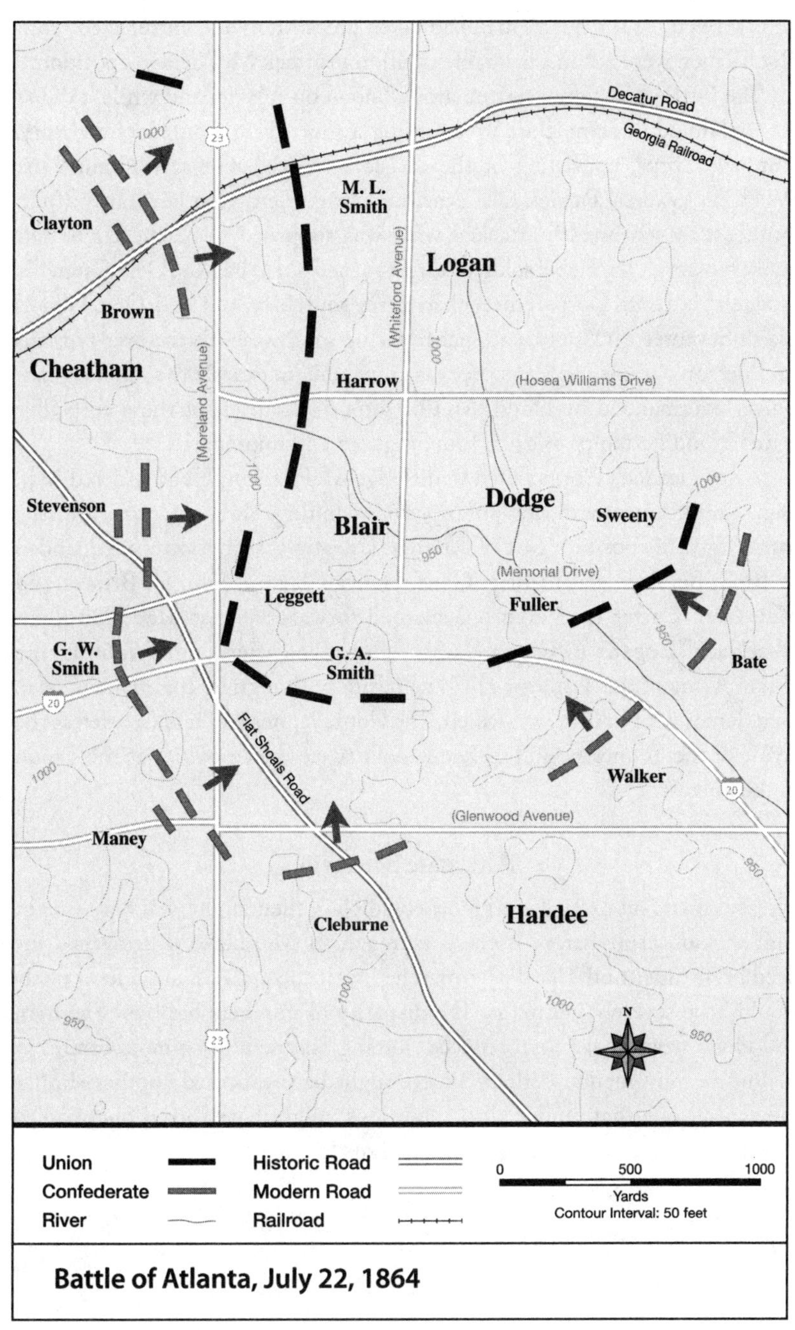

Battle of Atlanta, July 22, 1864

units arrived, McPherson's men had taken precautions and entrenched. Thus Hood's men were not in a favorable position to attack McPherson's position.[43]

The Battle of Atlanta started around noon on July 22, and while it didn't go as planned, it came close to achieving a short-term Confederate victory. Hardee's Corps, consisting of the divisions of Maj. Gens. William Bate, W. H. T. Walker, Patrick Cleburne, and Brig. Gen. George Maney (from southeast to southwest), attacked what was supposed to be the Union left flank. However, the Rebel soldiers' target turned out to be Maj. Gen. Grenville Dodge's Sixteenth Corps, entrenched facing southeast, and Maj. Gen. Francis Blair's Seventeenth Corps, entrenched facing southwest. To the ever-cautious McPherson's credit, he feared he was vulnerable to exactly the flanking maneuver commanded by Hood. McPherson's dispositions of these corps defeated Hood's attempt to catch him off guard and unprepared.[44]

After Hardee's Corps failed to dislodge McPherson, Hood ordered Maj. Gen. Frank Cheatham, temporarily commanding Hood's Corps, into the battle from his position east of Atlanta. Cheatham's divisions, commanded by (from north to south) Brig. Gens. Henry Clayton, John C. Brown, and Maj. Gen. Carter L. Stevenson, charged forward against Maj. Gen. John "Blackjack" Logan's Fifteenth Corps. After a long afternoon of fighting, the Union Army of the Tennessee held its position, though its commander, Maj. Gen. James McPherson, was killed. The Confederates had failed to defeat the Army of the Tennessee and suffered about twice the casualties as the Union in the process.[45]

Alternate Scenario

If rested men had carried out Hood's bold plan, they might well have caught McPherson's army before it could entrench. If McPherson's army had indeed been caught off guard as it marched west toward Atlanta, Hood likely would have severely injured it. The disparity of numbers between Sherman and Hood would have been reduced, forcing Sherman to be more careful in his future movements. Perhaps Hood might have executed another similar movement, one that, under ideal conditions, might have forced Sherman to slow his advance and prolong the campaign.[46]

CHAPTER 6

FINISHING THE CAMPAIGN, JULY 23–SEPTEMBER 2, 1864

Sherman realized that he could not realistically assault the Atlanta defenses and so ordered an all-out assault on the railroads still supplying the city. Hood continued to protect Atlanta from capture. However, Sherman made two final critical decisions resulting in the loss of Atlanta to the Confederacy.

Sherman Destroys the Railroad, Not Hardee

Situation

Maj. Gen. William T. Sherman recognized that the Atlanta defenses were too strong to attack and too extensive and lengthy to surround to conduct a proper siege. Thus he continued with his earlier critical decision to destroy the railroads. He began maneuvering against the two potential remaining railroads supplying Atlanta in order to completely stop the flow of supplies such as food and ammunition into the already beleaguered city. After Maj. Gen. James McPherson was killed, Sherman ordered Maj. Gen. Oliver O. Howard, now in command of the Army of the Tennessee, to march from east of Atlanta to the southwest, then south and east toward East Point. The Macon and Western, the sole remaining railroad serving Atlanta, merged at East Point with the temporarily useless Atlanta and West Point Railroad. Howard's force moved out on July 27 and proceeded to the Lick Skillet Road near the Ezra Church.[1]

When Hood was informed of Howard's initial approach toward East Point, he ordered Lieut. Gen. Stephen D. Lee, newly appointed commander of Hood's former corps, to march his corps to the Lick Skillet Road and "prevent him [Howard] from gaining the Lick Skillet Road." Lee advanced on July 28 only to discover that Howard had already arrived at this critical junction. Howard noted the presence of more Confederate cavalry in this area than was normal, and he ordered his men to entrench in case they were attacked. He directed that these entrenchments be placed on good ground, arranged in a horseshoe-like configuration.[2]

Upon arrival at the Lick Skillet Road near Ezra Church, Lee discovered that Howard had already beaten him to his assigned location, where he was to "hold the enemy in check." Lee was further ordered, "[You are] not to attack unless the enemy exposes himself in attacking us."[3]

Instead, Lee decided to assault the entrenched Union line. Within a few hours the combined Confederate losses were over three thousand compared to the Union's six hundred.[4]

The useless slaughter of irreplaceable Confederate soldiers appalled Davis when he learned of it. He cautioned Hood, who had lost eleven thousand men in eleven days, not to conduct any more direct assaults unless absolutely necessary. By issuing this warning to Hood, Davis effectively condoned Johnston's former strategy of avoiding direct combat.[5]

During late July, Maj. Gen. George Stoneman and Brig. Gen. Edward McCook carried out two unsuccessful cavalry raids. Stoneman decided to modify his orders in an attempt to free the Union prisoners at Andersonville. However, he and most of his men were captured some eighteen miles north of Macon, near the small town of Round Oak. McCook lost his fight near Newnan, southwest of Atlanta, and was lucky to escape. About ten days later, Hood sent most of Wheeler's Cavalry on a raid into northern Georgia and Tennessee, reducing his ability to track Union movements.[6]

The Confederates further entrenched southwest of the city to keep Sherman from capturing the Atlanta and West Point Railroad. A small battle at Utoy Creek ensued, and Rebel soldiers held off the Union attacks. In the fighting around Utoy Creek, the Union losses totaled about one thousand while the Confederate losses numbered, for once, not more than a couple of hundred.[7]

After failing to drive the Confederates from Atlanta by a three-week bombardment in August, Sherman continued in his attempt to destroy the sole remaining railroad. He sent the bulk of his infantry southwest of the city. On August 29, his men destroyed some thirteen additional miles of the Atlanta and West Point Railroad, which had operated between West Point, located on the Alabama-Georgia border, and Atlanta. Maj. Gen. Lovell Rousseau's

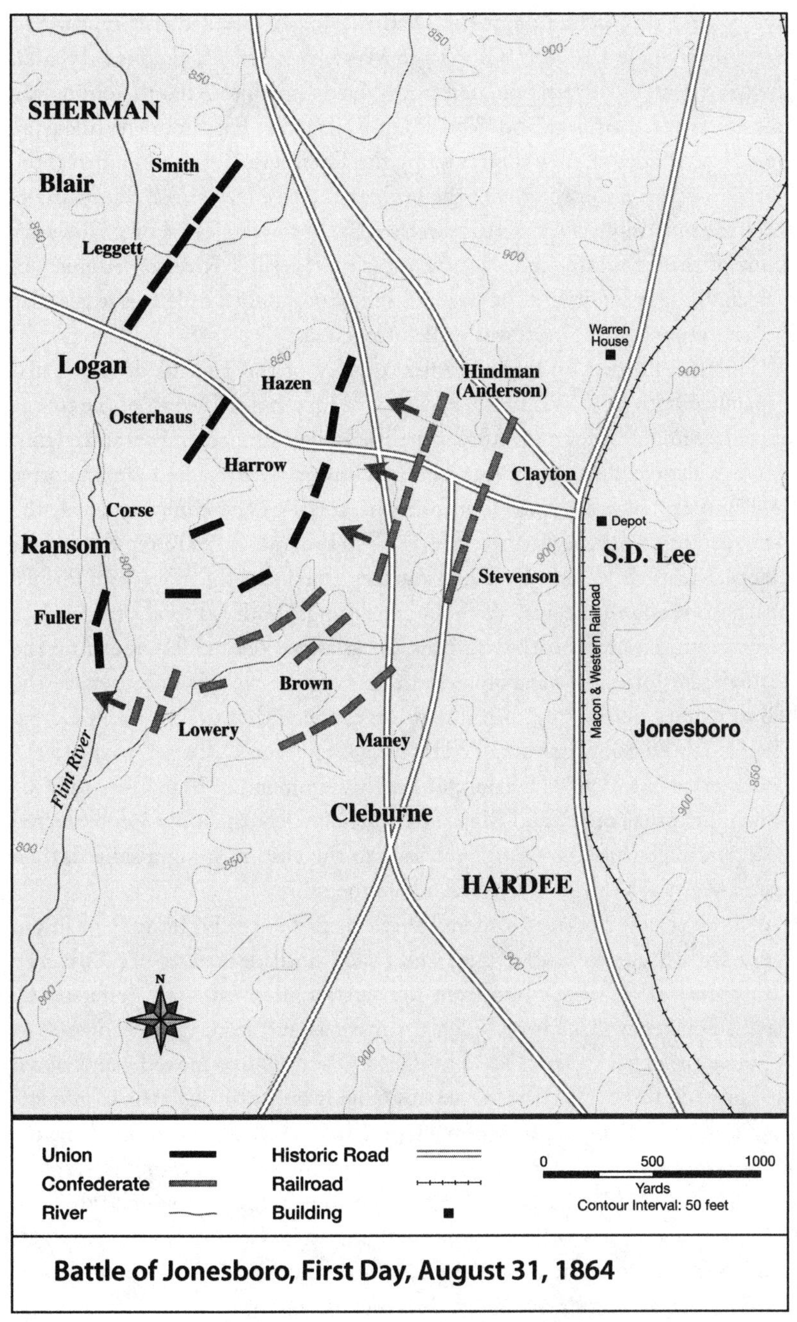

Battle of Jonesboro, First Day, August 31, 1864

cavalry west of Opelika, Alabama, had previously disabled this railroad so that only a single line, the Macon and Western Railroad, supplied Atlanta. The Macon and Western operated from Macon north to Atlanta, joining the now-interrupted Atlanta and West Point Railroad at East Point. While Maj. Gen. Henry Slocum, now commanding the Twentieth Corps, remained at the Chattahoochee River to protect the bridges and river crossings, Sherman ordered the remaining six corps to march southeast toward Jonesboro. Howard's Army of the Tennessee led the way, crossing the Flint River on August 30, digging in between it and the town of Jonesboro, only a mile to the east. By the next morning, Howard was well entrenched.[8]

Hood, informed by his remaining cavalry of the Federal deployments, dispatched both Lee's and Hardee's Corps to Jonesboro. The last of the troops arrived by midafternoon on August 31. The Rebels immediately attacked, but they had little chance of success against Howard's entrenched Union corps. Led by many new commanders from the corps to the company level, the Confederate troops performed poorly. The Federals quickly repulsed their attacks. Meanwhile, Hood had become concerned that the movement toward Jonesboro was only a feint. Without consulting Hardee, Hood ordered Lee to depart and march northward back to Atlanta, considerably reducing the Confederate force at Jonesboro. Hardee's situation was then desperate—he had to extend his already thin line to cover the withdrawal of Lee's Corps. Cheatham's Division, commanded by Brig. Gen. John C. Carter, manned the Confederate left. Bate's Division, under the command of Maj. Gen. John C. Brown, held the center, and Maj. Gen. Patrick Cleburne's division protected the right. Cleburne's Division bent back to the east, forming a salient, then passed near the Warren house and across the railroad.[9]

The next day, Sherman ordered three corps to attack Hardee's position. The assault began around 4 p.m. and lasted until dark. Logan's Fifteenth Corps attacked Hardee's line from the west, while Maj. Gen. Jefferson C. Davis's Fourteenth Corps provided the main assault from the northwest. At the same time, Maj. Gen. David Stanley's Fourth Corps moved south down the railroad. This overwhelming assault quickly broke through the Confederate line at the salient, capturing much of Brig. Gen. Daniel Govan's brigade, as well as the general himself. Union troops likewise overran the Orphan Brigade, commanded by Brig. Gen. Joseph Lewis. Hardee plugged this gap by rushing Vaughan's Brigade, now commanded by Col. Michael Magevney, into that position, holding off the Federals until dark. Had Sherman coordinated his attacks better, Hardee's Confederates might have easily been overrun and destroyed or captured. Meanwhile, elements of the Fourth Corps had arrived on the railroad near Rough and Ready and had begun to cut it.[10]

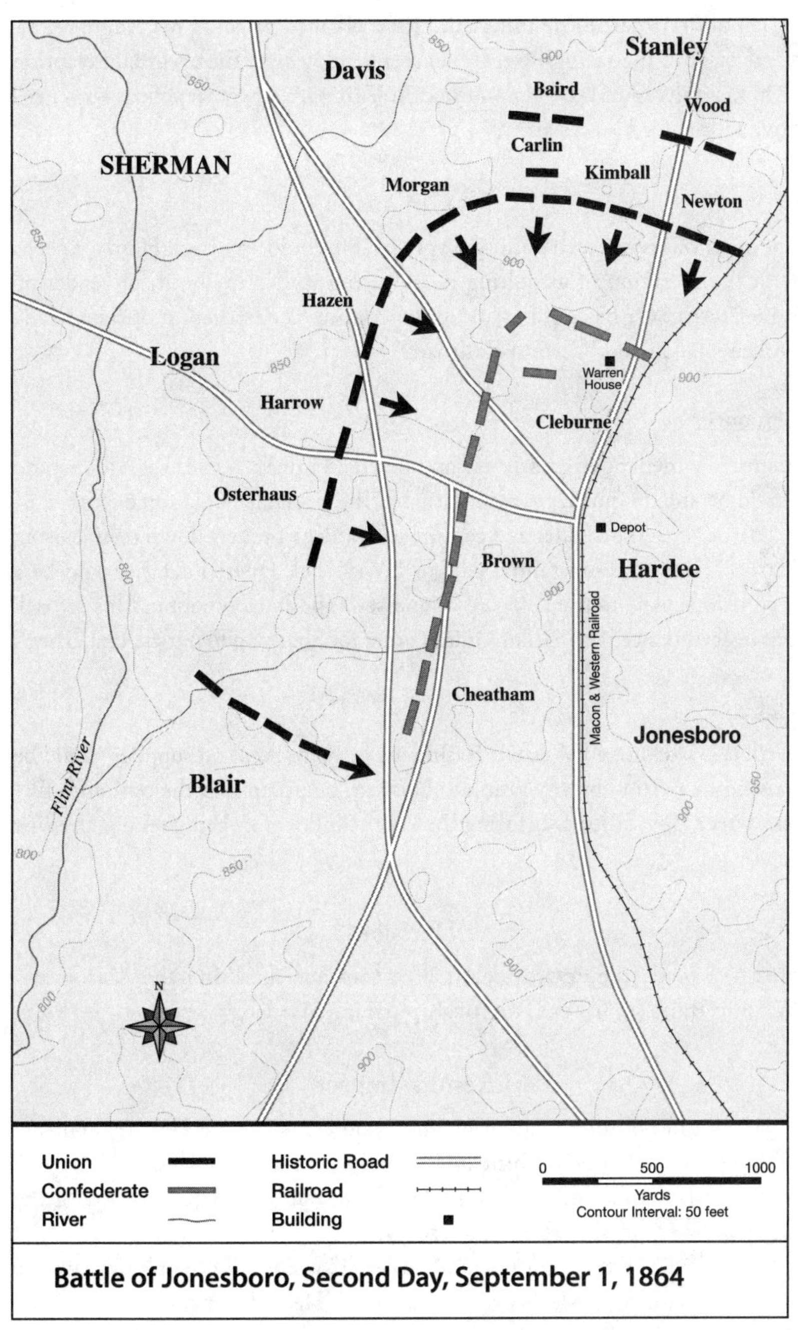

Battle of Jonesboro, Second Day, September 1, 1864

In all four battles he initiated, Hood planned to catch his Union opponents prior to their digging entrenchments. However, the eventual execution of his assaults found the Union forces at least partially entrenched, with negative results for Hood's army.[11]

Options

Sherman was now faced with two options: He could approach Hardee's corps with the intention of assaulting it, capturing it, destroying it, or rendering it ineffective. Or he could focus on the continued destruction of the already broken Macon and Western Railroad.[12]

Option 1

Sherman's men now greatly outnumbered Hardee's remaining troops and would be able to quickly surround them. The Federals could force either a final battle or the surrender and capture of Hardee's broken-down men. Losing Hardee's Corps, a substantial part of Hood's beleaguered army, would be a very serious blow to the Army of Tennessee's ability to function. This setback was in accordance with Grant's initial order for Sherman to pursue that army.[13]

Option 2

With the Macon and Western Railroad already broken, no supplies would be moving to Atlanta by any railroad. Even so, Sherman had the option to further wreck this railroad, ensuring the impossibility of its being rebuilt anytime soon.[14]

Decision

Sherman made the critical decision to continue wrecking the Macon and Western Railroad instead of actively pursuing Hardee.[15]

Results/Impact

Sherman did not follow up on his initial orders to pursue Hardee, and that evening the Confederates retreated unmolested six miles south to Lovejoy's Station. More miles of track were destroyed, but an isolated portion of the Confederate army was allowed to escape.[16]

Why did Sherman not pursue Hardee? Consider Sherman's own words: "I do not wish to waste lives by an assault." He did not possess the hard-charging, go-for-the-kill mentality of other combat generals such as Grant.[17]

Hood's army, reduced in numbers, was now less effective against Sherman or any Union army. Nonetheless, the soldiers were capable of some fighting,

Destroyed Confederate railroad. National Archives.

as demonstrated by Hood's later Tennessee Campaign at the Battle of Franklin on November 30, and the Battle of Nashville on December 15–16.[18]

Alternate Decision and Scenario

If Sherman had gone after Hardee, assuming a successful outcome, he could have destroyed or captured what was left of Hardee's Corps and crippled the Army of Tennessee. In doing so, Sherman would have somewhat complied with his original orders, and he might have virtually eliminated Hardee's Corps from further fighting. Sherman then could have returned to destroying more of the Macon and Western Railroad, satisfying both objectives.[19]

Sherman Ends the Pursuit of Hood, Captures Atlanta

Situation

Hood, finally realizing the railroads were lost, ordered the abandonment of Atlanta. On the morning of September 2, unbeknownst to Sherman, Mayor

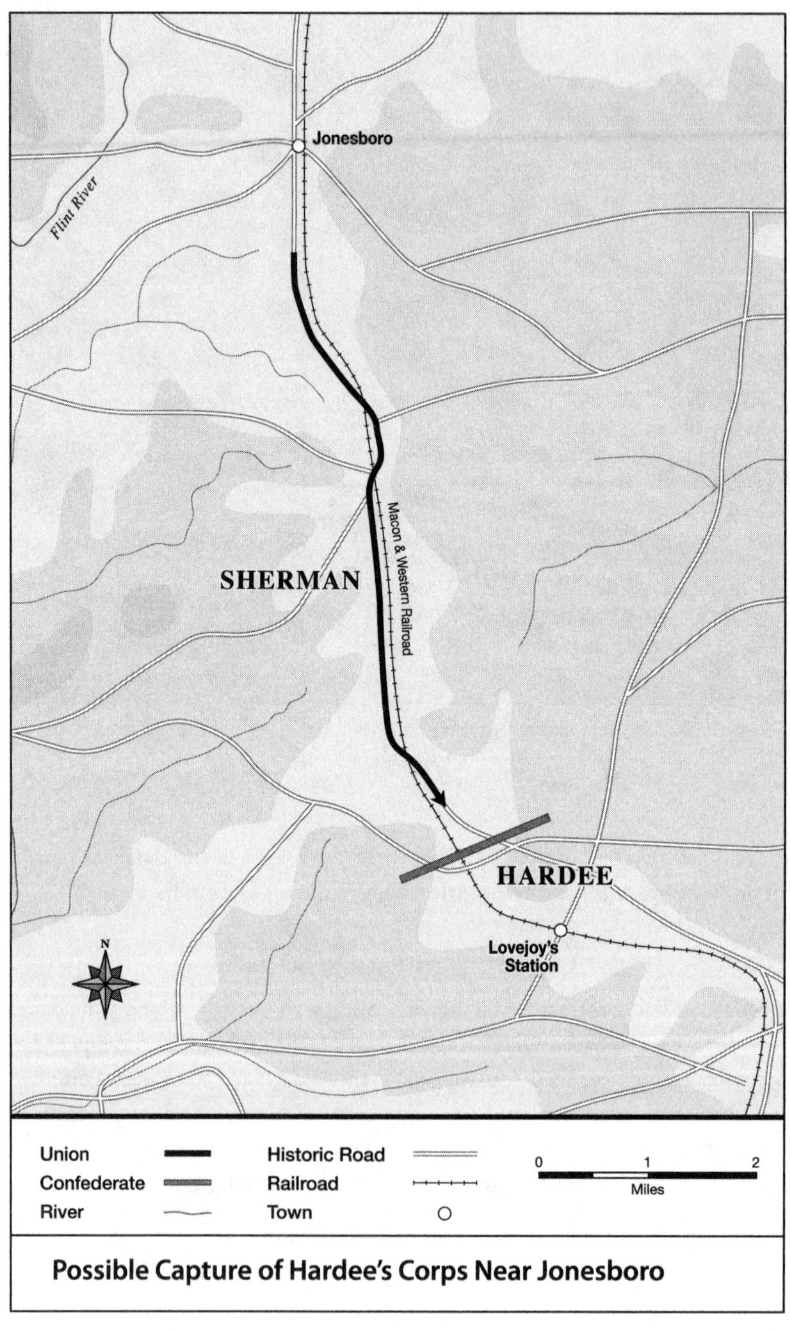

Possible Capture of Hardee's Corps Near Jonesboro

James Calhoun formally surrendered Atlanta to Brig. Gen. William T. Ward of the Twentieth Corps. The Twentieth was guarding the railroad bridge across the Chattahoochee River, and Ward was the first Union general officer the mayor encountered north of downtown. After hearing explosions the previous evening, when Hood had destroyed remaining military assets within Atlanta, Ward was leading a brigade south to observe conditions in the city.[20]

Options

Sherman was faced with two final options: he could pursue Hood and his Army of Tennessee, or he could rest and refit his armies in Atlanta.[21]

Option 1

Sherman could order the pursuit of Hood's army and attempt to do battle with it, capture part or all of it, and render it ineffective. However, this task would not be easy, as the Army of Tennessee had proven elusive. Hood could add to Sherman's woes by drawing him away from the railroad, and at the same time, friendly citizens and Rebel quartermasters could resupply Hood.[22]

Option 2

Sherman's other option was to enter Atlanta and rest and refit his men. After four months of constant marching and fighting, Sherman's soldiers were exhausted and in need of respite. Yet this option would allow Hood to escape to fight another day.[23]

Decision

Sherman made his final critical decision of the Atlanta Campaign when he ordered his men into Atlanta, allowing Hood to regroup and prepare to reengage.[24]

Results/Impact

The capture of Atlanta was an extremely positive event for President Lincoln, who would be reelected in November, and it also shed positive light on Grant and Sherman. However, Sherman faced some practical considerations. After four months of almost continual marching and fighting, his men were worn out. How much longer could he push them in pursuing Hood? Hood had the ability to retreat farther south, among Confederate supporters, and he could rely on a much shorter supply line. Therefore, Sherman realized the chase might become futile. Maintaining his railroad supply line all the way

The destroyed Atlanta car shed. *Photographic History*, Vol. III, 135.

to Atlanta appeared doable, but it would require continuous vigilance and defense from Confederate raids. Sherman needed to rest, refit, and resupply his armies before the next campaign began.[25]

Timing was a critical factor, as Sherman captured Atlanta two months before the Union presidential election, giving Northern voters enough time to realize that the end of the war was finally in sight. Sherman's continued pursuit of Hood's reduced army was essentially extraneous to the victory at Atlanta. Sherman had delivered to both Grant and Lincoln a significant prize and, more specifically, a strong display of Union dominance over the fading Confederate war effort.[26]

During this time, Sherman began devising the essence of the future March to the Sea, in which he marched away from his supply line. It would become Maj. Gen. George Thomas's responsibility to worry about Hood. Sherman ordered Thomas to guard the Union territory already seized. Thomas, along with the Fourth and Fourteenth Corps then marched to, and entrenched in Nashville, and prepared to counter Hood, should he advance in that direction.[27]

Supplying his large armies was a factor in Sherman's decision. Extending his already long supply line beyond Atlanta would have required even more men to protect it. Sherman realized that it was simply too impractical to lengthen the route even farther. Undoubtedly, concern over Forrest's or other Confederate forces' ability to launch raids and sever this line entered into his decision-making. Sherman's fears were proven correct shortly after the fall of Atlanta, as raids were conducted against the railroad north of the city. Although a failure, Hood's attack at Allatoona Pass on October 5, 1864, foreshadowed Sherman's concern over maintaining the railroad supply line.[28]

Alternate Decision and Scenario

Had Sherman continued pursuing Hood, he would have the opportunity to either destroy Hood's army in detail, or keep it from being resupplied with food, clothing, and ammunition. Yet Hood had remained elusive. He was unlikely to have been forced into a confrontation not of his own choosing. While Sherman's men were ready for a period of rest, had he been more aggressive, he might have at least tried to eliminate one of the two main Confederate armies. This accomplishment would have given the Union most of the Confederacy west of Virginia and the Carolinas. As noted, while the capture of Atlanta certainly provided more political capital to assist in President Lincoln's reelection, the elimination of a major Confederate army could only have furthered his cause and that of the Union.[29]

Other than a brief pursuit into North Georgia after the capture of Atlanta, had Sherman continued to pursue Hood's army, the elimination of, the severe reduction of, or the dispersal of the Army of Tennessee might have allowed Sherman to send extensive reinforcements to Grant in Virginia. This might have allowed Grant to break through Lee's Petersburg defenses and end the war in the fall of 1864, rather than continue into April of 1865. We will never know.[30]

Although beyond the scope of the Atlanta Campaign, Sherman's March to the Sea was certainly concocted as a methodology to eliminate his supply concerns and yet allow his troops to penetrate deeper into the heart of the Confederacy. This march ultimately proved to the Confederacy that it was unable to cope with this Union horde. The South's vulnerability to the movements of Union force was displayed for all to see. This was a severe blow to Confederate morale, if not the most severe one since the war had begun.[31]

CHAPTER 7

AFTERMATH AND CONCLUSIONS

The capture of Atlanta dealt a devastating blow to Confederate morale. Atlanta had already been stripped of most of its ability to provide necessary supplies to the rest of the Confederacy, and its loss as a railroad hub seriously impinged on the movement of supplies and troops throughout the South. The likelihood that the Confederacy could survive as a separate nation was now seriously in question: in fact, its end was only eight months away.

Gen. John B. Hood's horrific losses in his subsequent campaign against Nashville in late 1864 were diametrically opposed to Maj. Gen. William T. Sherman's triumphant March to the Sea. Lieut. Gen. Ulysses S. Grant accepted the surrender of Gen. Robert E. Lee's Army of Northern Virginia on April 9, 1865. Led once again by Gen. Joseph E. Johnston, the remnants of the Army of Tennessee, and other units, surrendered to Maj. Gen. William T. Sherman in North Carolina on April 26. Interestingly, Johnston surrendered more Confederate soldiers—some eighty-nine thousand, as his department included the Carolinas, Georgia, and Florida—than did Lee. Soon the small armies of Gen. Edmund Kirby Smith and Lieut. Gen. Richard Taylor also surrendered. The Civil War was over, and the Confederacy was no more.[1]

Ten of the critical decisions were tactical, four were personnel related, three were strategic, two were organizational, and one each was operational or logistical. Commanders at three different levels of authority made these twenty-one critical decisions. Six of the critical decisions were reached by the three men at the top of the chain of command, or the national level:

US president Abraham Lincoln, Confederate president Jefferson Davis, and General-in-Chief Ulysses S. Grant. President Lincoln made only one critical decision, and it concerned personnel. After establishing Grant as the general to coordinate the Union's military efforts, Lincoln allowed him to plan and conduct operations. Davis made three critical decisions; two involved selecting personnel, and one was organizational. Grant, as general-in-chief of the Union armies, made two critical decisions at the national level, one operational and one personnel related.

Sherman, as commander of the Military Division of the Mississippi and the overall commander of three separate armies in the field, made ten critical decisions at the departmental level. His choices ultimately gained him possession of Atlanta. Six were tactical, two were strategic, and one each were logistical and organizational. To some extent, most of Sherman's critical decisions involved supply, whether his or the Rebels, an often overlooked part of any campaign.

Gen. Robert E. Lee, who by the war's end was equivalent to Grant as general-in-chief of the Confederate armies, made no critical decisions concerning the Atlanta Campaign. He came closest to doing so in his marginal endorsement of Hood for army command. As army and department commander, before he was relieved of command, Johnston made three critical decisions, two tactical and one strategic. The rest of Johnston's decisions were reactions to Sherman's movements. Hood, who replaced Johnston, made only one critical decision, which was tactical.

Maj. Gen. James McPherson's tactical decision to retreat from Resaca was the only critical decision made at the Union army level of command.

Johnston's immediate subordinate commanders were corps commanders, none of whom made critical decisions. Had Johnston redirected Hood, Hood's failure to attack at Cassville could still have been rectified. Hood made one tactical critical decision when he ordered a flank attack on McPherson's army that, unfortunately for Hood and the Confederacy, failed. Had it been successful, the assault potentially might have altered the timetable in favor of the Confederacy.

In a review of the entire campaign, several events stand out. The Union's and Confederacy's appointments of army/department commanders prior to the Atlanta Campaign would strongly influence the results. An aggressive Sherman moving against a defensive-oriented Johnston boded ill for the Confederacy.

Sherman built up and maintained a huge supply system and supply line. He established repair crews equipped with prefabricated portions of railroad bridges to quickly repair ones that had been damaged or destroyed. Sherman's

Memoirs quotes Rebel soldiers who believed these repair crews even carried their own prebuilt tunnels! Early and continuous focus on his entire supply situation allowed Sherman to successfully carry out his campaign.[2]

The opponents' disparity in manpower rendered the outcome of the campaign predictable. The Union simply had more than enough men to eventually overwhelm the Confederate Army of Tennessee. For the most part, Sherman skillfully deployed his men, and by means of the flanking maneuver, he continually forced Johnston to retreat. Johnston seemed generally unwilling to attack Sherman as he waited for the Union general to expose a part of his immense force. Other than at Cassville, this opportunity never occurred.[3]

The appointment of Lieut. Gen. John Bell Hood, temporarily promoted to general, changed the Army of Tennessee's strategy from defensive to offensive. Though intended to benefit the Rebels, this change worked to the advantage of the Union armies, as they could absorb the loss of soldiers much more readily than could the Army of Tennessee. It is very unlikely that any Confederate general placed in the same situation could have held back Sherman. But it would have been possible to commit fewer men to battle with the resulting losses. To Hood's credit, he devised battle plans for attempting to catch Sherman's men before they entrenched and while they were vulnerable to assault. Unfortunately, these plans did not result in the desired victories. Hood's loss of irreplaceable Confederate officers and men doomed the Army of Tennessee and the Confederacy.[4]

According to Grant, Sherman's initial objective was the Army of Tennessee. As he conquered more territory and forced Johnston back, Sherman made Atlanta his objective, especially after Grant gave him the independence to do so. After Hood replaced Johnston, Sherman remained focused on the capture of Atlanta. Some scholarship tends to downplay the necessity of the accomplishment, but it was decisive enough to have a hand in Lincoln's reelection and foreshadowed the demise of the Confederacy. While this resolution to the Atlanta Campaign may not have been the best one, it was good enough. Had Sherman strictly sought the defeat or destruction of the Army of Tennessee and accomplished that goal, Atlanta (and other important cities) would then have been his for the taking. The downside to Sherman's occupying Atlanta to rest and refit his men was that the Rebel Army of Tennessee, though reduced in size, was able to fight another day. Had it been eliminated as an effective force, Sherman would have been able to send reinforcements to Grant at Petersburg. This support might have ended the war in the fall of 1864, saving the lives of thousands of Union and Confederate soldiers.[5]

Another way to view these critical decisions is to examine how many proved successful in the campaign, and how many eventually proved unsuccessful. Without specifically reviewing each one, some choices stand out. Interestingly, none of the battle critical decisions (or, for that matter, any of the other battles) seemed to have an overall effect on the outcome of the Atlanta Campaign. However, had the results of these battles been successful, they could well have had an effect on the campaign's final outcome. Johnston's failure to attack at Cassville, Sherman's assault at Kennesaw Mountain, and Hood's flank attack against McPherson's army might have either sped up or slowed down the campaign's timetable, had their objectives been met. Likewise, Sherman's failure at Snake Creek Gap resulted in a botched chance to defeat Johnston early in the campaign. Sherman's decision to leave the railroad before Allatoona Pass quickly proved unacceptable, although he did manage to avoid a confrontation there. Most other critical decisions seemed to bring at least partially positive results.

Not having served with Sherman from May to September 2, 1864, we cannot know how tired and worn out his men were. It is easy to assume that they would have continued to advance after Hood. Likewise, Hood's men were undoubtedly just as weary, if not even more so, given the reduced Confederate supply system. It might not have been so easy to destroy the Army of Tennessee or render it ineffective in combat. Neither of these outcomes would have been a forgone conclusion. Hood's smaller army was more mobile. In leaving the railroad while chasing after Hood, Sherman would have been forced to establish an even longer supply line. He decided against this plan, realizing its potential supply problems and the likelihood that Hood could escape. This mindset led Sherman to formulate his March to the Sea, whereby he cut his men off from any supply line and lived off the spoils of the land as he marched to Savannah. He designated Thomas to deal with Hood, should Hood decide to head north toward Nashville and the Ohio River, which the Confederate general did.[6]

Of all the critical decisions discussed and evaluated above, two stand out. The first was McPherson's failure to capture Resaca and sever the Western and Atlantic Railroad there. Had this turning maneuver been carried out successfully, the war might have ended sooner—a tantalizing thought. With the Army of Tennessee ineffectual at Resaca, Sherman could have easily marched to and captured Atlanta. He then could have moved some of his armies to reinforce Grant in Virginia, where they could have assisted in breaking the siege around Petersburg sooner and obtaining Lee's surrender. Like many historians, the author is singularly concerned by this failure by McPherson and Sherman.

Of equal consideration was Davis's critical decision to appoint Hood as Johnston's replacement to command the Army of Tennessee. Hood's shifting over to offensive operations resulted in Confederate losses and a much reduced Army of Tennessee defending Atlanta. This loss of effectiveness further increased with Hood's casualties at the Battles of Franklin and Nashville during his botched Tennessee Campaign in late 1864. Of course, had Sherman/McPherson disabled the railroad at Resaca and defeated the Army of Tennessee there, Hood probably would never have had the opportunity to be placed in command and take his subsequent actions.

The Atlanta Campaign was a critical episode of the American Civil War that provides us with important insight into the fighting and its conclusion. While authors and historians vie to select the actual turning point of the Civil War, the Atlanta Campaign certainly was a precursor to the end of the Confederacy. With the capture of Atlanta, Confederate soldiers and civilians had to realize that their fight for independence was unlikely to succeed. Men such as Maj. Gen. Patrick Cleburne (killed at the Battle of Franklin) attempted to further the Rebel cause by recommending the freeing of male slaves to fight on the Confederate side. These efforts were ignored, and slaves instead fled to the Union army—almost 200,000 of them eventually enlisted. The Confederacy simply had run out of soldiers to maintain its independence. As Rebel infrastructure continued to fail, especially in regard to the destruction of railroads and the virtual elimination of blockade-runners, the South was incapable of sustaining the fight much longer. Sherman and his conduct of the Atlanta Campaign contributed immensely to the Confederacy's impending defeat in the Civil War.[7]

After resting and refitting his men, and sending the ill and unfit ones back north, Sherman destroyed anything of military value within Atlanta. He then departed with some sixty thousand troops in two wings and began his March to the Sea. Sherman's marching essentially unimpeded through Georgia to Savannah demonstrated to the Confederacy its inability to confront a Union army deep within its territory. Reaching Georgia's east coast, Sherman then convinced Grant to allow his force to continue the march north through the Carolinas and join Grant and his men at Petersburg. However, before Sherman's force arrived, Grant finally outflanked and overcame Lee's entrenched army around Petersburg, forcing Lee to retreat. Shortly thereafter, Grant finally surrounded Lee near Appomattox Court House, west of Richmond. Lee had no reasonable choice but to surrender, and he did so formally on April 9, 1865. His capitulation effectively allowed Johnston and his cobbled-together force, which had been trying to slow Sherman's advance northward, to surrender as well. For all practical purposes, the Civil War had ended.

In conclusion, few things are more helpful in examining critical decisions than traveling to the sites where those decisions were made. These journeys are similar to walking a battlefield; both practices give those interested in a battle or campaign a clearer picture of the situation. To assist the student of the Atlanta Campaign, appendix I presents a brief driving tour guide of the sites where some of the critical decisions were made, along with commentary by some of those involved in the decision-making and resulting actions thereabouts. Please realize that this is not a tour of the battlefields per se, but of sites related to the campaign's critical decisions.

APPENDIX I

DRIVING TOUR OF THE CRITICAL DECISIONS OF THE ATLANTA CAMPAIGN

There is great value in visiting a site to better visualize the terrain that faced the Atlanta Campaign's decision-makers. "Boots on the ground" will enhance readers' understanding as to both the reasons for these decisions and their outcomes. Because of the scope of the Atlanta Campaign, any tour of the various sites requires many miles of driving. It is roughly 135 miles from Missionary Ridge in Chattanooga to Jonesboro if one drives only on I-75. This distance does not include leaving the interstate to visit any stops. Visiting these many locations will add considerable time and mileage to the tour, so plan accordingly.

As this tour of the campaign is an adjunct to a discussion of the critical decisions, this guide will direct you to some of the sites that you can still see today. What follows is not a complete tour of the Atlanta Campaign—guidebooks for this purpose have already been published. Instead, this tour guide leads the reader to some of the sites where commanders made critical decisions. However, many of these choices were reached away from northern Georgia or away from the battlefields. For instance, Lincoln appointed Maj. Gen. Ulysses S. Grant to overall command while in Washington, DC, and Jefferson Davis appointed Gen. Joseph E. Johnston to command while in Richmond, Virginia. It would be impractical to include these cities in this tour, so areas only immediately accessible from I-75 are included instead.

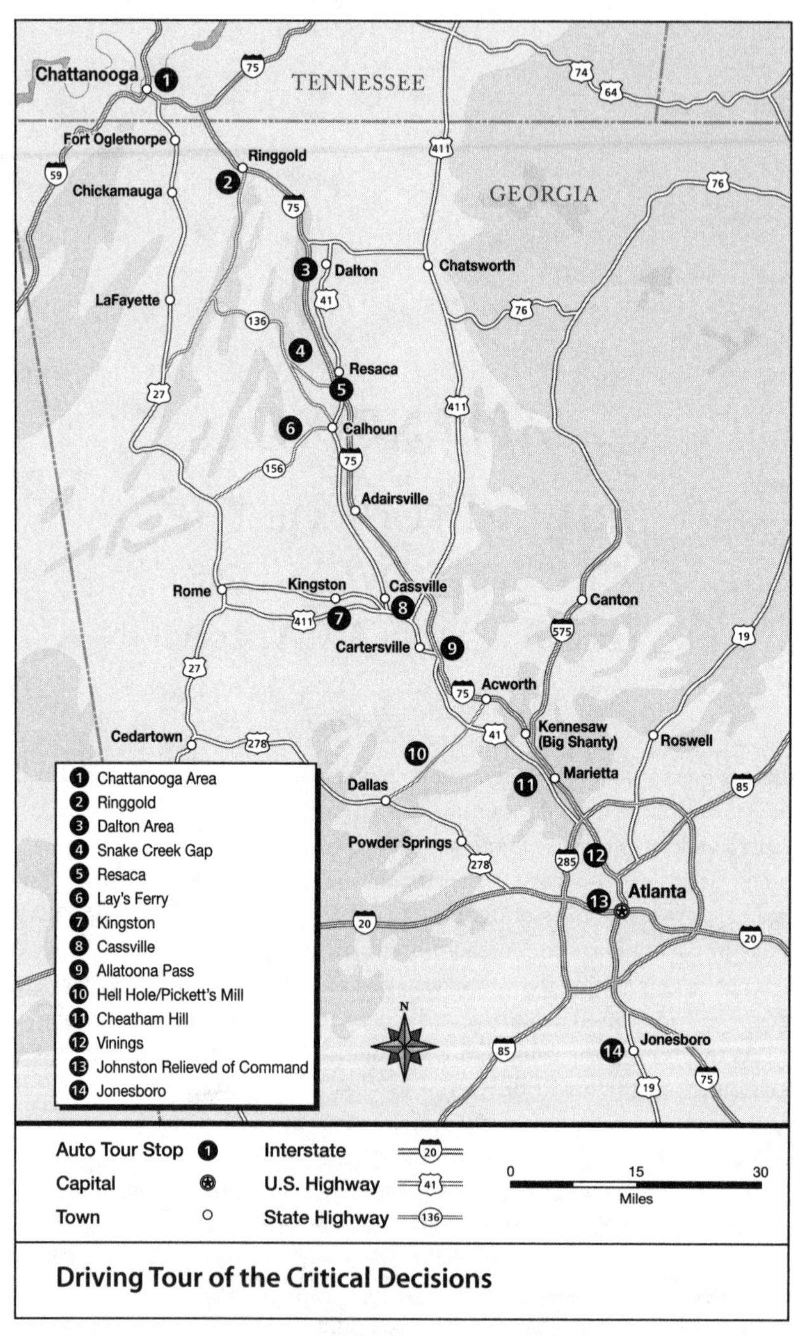

Driving Tour of the Critical Decisions

Therefore, we will briefly review the first five critical decisions made elsewhere at the stop at Ringgold. You can choose to visit whichever areas are of particular interest. The various areas are generally accessible from I-75, and the locations of the stops within each area are provided here. Also provided are directions back to I-75 or to the next tour stop(s) once you complete your visit to a site. With the exception of Stop 7 at Kingston, the tour is in chronological order. Starting in Chattanooga, the excursion will proceed south along I-75. You may join and depart the tour as you wish.

Please remember that your safety is paramount. Always park off of roads and highways so that you and your guests will not be struck by or obstruct traffic. Use common sense in respecting both government and private property. Do not read while driving; either pull over and stop to read, or have a passenger read. We don't need any more casualties along the campaign trail!

With these points in mind, take the opportunity to visualize what the commanders and soldiers saw in 1864. Making this effort will give you a much better understanding of the campaign. A brief review of what transpired at each stop is provided to help you relate the stop to the appropriate critical decision. Navigational instructions are given prior to the historical review at each stop. In most instances, mileages are provided between turns and stops. These distances are approximate, and vehicle odometers vary. It is best to be on the lookout for the next turn or stop before reaching the mileage indicated. Please reference the driving tour map for each stop.

Stop 1: Chattanooga Area (Optional)

As you begin the tour of the Atlanta Campaign, you may visit the Chickamauga and Chattanooga National Military Park if you have the time and interest. Here, you can learn about or review the climactic Battle of Chickamauga, which resulted in the only real victory for the Confederate Army of Tennessee. This battle also resulted in the Confederates' siege of Chattanooga. Likewise, you can study or review the actions of the Battle of Chattanooga (or Missionary Ridge), which resulted in the breakout of the Union force under siege and set the stage for the upcoming Atlanta Campaign. Time permitting, following the National Park Service tour of the Chickamauga Battlefield will enhance your appreciation of the Confederate victory. Following National Park Service directions, a visit to the crest of Missionary Ridge is also particularly insightful. This tour stop vividly illustrates the steep terrain the Union regiments had to climb, and the resulting breakout. For more information and visitor center hours of operation go to www.nps.gov/chch.

Return to your vehicle and drive to Stop 2.

From I-75 southbound, take Exit 348 north on GA 151 into Ringgold, then drive east about 0.6 mile to the *T* intersection, which is Nashville Street/US 41. (If touring from the south, take the same I-75 exit north to begin each tour). Turn right (southeast) onto Nashville Street/US 41, and proceed 0.9 mile to just before the railroad underpass. Turn left (northeast) into the depot parking lot. Leave your vehicle, walk onto the pedestrian bridge over US 41, and face south. You will have a good view of Ringgold Gap, which is a short distance beyond the depot.

Stop 2: Ringgold

Critical Decisions: (1) Davis Appoints Johnston to Command the Army of Tennessee, (2) Lincoln Appoints Grant General-In-Chief of All Union Armies, (3) Grant Attaches Himself to the Army of the Potomac as an Advisor, (4) Grant Appoints Sherman to Command in the West, (5) Sherman Strengthens and Improves His Railroad Supply Line

After the defeat at Missionary Ridge on November 25, 1863, the Army of Tennessee retreated southeast. This retreat continued all night, as the Confederates fell back through Ringgold, Georgia.

The old Western and Atlantic depot features damage from artillery fire during the engagement at Ringgold Gap. Built in 1849, this structure was in use for many years. Union and Confederate soldiers used the depot prior to the Atlanta Campaign, and it is one of few buildings that survived the war.

Ringgold Gap, directly in front of you, is where Cleburne's Division held back the Union forces pursuing the Army of Tennessee after its stunning defeat on Missionary Ridge. For his defense of that army here at Ringgold Gap, Cleburne received the thanks of the Confederate Congress. The Army of Tennessee wintered at Dalton, and the Union armies prepared for the 1864 campaign while quartered in the Chattanooga-Ringgold area.

Since the first five critical decisions of the Atlanta Campaign were made in locations outside of this tour, a brief review of these decisions follows. On December 16, 1863, President Jefferson Davis appointed Gen. Joseph E. Johnston commander of the Army of Tennessee. This appointment was Critical Decision 1, and it resulted in Johnston's defensive policy implemented from the beginning of the campaign and the resultant surrendering of northern Georgia to the Union. While this choice resulted in fewer casualties for the Army of Tennessee, it ultimately cost Johnston his command.

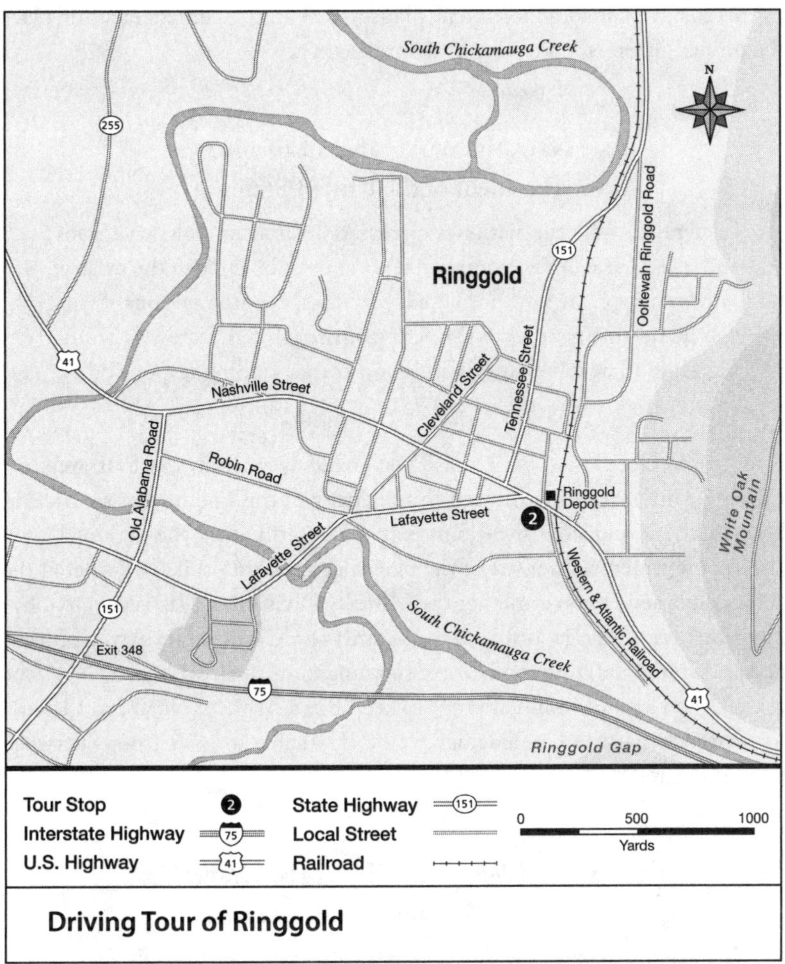

Driving Tour of Ringgold

Narrative of Gen. Joseph E. Johnston, CSA, Commanding Department and Army of Tennessee

I can see no other mode of taking the offensive here, than to beat the enemy when he advances, and then move forward.[1]

Critical Decision 2 of the campaign was President Lincoln's appointment of Maj. Gen. Ulysses S. Grant to the newly restored rank of lieutenant general, which made him the undisputed general-in-chief of the Union armies.

In this role, Grant could formulate plans to defeat the Confederacy and place the proper generals in position to assure victory.

Narrative of Abraham Lincoln, President of the United States

General Grant, the nation's appreciation of what you have done, and its reliance upon you for what remains to be done in the existing great struggle, are now presented, with this commission constituting you lieutenant-general in the Army of the United States. With this high honor, devolves upon you, also a corresponding responsibility.[2]

Critical Decision 3, which also was made away from the tour area, involved Grant's attaching himself to the Army of the Potomac as an advisor. He quickly developed a five-point plan for coordinating the various Union armies' movements. The part of the plan that applies to this tour ordered the three combined Union armies of the Military Division of Mississippi to move into northern Georgia and advance against the Confederate Army of Tennessee. Grant would not be in direct command of these western troops. The other Union armies would attempt to keep Lee's Army of Northern Virginia so occupied that the Confederacy would be unable to shift troops between them if desired.

Narrative of Lieut. Gen. Ulysses S. Grant, USA, General-in-Chief, Union Armies

My general plan now was to concentrate all the force possible against the Confederate armies in the field. There were but two such, as we have seen, east of the Mississippi River and facing north. The Army of Northern Virginia, General Robert E. Lee commanding, was on the south bank of the Rapidan, confronting the Army of the Potomac; the second, under General Joseph E. Johnston, was at Dalton, Georgia, opposed to Sherman who was still at Chattanooga.[3]

Grant also made Critical Decision 4 of the Atlanta Campaign, placing Maj. Gen. William T. Sherman in command of the Military Division of the Mississippi. Grant trusted Sherman and deemed him more capable than other generals who had more seniority.

Narrative of Lieut. Gen. Ulysses S. Grant, USA, General-in-Chief, Union Armies

You [Sherman] I propose to move against Johnston's army, to break it up, and to get into the interior of the enemy's country as far as you can, inflicting all the damage you can against their resources.[4]

Sherman made Critical Decision 5, adequately preparing his supply line and especially concentrating on that part of the Western and Atlantic Railroad as he advanced. It was critical that Sherman be able to continuously supply his more than one hundred thousand men and his forty-five thousand horses and mules. This preparation was a giant undertaking.

Narrative of Maj. Gen. William T. Sherman, USA, Commanding Military Division of the Mississippi

The problem then was to deliver at Chattanooga and beyond one hundred and thirty car-loads daily, leaving the beef-cattle to be driven on the hoof, and all the troops in excess of the usual train guards to march by the ordinary roads.[5]

The Army of Tennessee wintered at Dalton, while the Union armies prepared for the 1864 campaign while quartered in the Chattanooga-Ringgold area.

Return to your vehicle for the drive to Stop 3.

Leaving the parking lot, turn left (south), and continue to follow US 41 south out of Ringgold approximately 3.2 miles to the junction with I-75. Enter I-75 South, and continue south to Exit 336, exiting onto the intersection with Chattanooga Road/US 41 North (do not drive into Dalton). Turn left (northwest) on Chattanooga Road/US 41, and drive approximately 0.8 mile to the Georgia State Patrol Headquarters building on the left. Carefully turn left into the parking lot in front of the building where one of the "pocket parks" and information signs are located. Leave your vehicle, face northeast across Chattanooga Road, and look up at Rocky Face Ridge.

Stop 3: Dalton Area

Critical Decisions: (6) Johnston Decides to Defend the Dalton Area from Attack, (7) Davis Orders Reinforcements to Johnston, (8) Sherman Orders McPherson to Sever the Railroad at Resaca

After you exited I-75, you again passed through Mill Creek Gap, also called Buzzard Roost. The terrain of Rocky Face Ridge, which you are now observing, reminds us of the old adage "One picture is worth a thousand words." You can observe why Maj. Gen. William T. Sherman did not plan to directly assault the Confederate position here, resulting in Critical Decision 8 to try to sever Johnston's supply line at Resaca.

With Critical Decision 6 of this campaign, Johnston determined to defend the town of Dalton. The Army of Tennessee had fallen back to Dalton after being defeated at Missionary Ridge. When Federal pursuit was stopped at Ringgold, the army encamped at Dalton during the winter of 1863–64. After Johnston assumed command of the Army of Tennessee, he ordered defensive works built around Dalton, utilizing the natural fortifications provided by Rocky Face Ridge. He did not like the Dalton defensive position. However, Johnston realized that retreating to a better location would not be a good political move. Leaders, soldiers, and citizens were all likely to see the retreat as a failure to defend northern Georgia, and Confederate morale would be dealt a mighty blow.

Narrative of Gen. Joseph E. Johnston, CSA, Commanding Department and Army of Tennessee

The position at Dalton had little to recommend it as a defensive one. It had neither intrinsic strength nor strategic advantage. It neither fully covered its own communications, nor threatened those of the enemy. The railroad from Atlanta to Chattanooga [Western and Atlantic Railroad] passes through Rocky-Faced [*sic*] Ridge by Mill-Creek Gap, three miles and a half beyond Dalton, but very obliquely, the course of the road being about thirty degrees west of north. As it [the Ridge] terminates but three miles north of the gap, it offers little obstacle to the advance of a superior force from Ringgold to Dalton. Between Mill-Creek and Snake-Creek Gaps, this ridge protects the road to Atlanta on the west, but at the same time covers any direct approach from Chattanooga to Resaca or Calhoun—points on the

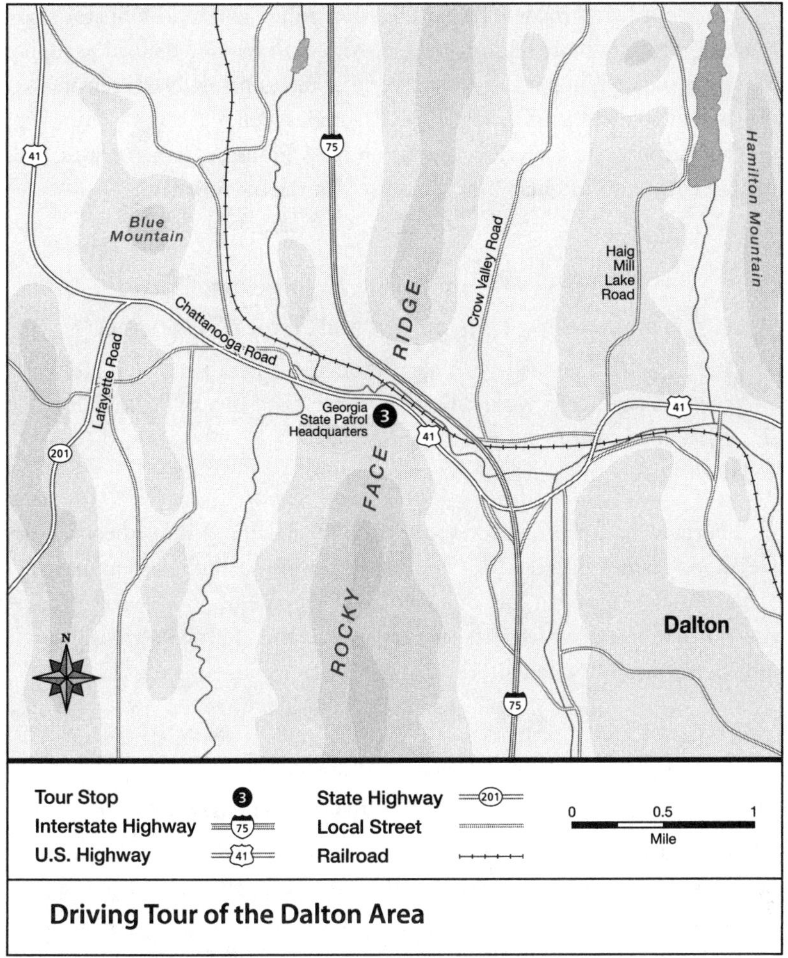

Driving Tour of the Dalton Area

route from Dalton to Atlanta—or flank movement in that direction, by an army in front of Mill-Creek Gap. These considerations would have induced me to draw the troops back to the vicinity of Calhoun, to free our left flank from exposure, but for the earnestness with which the President and Secretary of War, in their letters of instructions, wrote of early assumption of offensive operations and apprehension of the bad effects of a retrograde movement upon the spirit of the Southern people.[6]

President Davis made Critical Decision 7 in response to Johnston's continued appeals for more reinforcements. Although seldom inclined to support Johnston, with whom he had a poor working relationship, Davis relented and dispatched soldiers from Lieut. Gen. Leonidas Polk's Army of Mississippi for this purpose. As a previous quotation from Johnston demonstrates, these reinforcements would help him immensely in the coming days:

Narrative of Gen. Joseph E. Johnston, CSA, Commanding Department and Army of Tennessee

I see no other mode of taking the offensive here than to beat the enemy as he advances, and then move forward. But, to make victory possible, the army must be strengthened.[7]

Sherman had planned for some time to make and implement Critical Decision 8, which ordered McPherson's Army of the Tennessee to march via Snake Creek Gap to cut Johnston's railroad supply line at or near Resaca. As you can see, Sherman knew it was not worth the effort to seriously assault Johnston's entrenchments here.

Narrative of Maj. Gen. William T. Sherman, USA, Commanding Military Division of the Mississippi

From Tunnel Hill I could look into the gorge by which the railroad passed through a straight and well-defined range of mountains, presenting sharp palisade faces, and known as "Rocky Face." The gorge itself was called the "Buzzard Roost" [now Mill Creek Gap]. We could plainly see the enemy in this gorge and behind it, and Mill Creek which formed the gorge, flowing towards Dalton, had been dammed up, making a sort of irregular lake, filling the road, thereby obstructing it, and the enemy's batteries crowned the cliffs on either side. The position was very strong, and I knew that such a general as was my antagonist (Jos. Johnston) who had been there six months, had fortified it to the maximum. Therefore I had no intention to attack the position seriously in front, but depended on McPherson to capture and hold the railroad to its rear, which would force Johnston

> to detach largely against him, or rather, as I expected, to evacuate his position at Dalton altogether.[8]

As a result, the campaign began with Sherman's assaulting Johnston's works and being rebuffed, although Sherman had no intention of seriously attempting to carry these works. The Union general had another plan in mind.

Return to your vehicle and drive to Stop 4.

Carefully turn left (northwest) back onto Chattanooga Road/US 41 North (during busy traffic, turn right, and find a convenient location to turn around). Drive about 1.0 mile to the intersection with GA 201 (LaFayette Highway) on the left. Turn left (southwest) onto GA 201, and continue southwest on GA 201 about 11.3 miles to the small town of Villanow. Pull over and park just prior to the intersection with GA 136, and remain in your vehicle. This is a brief, intermediate pause, to enlighten you as you drive to Stop 4.

At his headquarters in Chattanooga prior to the campaign, Sherman had made Critical Decision 8 to divert Johnston's attention via a series of minor assaults against Rocky Face Ridge. Sherman had also sent Maj. Gen. James B. McPherson's Army of the Tennessee via Villanow through Snake Creek Gap to cut Johnston's line of supply at Resaca. Maj. Gen. George Thomas originally proposed this plan, and Sherman modified it to use McPherson's army.

From Villanow you are going to follow McPherson's line of march that began at LaFayette. He and his army marched through Villanow, which is directly in front of you, and continued through Snake Creek Gap. It will quickly become obvious how marvelous this approach to Resaca and Johnston's all-important railroad line of supply was. After Sherman made Critical Decision 8, this march was the result.

At Villanow turn left (southeast) onto GA 136, and follow it for 8.0 miles. Just prior to the intersection with GA Conn 136, look to your left (east), carefully turn left, and park at the historical marker describing Snake Creek Gap. Leave your vehicle, walk to and read the marker, and observe the terrain around this gap.

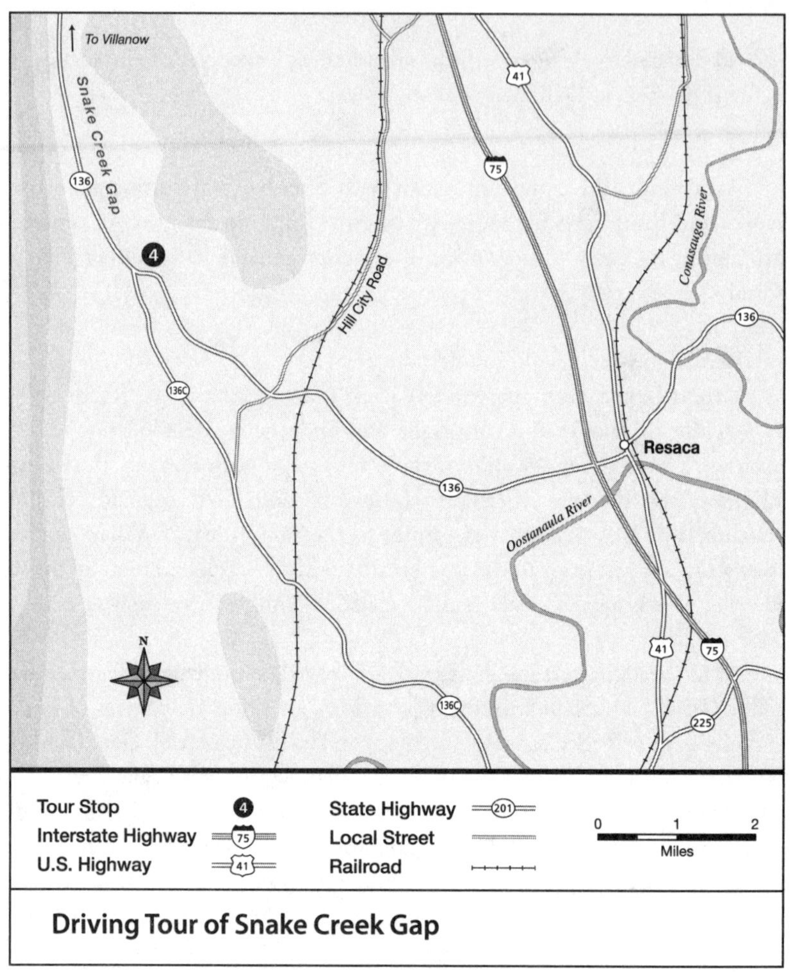

Driving Tour of Snake Creek Gap

Stop 4: Snake Creek Gap

Critical Decisions: (8) Sherman Orders McPherson to Sever the Railroad at Resaca, (9) Sherman Fails to Support McPherson's Turning Movement

Snake Creek Gap provided an excellent route for Sherman to make a turning maneuver by marching through it and continuing to the small town of Resaca, located on the Western and Atlantic Railroad. If Sherman could sever Johnston's only real supply line there, the Western and Atlantic Railroad, he would have an excellent chance of forcing Johnston to fight for his army's existence. For whatever reason, the Confederate cavalry did a poor job of scouting this area. Johnston believed that a Union movement here would be toward Rome, not Resaca, which is just what Sherman had hoped for. On Sunday, May 8, the leading units of McPherson's Army of the Tennessee reached the gap, and the rest of his army eventually followed. It was only about a half-dozen miles from the gap to Resaca. So far, Sherman's plan was working.

Narrative of Maj. Gen. William T. Sherman, USA, Commanding Military Division of the Mississippi

Therefore I had no intention to attack the position seriously in front [Rocky Face Ridge], but depended on McPherson to capture and hold the railroad to its rear, which would force Johnston to detach largely against him, or rather, as I expected, to evacuate his position at Dalton altogether.[9]

Return to your vehicle to drive to Stop 5.

This stop has three positions: 5A, 5B, and 5C. Carefully reenter GA 136, and immediately turn left (east). Do NOT go south on GA Conn 136. Remain on GA 136 for about 5.7 miles toward Resaca—you are driving through Snake Creek Gap. Watch for Pine Road. About 0.1 mile (east) past the intersection with Pine Road, turn left (north) onto Fain Brown Road, and park near the interpretive signs on the left (Position 5A). Carefully walk to and read the interpretive signs.

Stop 5: Resaca

Critical Decisions: (9) Sherman Fails to Support McPherson's Turning Movement, (10) McPherson Fails to Capture Resaca

From this location, McPherson's troops continued east toward Resaca until some Georgia militia and the men of Cantey's Brigade fired on them. Near here, McPherson made Critical Decision 9 to withdraw, as he was unsure of his opponents' strength. Had Sherman reinforced McPherson and/or accompanied him on this movement, the outcome might have turned much more to the Union's favor.

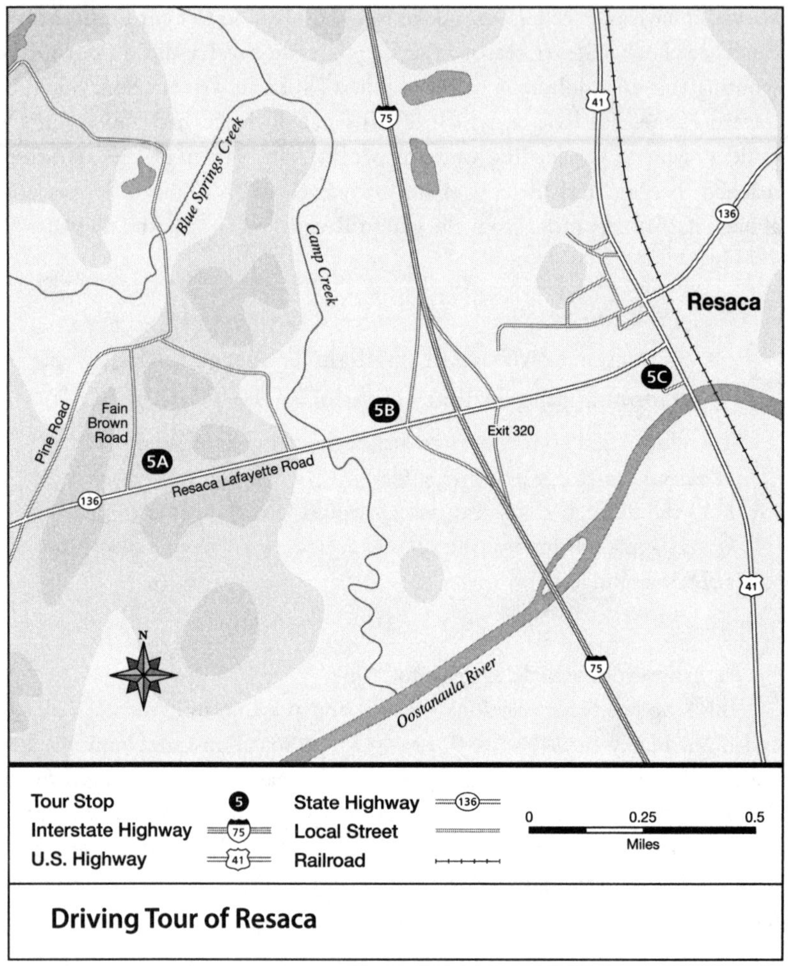

Driving Tour of Resaca

Report of Maj. Gen. James B. McPherson, USA, Commanding Army of the Tennessee, Military Division of the Mississippi

The enemy have a strong position at Resaca naturally, and, as far as we could see, have it pretty well fortified. They displayed considerable force, and opened on us with artillery. After skirmishing till nearly dark, and finding that I could not succeed in cutting the railroad before dark, or getting to it, I decided to withdraw the command and take a position for the night between Sugar Valley and the entrance to the gap for the following reasons: First. Between this point and Resaca there are a half dozen good roads leading north toward Dalton down which a column could march, making our advanced position a very exposed one. Second. General Dodge's men are all out of provisions, and some regiments have had nothing today. . . . If I could have had a division of cavalry I could have broken the railroad at some point.[10]

The decision not to follow through and sever the railroad here was truly a critical one. Had McPherson sent more units on the attack, he would have been able to reach and sever the railroad at Resaca. In turn, this accomplishment would have significantly affected this campaign. When he met McPherson several days later, the first thing Sherman said was, "Mac, you have lost the opportunity of a lifetime!"

Report of Maj. Gen. Patrick Cleburne, CSA, Commanding Cleburne's Division, Hardee's Corps, Army of Tennessee

How this gap which opened upon our rear and line of communications was neglected I cannot imagine. General Mackall, Johnston's Chief-of-Staff, told me it was the result of a flagrant disobedience of orders, by whom he did not say. Certainly the commanding general never could have failed to appreciate its importance. Its loss exposed us at the outset of the campaign to a terrible danger and . . . forced us to retreat from a position where we might have detained the enemy for months.[11]

Return to GA 136. Turn left (east), and proceed about 0.5 mile to a point just short of I-75. Pull over at the entrance to the Resaca Battlefield on the left (north), and park (Position 5B). Leave your vehicle, and face north at the battlefield proper.

At this location, Sherman maintained two of his options: holding Johnston in position and keeping him there with some assaults while waiting for Sweeney's outflanking maneuver via Lay's Ferry. (If interested in visiting, drive into the battlefield if it is open, or to learn when the battlefield is open for visitors, go to www.resacabattlefield.com.)

Turn around, face south, and view the hill just south of GA 136. This is Bald Hill.

Originally defended by the Confederates, Bald Hill was captured by McPherson's men on May 14.

Report of Maj. Gen. John Logan, USA, Commanding Fifteenth Corps, Army of the Tennessee

This position, if in our possession, would bring us within three-eighths of a mile of the enemy's nearest fort, and within half a mile of the railroad bridge, thus practically cutting the railroad. To gain this position had been the work intended for the next day, and a number of bridges were to have been thrown over Camp Creek on the night of the 14th instant to facilitate the passage of troops, but the continuous artillery and musketry fire on the left, and the nescessity for us to make a further diversion, precipitated the movement, and at 5:30 p.m. of the 14th the assaulting column crossed Camp Creek as best they could, some over the bridge, others on logs, and others wading, with their arms and equipments held over their heads. The assaulting force consisted of Brig. Gen. Charles R. Woods brigade, of the First Division; the Third Missouri lnfantry, of the Third Brigade, being substituted for the Twenty-sixth Iowa Infantry, which, being engaged as skirmishers, was un-available, on the left, and Brig. Gen. Giles A. Smith's brigade, of the Second Division, on the right. Both brigades were formed in double lines, and in front and on time left of Woods brigade the Twelfth Missouri Infantry, disposed as skirmishers, accompanied the assaulting columns. The average distance to the objective point was about one-third of a mile, over a marshy bottom, nearly clear of standing timber, but full of fallen tree trunks and thickets, and intersected with miry sloughs. At ten minutes before 6 p.m. the advance sounded, and the lines of gallant men started at the double, quick over the difficult ground, followed by the cheers of their fellow soldiers on the Camp Creek hills, and met by a storm of lead and iron from the enemy. The rebel infantry poured in from the hills in front a close, destructive, and well-directed fire. The artillery from their forts opened in one continuous roar. The direction of most of their artillery fire was at first diagonally across the lines, the angle growing less as the storming column advanced, until it nearly enfiladed

> them. Their practice was excellent, the bursting of shells directly over the devoted lines seemed continuous, but neither thicket, nor slough, nor shot, nor shell, distracted for a moment the attention of the stormers from their objective point. Lines temporarily disarranged were reorganized without slackening the speed, until, without firing a shot, they, at the point of the bayonet, planted their colors on the summits of the conquered hills. Under the soldierly and efficient direction of their brigade commanders the troops were at once disposed in the most advantageous positions for holding the ground, and for protection from the artillery fire still furiously kept up. Pioneers and intrenching tools were sent over, and work was immediately commenced making rifle-pits. The indications being that additional troops had been brought up by the enemy, and that an attempt would be made to retake the hills, the vigilant brigade commanders kept their troops ready for every emergency, and the line of skirmishers well advanced and on the alert. The indications proved true, and about 7.30 o'clock in the evening the skirmishers came in, and shortly after them a large force of the enemy, in column of regiments, advanced to the assault. They were met by a withering fire, which, at first, they received steadily, soon shook, and finally broke their lines and forced them to retire and reform.[12]

Continue east on GA 136, crossing over I-75, about 0.6 mile to the intersection with US 41. Turn right (south) onto US 41, and park (Position 5C). Leave your vehicle and carefully look to your left (east), and observe the railroad tracks. These are representative of the tracks McPherson was supposed to sever. Look forward (south), and observe the highway and railroad bridges crossing the Oostanaula River, just ahead of you.

The modern bridge and the modern railroad bridge to your left are representative of the two period bridges that were major targets for Sherman's armies. The stone abutments at either end of the railroad bridge are original to the time of the battle. Sherman's fighting at Resaca aimed to destroy the road and railroad bridges across the Oostanaula River to cut Johnston off from his supply line.

Reenter your vehicle and drive to Stop 6.

Continue driving south on US 41. In 1.5 miles you will pass under I-75 at Exit 318. Continue south on US 41 for another 1.9 miles until you reach the intersection with GA 225. Continue southwest on US 41/Wall Street 1.8 miles to the intersection with Line Street. Turn right (west) onto East Line Street, which becomes GA 156, and continue west about 1.3 miles to Herrington Bend Road on the right. Turn right (northwest) onto Herrington Bend Road, and drive 1.1 miles to Hunt Road on the left. Park safely, and walk to and read the marker labeled Lay's Ferry.

Stop 6: Lay's Ferry

Critical Decision: (11) Sherman Outflanks Johnston at Resaca

While engaged in combat on May 14 and 15, Sherman made Critical Decision 11 on the Resaca Battlefield. Rather than continue to assault Johnston, Sherman decided to outflank him. On May 14, he ordered Brig. Gen. Thomas W. Sweeny's division to cross the Oostanaula River at Lay's Ferry. However, fearful of Confederate forces discovered there, Sweeny returned later in the day. On the fifteenth, Sweeny successfully crossed the river once more and held his position. Johnston realized he was in danger of being outflanked by losing the bridges crossing the Oostanaula, which were now subject to Union artillery fire. His line of retreat was being threatened, and he was forced to withdraw. You are now near the site near Lay's Ferry connected with that critical decision.

Though its exact site is inaccessible, Lay's Ferry was located about half a mile north of the sign. Johnston assigned Confederate Maj. Gen. W. H. T. Walker and his division to guard this area, and the troops sent Johnston word that elements of the Union army had crossed the river. Realizing that he was being flanked, Johnston immediately began planning his army's withdrawal. This decision was a reaction to Sherman's critical decision to attempt to outflank Johnston at Resaca, rather than continue to fight there. Johnston successfully completed his withdrawal early on May 16.

Narrative of Maj. Gen. William T. Sherman, USA, Commanding Military Division of the Mississippi

During the 15th we had a day of continual battle and skirmish. At the same time I caused two pontoon-bridges to be laid across the Oostanaula River at Lay's Ferry, about three miles below the town, by which we could threaten Calhoun, a station on the railroad seven miles below Resaca.[13]

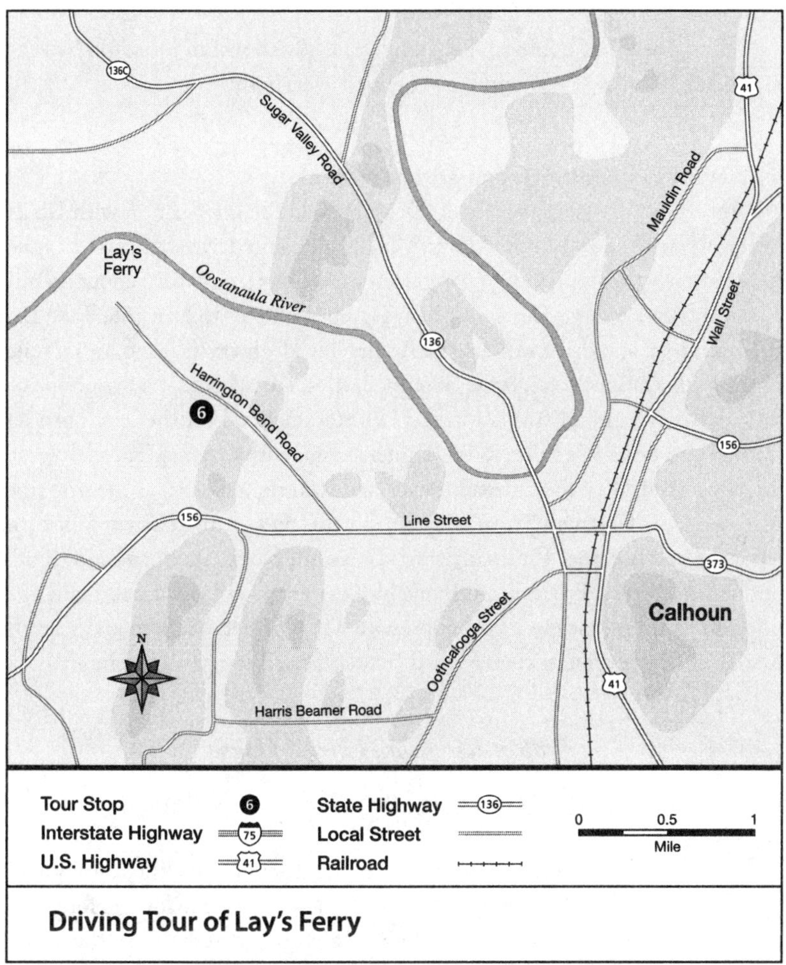

Driving Tour of Lay's Ferry

Narrative of Col. Henry Stone, USA, On Staff, Maj. Gen. George H. Thomas, Commanding Army of the Cumberland

It is hardly possible to imagine a more successfully managed movement than that of Johnston. As late as 11 o'clock the skirmishers of both armies were within speaking distance of each other. Yet at daylight, as early as 4 o'clock in the morning, the whole place was as deserted as though no soldiery had occupied it for a month. Not a box of ammunition, not a barrel of hard-tack, not a wagon, not an animal was left behind. The completeness with which Johnston had made his escape profoundly impressed everybody.[14]

Return to your vehicle and drive to Stop 7.

Return to GA 156/Line Street. Drive back to the intersection with US 41/Wall Street. Turn right onto US 41/Wall Street, and drive southeast 2.1 miles to the intersection with GA 53. Angle left onto GA 53, and drive about 1.0 mile to the entrance to I-75. Drive south on I-75 for 6.3 miles to Exit 306. Take Exit 306 from I-75, and drive west on the Adairsville Highway/GA 140 for 1.6 miles to the Hall Station Road. After about 1.2 miles, cross US 41, and continue 0.4 mile past the railroad tracks to the Hall Station Road on the left. Turn left (south), and drive 10.2 miles to the T intersection with GA 293. Turn left (east), drive 300 yards over the railroad tracks, and turn right (south) at the first right turn, which is Coleman Street. Drive 100 yards on Coleman Street as it turns left (east) and becomes Railroad Street. Drive one block, and turn right (south) on Johnson Street. Proceed south one block over the railroad tracks, and park safely to your right at the intersection with Main Street. Walk to and read the marker on the northeast corner titled "House Site, Thomas V. B. Hargis."

Stop 7: Kingston, Hargis House

Critical Decision: (13) Sherman Decides to Leave the Railroad

Note that this stop should follow the next stop, Cassville, chronologically. Sherman first dealt with Johnston at Cassville (see below) before retiring to the Hargis House later on the nineteenth and remaining there until the twenty-third. This stop is designed to make travel easier and to avoid a repeated trip over the same roads.

Sherman made Critical Decision 13 at Kingston. Opting not to assault Johnston at Allatoona Pass, he instead left the railroad supply line and moved south toward Dallas and New Hope Church.

Kingston was the site of the Hargis House, where Sherman allowed his armies a few days to rest and refit while he made plans. Realizing the futility of attacking Johnston and his men entrenched at Allatoona Pass, Sherman made the critical decision to leave his supply line and attempt to outflank Johnston by moving south toward Dallas, Georgia. The consequences of this choice were immense. Union forces would have to be supplied with thousands of wagons from the railhead. Eventually, Sherman and his armies benefited

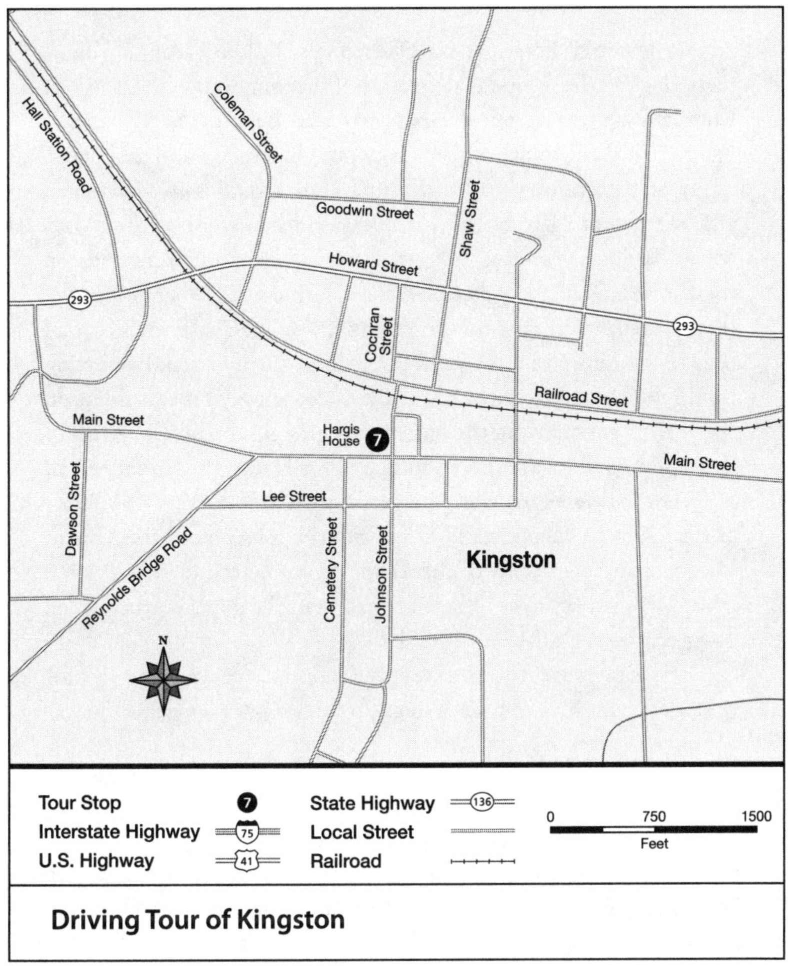

from this decision. Note that the location of the Hargis House is identified as south of the main street in Kingston; during the Civil War, Kingston's main street was Railroad Street.

Narrative of Maj. Gen. William T. Sherman, USA, Commanding Military Division of the Mississippi

In early days (1844), when a lieutenant of the Third Artillery, I had been sent from Charleston, South Carolina, to Marietta, Georgia, to assist Inspector-General Churchill to take testimony concerning certain losses of horses and accoutrements by the Georgia Volunteers during the Florida War; and after completing the work at Marietta we transferred our party over to Bellefonte, Alabama. I had ridden the distance on horseback, and had noted well the topography of the country, especially that about Kennesaw, Allatoona, and the Etowah River. On that occasion I had stopped some days with a Colonel Tumlin, to see the remarkable Indian mounds on the Etowah River, usually called the "Hightower." I therefore knew that the Allatoona Pass was very strong, would be hard to force, and resolved not even to attempt it, but to turn the position, by moving from Kingston to Marietta *via* Dallas; accordingly I made orders on the 20th to get ready for the march to begin on the 23d. The Army of the Cumberland was ordered to march for Dallas, by Euharlee and Stilesboro'; Davis's division, then in Rome, by Van Wert; the Army of the Ohio to keep to the left of Thomas, by a place called Burnt Hickory; and the Army of the Tennessee to march for a position a little to the south, so as to be on the right of the general army, when grouped about Dallas.[15]

The Etowah is the Rubicon of Georgia. We are now in motion like a vast hive of bees, and expect to swarm along the Chattahoochee in a few days.[16]

Return to your vehicle and drive to Stop 8.

This stop features two positions: 8A and 8B. Usually, you cannot actually stop at 8B, but observe it while moving along in traffic. Enter Main Street eastbound, then drive two blocks to Church Street, and turn left (north). Cross the railroad tracks, and turn right (east) onto Railroad Street. Drive 0.6 mile to the intersection with the Kingston Highway/GA 293. Turn right, and continue east about 3.5 miles to a left turn onto Firetower Road. Proceed east/northeast on Firetower Road 1.3 miles to the intersection with Joe Frank Harris Parkway/US 41. Cross over this highway, and continue 0.2 mile to the next intersection with the Cassville Road. Turn left (north) onto the Cassville Road, and drive 0.2 mile to the intersection with the Cassville White Road on the right (east). Turn right (east), and follow the road about 0.2 mile around a curve to the Cassville Cemetery on the right (south). Park at the cemetery (Position 8A), leave your vehicle, and face north.

Stop 8: Cassville

Critical Decision: (12) Johnston Plans to Attack Near Cassville

Narrative of General Joseph E. Johnston, CSA, Commanding Department and Army of Tennessee

The breadth of the valley here [Adairsville] exceeded so much the front of our army properly formed for battle, that we could obtain no advantage of ground, so after resting about eighteen hours, the troops were ordered to move to Cassville.

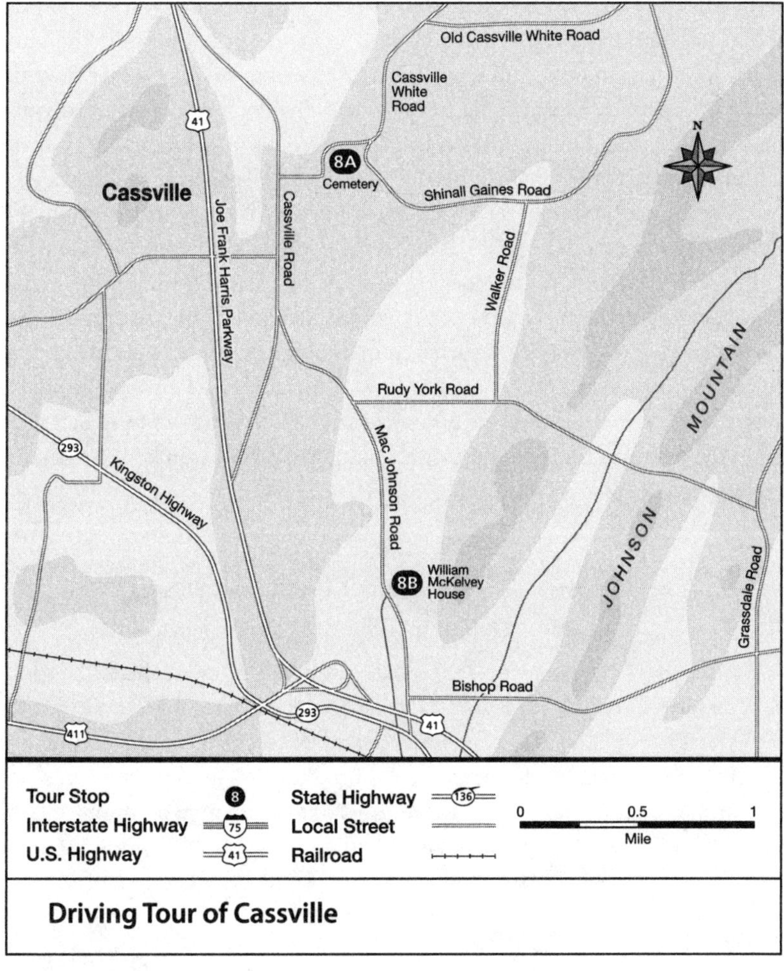

Driving Tour of Cassville

> Two roads lead southward from Adairsville, one following the railroad through Kingston, and, like it, turning at almost right angles to the east at that place, the other, quite direct to the Etowah Railroad-bridge, passing through Cassville, where it is met by the first. The probability that the Federal army would divide-a column following each road-gave me hope of engaging and defeating one of them before it could receive aid from the other.[17]

After formulating Critical Decision 12 to prepare his army to attack, Johnston ordered Hardee's Corps, along with the rest of the army's supply wagons and ambulances, to march straight south from Adairsville to Kingston. Hardee's Corps and the logistical elements were the decoy force, making it appear that Johnston's entire army was following this route. At the same time, Johnston ordered Polk's and Hood's Corps to take a shorter road directly to Cassville. Sherman did exactly what Johnston had hoped and divided his armies to march more efficiently. He ordered Thomas's large Army of the Cumberland to Kingston. McPherson's Army of the Tennessee was dispatched southwest along another road through Barnsley Gardens to Kingston. Finally, Sherman sent Schofield's Twenty-Third Corps and Hooker's Twentieth Corps to Cassville. On the morning of May 19, upon learning of Sherman's movements, Johnston carried out his critical decision by positioning Hardee east of Kingston to protect his army from Thomas's and McPherson's armies. Johnston positioned Polk's Corps to block/defend Cassville from the northwest. He also placed Hood's Corps northeast of Cassville to ambush Schofield and Hooker and attempt to destroy them in detail. Johnston issued a stirring general order:

> **Narrative of Gen. Joseph E. Johnston, CSA, Commanding Department and Army of Tennessee**
>
> Soldiers of the Army of Tennessee, you have displayed the highest quality of the soldier—firmness in conduct, patience under toil. By your courage and skill you have repulsed every assault of the enemy. By marches by day and by marches by night you have defeated every attempt upon your communications. Your communications are secured. You will now turn and march to meet his advancing columns. Fully confiding in the conduct of the officers, the courage of the soldiers, I lead you to battle. We may confidently trust that the Al-

mighty Father will still reward the patriot's toils and bless the patriot's banners. Cheered by the success of our brothers in Virginia and beyond the Mississippi, our efforts will equal theirs. Strengthened by His support, those efforts will be crowned with the like glories.[18]

Once all divisions were in position, Johnston had Hood facing west and prepared to ambush Schofield as he moved south along today's US 41 toward Cassville. However, unbeknownst to the Confederates, a division of Federal cavalry under the command of Brig. Gen. Edward McCook was on the move. Ordered to hit the railroad south of Cassville, McCook failed to find a direct road around Cassville to the east. He then joined today's Old Cassville White Road and stumbled into Stevenson's Division. Stevenson quickly faced the new, unexpected adversary from the east and pushed McCook and his men back. Hood, told of the attack on Stevenson, faced his entire corps east. Additionally, he ordered Stewart's Division to move east and then south through a gap to negate any further threat from that direction. Hood's redeployment frustrated the proposed ambush.

Narrative of Gen. Joseph E. Johnston, CSA, Commanding Department and Army of Tennessee

When General Hood's column had moved two or three miles, that officer received a report from a member of his staff to the effect that the enemy was approaching on the Canton Road in the rear of the right of the position from which he had marched. Instead of transmitting this report to me, and moving on in obedience to his orders, he fell back to that road and formed his corps across it, facing to our right and rear, towards Canton, without informing me of this strange departure from the instructions he had received. I heard of this [Hood's] erratic movement after it had caused such a loss of time as to make the attack intended impracticable, for its success depended on accuracy in timing it. The intention was therefore abandoned.[19]

Johnston then retreated about a mile south to his second position: Located west of where you are standing, Cassville was situated on favorable high ground. Hood's Corps entrenched from the area of this cemetery to the northeast. Polk's Corps continued the Confederate line almost due south, just east of today's US 41, to where US 41 turns southeast. Hardee's Corps continued Johnston's line south and then east. Schofield's Army of the Ohio was deployed north of the cemetery facing Hood, while Thomas's Army of the Cumberland was deployed roughly in a north-to-south line facing Polk and Hardee. Johnston believed that this was a strong defensive position.

Narrative of Gen. Joseph E. Johnston, CSA, Commanding Department and Army of Tennessee

To be prepared for it [further Union attack], the Confederate army was drawn up in a position that I remember as the best that I saw occupied during the war, the ridge immediately south of Cassville, with a broad, open, elevated valley in front of it completely commanded by the fire of troops occupying its crest.[20]

Johnston believed his position was a good one, but Lieutenant Generals Hood and Polk disagreed, feeling that Union artillery could enfilade their lines. As a result of this belief they asked for a meeting with Johnston, which Hardee did not attend.

After exploring the cemetery, turn left (southwest) out of the cemetery back onto the Cassville White Road. Continue about 0.4 mile (eventually heading west) to the intersection with the Cassville Road. Turn left onto the Cassville Road, and in about 0.5 mile, veer left (southeast) onto Mac Johnson Road.

As you drive south along Mac Johnson Road, you are now behind Polk's Corps' line and moving toward his headquarters.

Continue southeast on Mac Johnson Road past the intersection with River Birch Road 1.0 mile on the left and Camden Woods Road on the right. Continue about 0.1 mile to where the road bends slightly to the left (Position 8B). TREAT THIS AS A ROLLING STOP. BE EXTREMELY CAREFUL, and watch for traffic behind you. There is no close-by place to park! The old house on the left (east) of Mac Johnson Road was Polk's headquarters while he was at Cassville. The William McKelvey House is located before you cross over the small stream.

The William McKelvey House was Polk's headquarters after the army took up its second position at Cassville. It was here that Polk and Hood, fearing their new positions were vulnerable to Union artillery fire, talked Johnston into retreating again.

Narrative of Gen. Joseph E. Johnston, CSA, Commanding Department and Army of Tennessee

On reaching my tent soon after dark, I found in it an invitation to meet the Lieutenant-Generals at General Polk's quarters. General Hood was with him, but not General Hardee. The two officers, General Hood taking the lead, expressed the opinion very positively that neither of their corps would be able to hold its position next day; because, they said, a part of each was enfiladed by Federal artillery. The part of General Polk's corps referred to was that of which I had conversed with Brigadier-General Shoupe [(*sic*) Shoup was Johnston's chief of artillery]. On that account they urged me to abandon the ground immediately, and cross the Etowah.

A discussion of more than an hour followed, in which they very earnestly and decidedly expressed the conviction that when the Federal artillery opened upon them the next day it would render their positions untenable in an hour or two.

Although the position was the best we had occupied, I yielded at last, in the belief that the confidence of the commanders of two of the three corps of the army, of their inability to resist the enemy, would inevitably be communicated to their troops, and produce that inability. Lieutenant-General Hardee, who arrived after this decision, remonstrated against it strongly, and was confident that his corps could hold its ground, although less favorably posted. The error was adhered to, however, and the position abandoned before daybreak.[21]

Narrative of Capt. Walter J. Morris, CSA, Engineer Corps, Chief Engineer, Army of the Mississippi (Polk's Corps)

He [Lieut. Gen. Polk] then requested me to go at once, and examine the extreme right of his line, as he considered it untenable for defense. . . . At the time I arrived about the centre of Genl Polk's right, where the open crest of the ridge commenced, I found a very heavy enfilading & cross fire, going on from the enemy's batteries. There were but a few sentinels remaining upon the crest, the main body of men, intended to occupy this part of the line, were compelled to withdraw to the right and left at the foot of the ridge, out of sight, but not out of range of the enemy's batteries.[22]

Johnston's critical decision at Cassville to first cancel the planned ambush and later abandon a strong defensive line resulted in more retreating and loss of confidence in his ability to confront Sherman. We will never know if Johnston's planned attack would have succeeded.

Continue driving to Stop 9.

Continue driving south about 0.5 mile to the intersection with US 41/SR 3. Turn left onto US 41/SR 3, and drive about 2.7 miles to the exit for US 411/GA 20. After exiting right, turn left at the bottom of the hill, and drive under the highway you were just on. Just past the northbound exit ramp, turn right onto GA 20/Canton Highway. Be careful NOT to take the first right turn after passing under the overpass. Continue 2.1 miles to I-75. Drive 7.0 miles south on I-75 to Exit 283. From I-75 South, take Exit 283. Turn left (east) onto the Old Allatoona Road, proceed east about 1.5 miles to the parking lot on your left, and park. Leave your vehicle, and walk northwest to where a series of signs and monuments are placed.

Stop 9: Allatoona Pass

Critical Decisions: (13) Sherman Decides to Leave the Railroad, (14) Johnston Decides Not to Order His Cavalry to Sever Sherman's Supply Line

Note that this is a second stop connected with Sherman's critical decision to leave his railroad line of supply. This stop will provide an excellent visual reason why Sherman did not want to assault Johnston here.

Immediately east of the parking lot, Allatoona Lake obscures much of the terrain. Look northwest. You can still see the railroad cut north of the parking lot. It is easy to envision how difficult it would have been for Sherman to attack Johnston in this area. Sherman realized that the odds simply were not in his favor, and that Johnston would have the benefit of easily defensible terrain. Union troops' alternative of leaving the railroad and outflanking Johnston to the southwest seemed like a good idea. Several monuments and historical markers relate to the October 1864 Battle of Allatoona Pass that took place here. Realize that this battle was not part of the Atlanta Campaign but a result of it. After Atlanta's capture, Hood tried and failed to sever the railroad supplying Sherman here.

Sherman knew from having traveled the area in the 1840s that the countryside around Allatoona Pass would heavily favor the defense. He therefore made Critical Decision 12 in Kingston at the Hargis House not to confront Johnston at Allatoona Pass, but to attempt to outflank him by marching

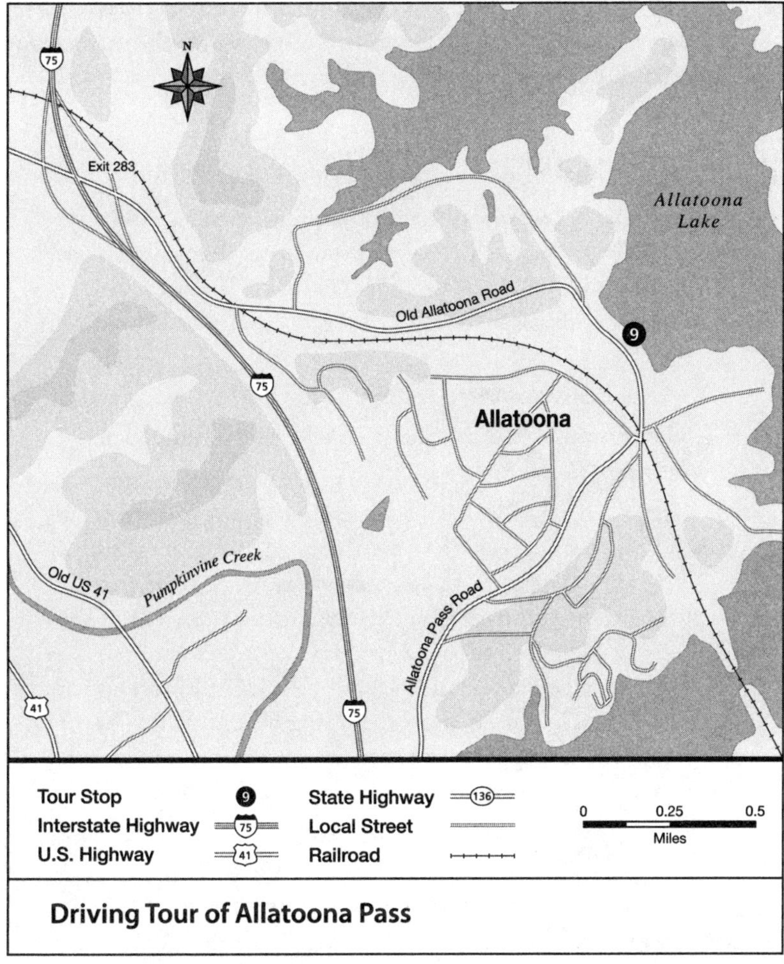

Driving Tour of Allatoona Pass

south to the Dallas area. Sherman realized that this plan would entail leaving the Western and Atlantic Railroad, which would create supply problems. Wagons would have to move supplies a greater distance from the railroad. You can now visualize this difficulty.

This stop is also representative of another critical decision concerning the Western and Atlantic Railroad. The railroad served as Sherman's supply line as he progressed southward. If the line could be severed, it was obvious to both sides of the conflict that Sherman would be forced to defer a sizeable number of his troops to repair the damage. In this event, the numbers of the opposing armies would be somewhat evened. Johnston might even have the edge. Johnston had begun a campaign of requests to President Davis, asking him to order Maj. Gen. Nathan B. Forrest's cavalry to sever Sherman's supply line. However, Davis had other duties for Forrest.

Comment by Historian/Author Bruce Catton

When Forrest hit a railroad line with serious intent, that line was obliterated, with as much time, care and effort devoted to its destruction as had gone into its original building. If Forrest ever got on Sherman's railroad line, Sherman was likely in serious trouble.[23]

Narrative of Gen. Joseph E. Johnston, CSA, Commanding Department and Army of Tennessee

Early in the campaign, the accounts of the number of cavalry in Mississippi given by Lieutenant-General Polk, just from the command of that department, and my correspondence with his successor, Lieutenant General S. D. Lee, gave me reason to believe that an adequate force to destroy the railroad communications of the Federal army could be furnished in Mississippi and Alabama, under an officer fully competent to head such an enterprise, General Forrest. . . . I made these suggestions in the strong belief that this cavalry would serve the Confederacy far better by contributing to the defeat of a formidable invasion, than by waiting for and repelling raids.[24]

Narrative of President Jefferson Davis, Confederate States of America

Forrest's command is now operating on Sherman's lines of communication and is necessary for other purposes in his present field of service. I do not see that I can change the disposition of our forces so as to help General Johnston more effectually than by the present arrangement.[25]

Johnston made Critical Decision 14 not to dispatch his own cavalry to sever the railroad behind Sherman. Maj. Gen. Joseph Wheeler's cavalry corps was certainly not as renowned as Forrest's. However, Johnston had the authority to order Wheeler to sever Sherman's supply line. Johnston decided not to do so for fear of reducing his command in front of Sherman while his own cavalry rode off to cut the railroad. Yet the potential benefit of cutting the line was huge. As noted above, a complete severing of Sherman's supply line would have forced Sherman to continue the campaign differently. While

Johnston was extremely vocal in requesting aid from Forrest (see above), he apparently was more cautious when it came to utilizing his own cavalry.

Return to your vehicle and drive to Stop 10.

Return 1.5 miles to I-75. Continue driving under I-75 at Exit 283, and drive 0.6 mile to the intersection with GA 41. Turn left (south), and drive about 4.6 miles until you reach the intersection with the Dallas Acworth Highway (GA 92). Bear right (southwest), and proceed about 6.4 miles to the intersection on the left (east) with Mount Tabor Road. Turn left (east) onto Mount Tabor Road, and follow it southeast 1.4 miles to the entrance to Pickett's Mill Battlefield Historic Site on your left (north). Turn left (north), and if open (go to https://gastateparks.org/PickettsMillBattlefield for hours), drive the short distance to the visitor center parking lot. Park, leave your vehicle, and observe the terrain. If the site is closed, leave your vehicle and examine the terrain.

Stop 10: "Hell Hole" and Pickett's Mill

Critical Decision: (13) Sherman Decides to Leave the Railroad

Once Sherman left the railroad, his armies plunged into what became known as the "Hell Hole"—the area around Dallas, New Hope Church, and Pickett's Mill. Here, the heavily wooded terrain allowed opposing soldiers to remain in almost constant contact with one another. Sherman failed to outflank Johnston to the southwest around Dallas as he had envisioned; the terrain played havoc with Sherman's transportation requirements. Additionally, Sherman proved unable to outflank Johnston. The Union general therefore abandoned his efforts in that regard and returned to his reliable supply line, the Western and Atlantic Railroad.

This resultant decision to return was not made at Pickett's Mill, but this location is an excellent example of the rough terrain the soldiers of both sides had to maneuver through. The purpose of the visit to Pickett's Mill is not to examine the battlefield (although you certainly may), but to see the terrain that influenced Sherman's critical decision to return.

Narrative of Maj. Gen. William T. Sherman, USA, Commanding Military Division of the Mississippi

On the other side of the Allatoona range, the Pumpkin-Vine Creek, also a tributary of the Etowah, flowed north and west; Dallas, the point aimed at, was a small town on the other or east side of this

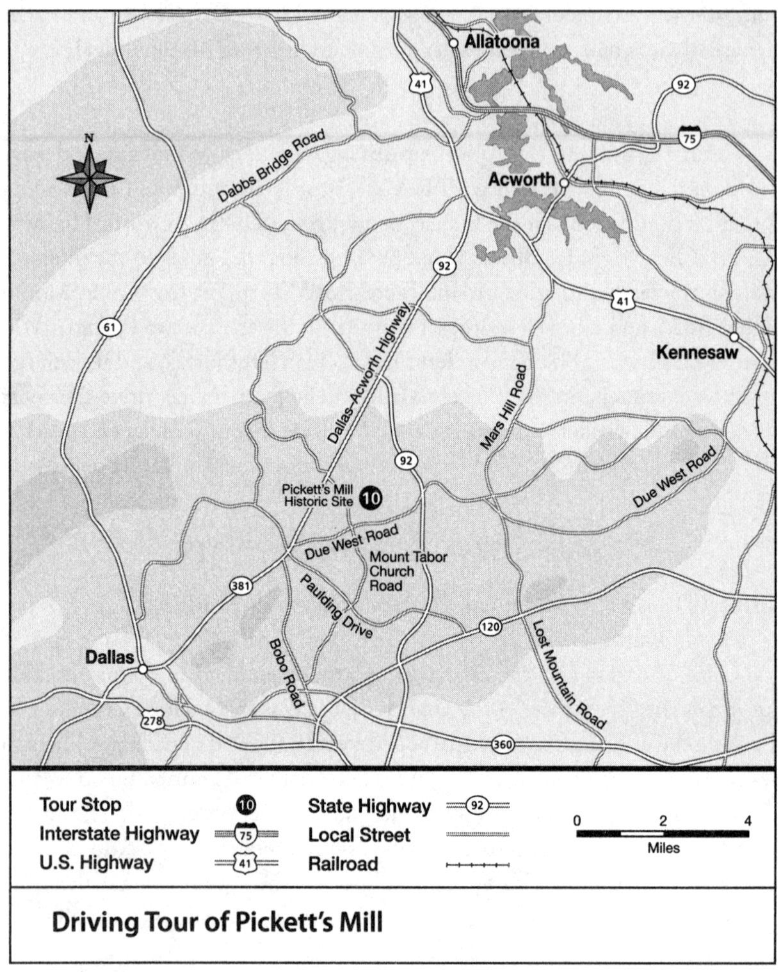

Driving Tour of Pickett's Mill

> creek, and was the point of concentration of a great many roads that led in every direction. Its possession would be a threat to Marietta and Atlanta, but I could not then venture to attempt either, till I had regained the use of the railroad, at least as far down as its *debouche* from the Allatoona range of mountains. Therefore, the movement was chiefly designed to compel Johnston to give up Allatoona.[26]

The Battle of Pickett's Mill was a one-sided victory for the Confederates. While Union troops suffered 1,732 casualties, Cleburne lost 448 men. Sherman failed to document this fiasco, as it was such a defeat for him. The loss reinforced his decision to move his forces back to the railroad.

Sherman's attempt to outflank Johnston at or around Dallas had failed, so not only did he need to try something else, but he also needed to get back to his supply line before he literally ran out of provisions. Although he had not outmaneuvered Johnston, Sherman had managed to get past Allatoona Pass, a necessary step for maintaining his supply line, without having to fight for it.

Return to your vehicle and drive to Stop 11.

This stop has two positions: 11A and 11B. From the entrance to Pickett's Mill Battlefield Historic Site, turn left (south) onto Mount Tabor Church Road, and drive 1.8 miles to the intersection with East Paulding Drive. Turn left (east) onto East Paulding Drive, and follow it about 2.8 miles to the intersection with the Dallas Highway (GA 120). Turn left (east) on GA 120, and drive about 6.1 miles toward Marietta until you reach the intersection with the Barrett Parkway. Continue through the intersection with the Barrett Parkway on GA 120 about 0.8 mile to the intersection with John Ward Road on the right (south). Turn right (south) onto John Ward Road, and drive about 0.3 mile to the intersection on the left with Cheatham Hill Road. Turn left (southeast) onto Cheatham Hill Road, and follow it about 0.2 mile to the Kennesaw Mountain National Battlefield Park parking lot on the right (west). Park there, leave your vehicle, and walk to the historical marker labeled "Sherman's Headquarters" (Position 11A). Face east after reading the marker.

Stop 11: Cheatham Hill

Critical Decision: (15) Sherman Orders a Direct Attack on the Kennesaw Mountain Line

Weary of outflanking Johnston, Sherman decided to try another tactic—a direct assault.

This was the location of Sherman's headquarters during part of the confrontation at the Kennesaw Mountain Line. Sherman had tired of his soldiers' continuous flanking movements and Johnston's blocking them. He then decided on another form of maneuver, a direct assault against Johnston's Kennesaw Mountain Line. Sherman reasoned that Johnston's line must be stretched thin, especially in the middle, as he protected the Confederate flanks. Consequently, Sherman hoped for a breakthrough in Johnston's center at the salient soon known as the Dead Angle on Cheatham Hill. The Federals carried out Critical Decision 15 to assault Johnston's Kennesaw Mountain Line on June 27.

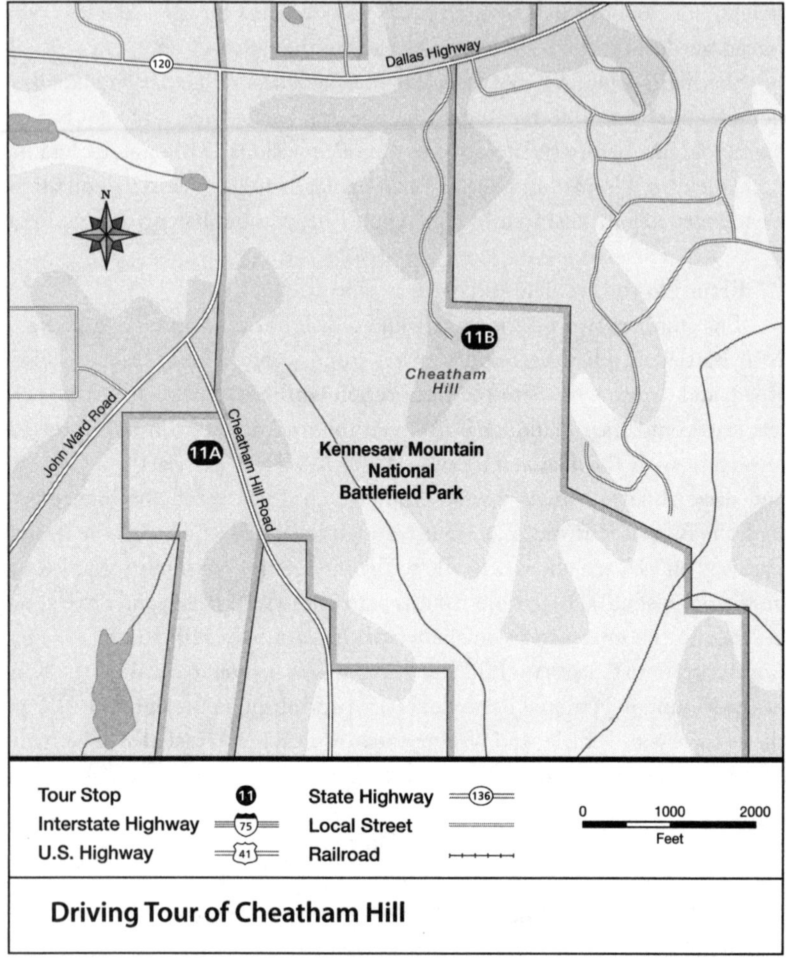

Driving Tour of Cheatham Hill

Narrative of Maj. Gen. William T. Sherman, USA, Commanding Military Division of the Mississippi

During the 24th and 25th of June General Schofield extended his right as far as prudent, so as to compel the enemy to thin out his line correspondingly, with the intention to make two strong assaults at points where success would give us the greatest advantage. I had consulted Generals Thomas, McPherson, and Schofield, and we all agreed that we could not with prudence stretch out any more, and therefore had no alternative but to attack "fortified lines," a thing carefully avoided up to that time. I reasoned, if we could make a

> breach anywhere near the rebel center, and thrust in a strong head of column, that with one moiety [part or position] of our army we could hold in check the corresponding wing of the enemy, and with the other sweep in flank and overwhelm the other half. The 27th of June was fixed as the day for the attempt.[27]

The diversionary attack against Pigeon Hill by Maj. Gen. John A. Logan's Fifteenth Corps commenced about 9 a.m. on June 27, with Brig. Gen. Charles Walcutt's brigade on the Union left (north), Brig. Gen. Giles A. Smith's brigade in the center, and Brig. Gen. Joseph Lightburn's brigade on the right, south of Burnt Hickory Road. At the same time, the Sixteenth and Seventeenth Corps made diversionary assaults against the Confederate right to prevent the shifting of Confederate troops toward the main Union attack farther south. The assault against Pigeon Hill was a supporting attack to keep the Confederates from shifting forces. The terrain around Pigeon Hill did not favor the assaulting forces.

The main assault was against a salient that quickly came to be known as the Dead Angle. The Dead Angle was located on what was later named Cheatham Hill after Maj. Gen. Benjamin F. Cheatham, the division commander of this part of the Kennesaw Mountain Line. Although the Union assault from the creek bottom a few hundred yards east of your position would only have to cover a few hundred yards of open ground, the terrain strongly favored the defense. Brig. Gen. George Maney's brigade defended the salient at and to the left (south) of it, while Brig. Gen. Alfred Vaughan's brigade was stationed to the salient's right (north). This strong defensive position included deep entrenchments, head logs, abatis, and cleared fields of fire. (For those interested, a short trail extends from this location across the road to the east, following the attack up on Cheatham Hill.)

For the drive to Position 11B, return to your vehicle, and retrace your drive by turning left (north) onto Cheatham Hill Road and driving back to the intersection with John Ward Road. Turn right (northeast) onto John Ward Road, and drive back to GA 120, which will become Whitlock Avenue. Turn right (east) onto Whitlock Avenue, and drive a short distance, about 0.3 mile, to the entrance to Cheatham Hill. Turn right (south) onto the Cheatham Hill Road, and follow it to the parking lot at the end. Park, leave your vehicle, and walk south along the trail at the southern end of the parking lot for several hundred yards to the large Illinois Monument (Position 11B). Face west, and observe the terrain.

This view imparts to you the huge obstacle faced by the Union soldiers assigned to attack this salient. While the Dead Angle was exposed, it was well protected. It is a wonder that the Union didn't suffer more casualties than it did. Although Sherman's theory that the Confederate line would likely be weak in the center had some merit, one must wonder if an attack at this location ever really had a chance.

The assault on the Dead Angle was conducted by elements of Thomas's Army of the Cumberland. The main attack was made against Vaughan's defenders, slightly north of the actual angle, by Brig. Gen. Charles Harker's brigade. Col. Daniel McCook's and Col. John G. Mitchell's brigades attacked Maney's position at the Dead Angle and south of it. Brig. Gen. John W. Geary's division was to attack the Confederate line to the right (south) of Mitchell, but artillery fire prevented it from reaching the Confederate line.

The attack commenced with the Union regiments in a compact column formation and following orders not to fire until the soldiers had successfully advanced into the Confederate trenches. After a short Union artillery barrage, the assault commenced, but it quickly became a slaughter. Cheatham had concealed several batteries, unknown to the Union high command, that opened fire, killing or wounding many of the Union attackers. These defenders fired and reloaded as fast as they could, and it was almost impossible for them to miss. The fighting did not last very long. A brief lull occurred when gunfire ignited the underbrush and threatened to burn many wounded Union soldiers. Men from both sides helped remove the injured troops.

Narrative of Col. George W. Gordon, CSA, Commanding Eleventh Tennessee, Vaughan's Brigade, Cheatham's Division, Hardee's Corps, Army of Tennessee

In this charge the first line of the enemy came with guns uncapped, to take us with the bayonet; but when it reached our dense abatis, extending thirty paces in front of our line, well fortified and provided with head-logs, they halted and staggered with considerable confusion. Their other lines closed upon their first, and in this condition we swept them down with great slaughter, although our line had been so attenuated by being extended that we had not as much as one full rank in our works. The enemy was severely punished. They were exposed to a flank as well as a front from our lines, which being provided with head-logs, the men were not only protected from actual danger, but being also free from the fear of it, delivered their fire with terrible accuracy.[28]

To retreat meant exposing Union troops to the defenders' deadly fire. Rather than risk being shot in the back while retreating, many Federals took cover where a dip in the terrain provided some shelter a short distance from the Confederate line. The Union strengthened this line, kept the enemy on edge for the next several days, and began to tunnel under the Confederate position. This tunnel entrance can be seen at the foot of the Illinois Monument.

Narrative of Brig. Gen. Alfred J. Vaughan Jr., CSA, Commanding Vaughan's Brigade, Cheatham's Division, Hardee's Corps, Army of Tennessee

In column seven lines deep, with not a cap on the guns of the first two lines, he attempted to storm our position. Never did men march into the very jaws of death with a firmer tread and with more determination than did the Federals to this attack. But they met intrenched [*sic*] infantry, and the concentrated fire of musketry, canister, grapeshot and shell mowed them down at every step. Yet they struggled forward, but every Confederate stood at his post, and in a short time it was more than mortals could stand and they broke and fled.[29]

Narrative of Pvt. Sam Watkins, CSA, Company H, First Tennessee, Maney's Brigade, Cheatham's Division, Hardee's Corps, Army of Tennessee

I had shot one hundred and twenty times that day [June 27]. My gun became so hot that frequently the powder would flash before I could ram home the ball, and I had frequently to exchange my gun for that of a dead comrade. . . . When the Yankees fell back, and the firing ceased, I never saw so many broken down and exhausted men in my life. I was sick as a horse, and as wet with blood and sweat as I could be, and many of our men were vomiting with excessive fatigue, over exhaustion, and sunstroke; our tongues were parched and cracked for water, and our faces blackened with powder and smoke, and our dead and wounded were piled indiscriminately in the trenches. There was not a single man in the company who was not wounded, or had holes shot through his hat and clothing.[30]

This was a staggering defeat for Sherman, who lost some three thousand men compared to the Confederates' loss of about six hundred. Some one thousand dead Union soldiers lay in front of the Dead Angle. Sherman would not again attack a line of this nature. His critical decision to vary successful but time-consuming flanking movements with an all-out frontal assault against the enemy's entrenched center failed miserably. Sherman would revert to what worked—outflanking Johnston.

Even so, concerned that he should continue the attacks to create a breakthrough, Sherman consulted with Thomas. Thomas famously replied, "We have already lost heavily today without gaining any material advantage. One or two more such assaults would use up this army!"[31] Sherman returned to maneuvering.

Return to your vehicle and drive to Stop 12.

Return to I-75 from Cheatham Hill by turning right (east) onto Whitlock Avenue. Drive about 2.9 miles to the intersection with North Marietta Parkway. Turn left (north and then east) onto North Marietta Parkway, and follow it for less than 2.0 miles to I-75. Drive south on I-75 to Exit 259. Exit I-75 onto I-285 (Atlanta Bypass) southwest (toward Montgomery and Birmingham), and proceed to Exit 18. Exit I-285, and turn left (east) onto Paces Ferry Road. Drive east on Paces Ferry Road through the intersection with Cumberland Parkway, then continue about 0.3 mile past the right intersection with Vining's Slope. At the next left intersection, turn left (north) onto Overlook Parkway. Continue to the next right turn, which is a parking lot. Turn right into the parking lot, park safely, and walk to where you can look south at the Atlanta skyline.

Stop 12: Vinings

Critical Decisions: (16) Sherman Makes Atlanta His Objective, (17) Sherman Decides to Destroy the Railroads Supplying Atlanta

This site is where Sherman first viewed Atlanta and, perhaps, where he first considered making it his primary objective.

On July 5, as the Confederate retreat continued, Sherman climbed to the top of Vining's Hill (also known as Mount Wilkinson) and viewed Atlanta for the first time. The city was nine miles away. This may not have been the point at which Sherman made Critical Decision 16 of the campaign, focusing on Atlanta's capture as his primary objective. However, the view from Vining's Hill certainly would have stimulated Sherman to make or reinforce that critical decision. Though it differs from the one Sherman viewed in 1864, today's skyline is still an inspirational sight.

Behind you to the north is the top of Vining's Hill, where Sherman had his initial view of Atlanta. Today the site is covered with a parking lot and

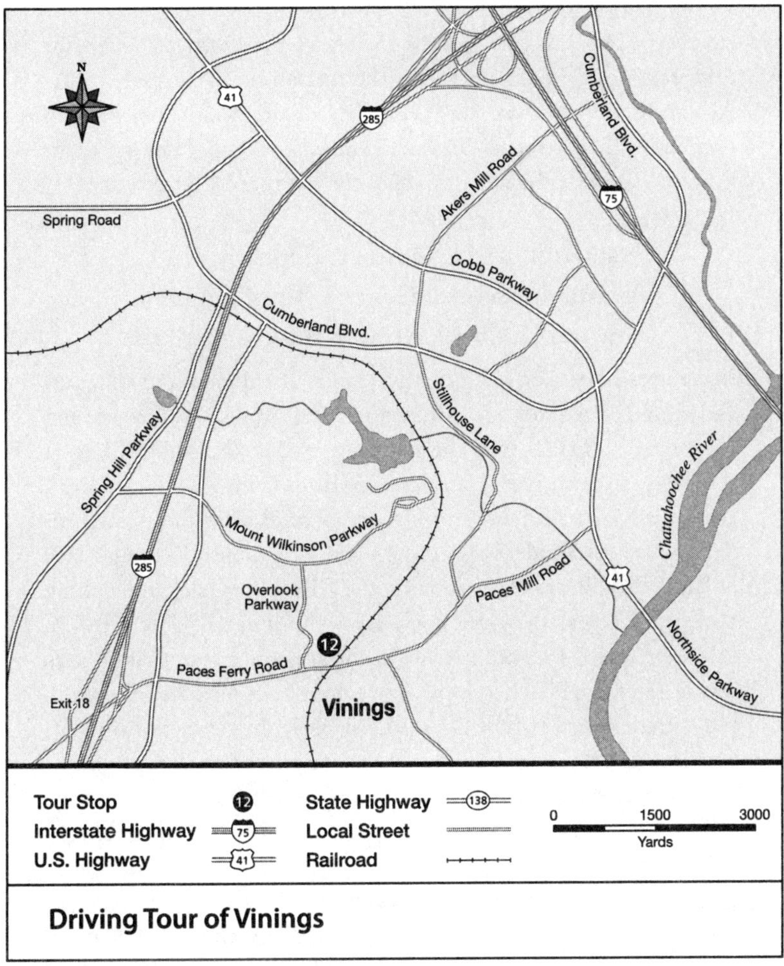

Driving Tour of Vinings

buildings. On a weekend or after business hours, it may be possible to walk or drive further up the hill, but buildings black its top.

Narrative of Maj. Gen. William T. Sherman, USA, Commanding Military Division of the Mississippi

I always expected to have a desperate fight to get possession of the Macon [rail]road, which was then the vital objective of the campaign. Its possession by us would, in my judgement, result in the capture of Atlanta, and give us the fruits of victory, although the destruction of Hood's army was the real object to be desired. Yet Atlanta was known as the "Gate-City of the South," was full of founderies [*sic*], arsenals, and machine, shops, and I know that its capture would be the death-knell of the Southern Confederacy.[32]

Narrative of Maj. James A. Connally, USA, Assistant Inspector General, Third Division, Fourteenth Corps, Army of the Cumberland

Mine eyes have seen the promised land! The domes and minarets and spires of Atlanta are glittering in the sunlight before us, and only 8 miles distant. On the morning of the 5th, while riding at the extreme front with the General [Brig. Gen. Absalom Baird], and eagerly pressing our skirmishers forward after the rapidly retreating rebels, suddenly we came upon a high bluff [Vining's Hill or Mount Wilkinson] overlooking the Chattahoochee, and looking southward across the river, there lay the beautiful "Gate City" in full view, and as the soldiers caught the announcement that Atlanta was in sight, such a cheer went up as must have been heard even in the entrenchments of the doomed city itself. In a very few minutes Generals Sherman and Thomas (who are always with the extreme front when a sudden movement is taking place) were with us on the hill top, and the two veterans, for a moment, gazed at the glittering prize in silence. I watched the two noble soldiers—Sherman stepping nervously about, his eyes sparkling and his face aglow—casting a single glance at Atlanta, another at the River, and a dozen at the surrounding valley to see where he could best cross the River, how he could best flank them. Thomas stood there like a noble Roman, calm, soldierly, dignified; no trace of excitement about the grand old soldier who had ruled the storm at Chickamauga.[33]

Sherman had tired of outflanking Johnston and had been unable to force a confrontation. As he closed in on Atlanta itself, Sherman changed his objective to capturing the city. He instinctively knew that Federal possession of Atlanta would send a strong signal to both sides that the Union was capable of winning the war. At some point, Sherman decided that possession of the city outweighed trying to catch Johnston's army, and Grant had also changed Sherman's orders to allow him more leeway in conducting his campaign.

Likely at the same time, Sherman decided that the best way to capture Atlanta was to cut off supplies by destroying the railroads that brought many necessities to both the Confederate army and the remaining civilians in the city. Of the four lines feeding into Atlanta, Sherman already controlled the Western and Atlantic Railroad. Once he outflanked Johnston's Chattahoochee River Line, he sent McPherson's Army of the Tennessee to destroy the railroad leading east out of Atlanta, the Georgia Railroad, from Decatur to Atlanta. Two other railroads remained, the Atlanta and West Point and the Macon and Western, which approached Atlanta from the west and south respectively. Near here, Sherman concurrently made Critical Decision 17 to destroy these other two supply lines to the beleaguered city.

After fighting the Battles of Peachtree Creek, Atlanta, and Ezra Church, Sherman circled around Atlanta and further disabled the already damaged Atlanta and West Point Railroad, leaving only one line to supply Atlanta. Before this event, however, a significant command change occurred.

Return to your vehicle and drive to Stop 13.

Depart the parking area, and drive south back to Paces Ferry Road. Turn left (east), and drive about 0.2 mile to where Paces Ferry Road turns right (southeast). Do NOT continue straight ahead or east on Paces Mill Road. Drive about 2.0 miles on Paces Ferry Road until it intersects with I-75 at Exit 255. Drive on to I-75, and drive south to Exit 251. Exit I-75 at Exit 251, and follow the signs south to the intersection with Fourteenth Street. Turn right (west) on Fourteenth Street, and continue about 0.6 mile to the intersection with Northside Drive. Pass through that intersection, and continue west 0.2 mile to Howell Mill Road. Turn left (south) onto Howell Mill Road. Proceed southbound on Howell Mill Road to the intersection with Eighth Street. Turn right (west) onto Eighth Street, and drive one block to the intersection with West Marietta Street. Turn slightly right, and continue northwest on West Marietta Street 0.6 mile (0.3 mile after crossing the railroad tracks) to 1040 (or thereabouts) West Marietta Street and park. Eventually markers may return to this location.

Stop 13: Johnston Relieved Of Command

Critical Decisions: (18) Davis Appoints Hood to Command the Army of Tennessee, (19) Hood Orders a Flank Attack against McPherson

President Davis increasingly believed that Johnston would not defend Atlanta or prevent its capture. After much contemplation and consultation, he made Critical Decision 18 to elevate Lieut. Gen. John Bell Hood to the temporary rank of general and place him in command of the Army of Tennessee. This site is near where Johnston's headquarters were located when he received word of his removal and Hood's promotion. Recall that this event preceded the Battle of Peachtree Creek.

In mid-July Johnston's headquarters were at the Dexter Niles House, which was located a short distance west of this location but no longer exists. It was here on the evening of July 17 that Johnston received the following dispatch from Confederate adjutant and inspector general Samuel Cooper in Richmond:

Report of Gen. Samuel Cooper, CSA, Adjutant and Inspector General, Confederate States of America

Lieut. Gen. John B. Hood has been commissioned to the temporary rank of general under the late law of Congress. I am directed by the Secretary of War to inform you that as you have failed to arrest the advance of the enemy to the vicinity of Atlanta, far in the interior of Georgia, and express no confidence that you can defeat or repel him, you are hereby relieved from the command of the Army and Department of Tennessee, which you will immediately turn over to General Hood.[34]

President Jefferson Davis's critical decision would quickly change the strategy of the Army of Tennessee from that of defense to offense. This shift was not lost on the soldiers of that army.

Narrative of Pvt. Philip D. Stephenson, CSA, Company K, Thirteenth Arkansas, Govan's Brigade, Cleburne's Division, Hardee's Corps, Army of Tennessee

General Johnston's dismissal took place July 18, 1864. To say that this was a shock to the whole army but feebly expresses the thought. It was a crushing blow, stunning men at first. The whole army reeled. Men looked into each other's eyes appalled and saw there what was in their own hearts, despair, the foreshadowing of calamity and ruin. Faith and hope for their own future and for the cause went away from the Army of Tennessee when Johnston went. Some wept

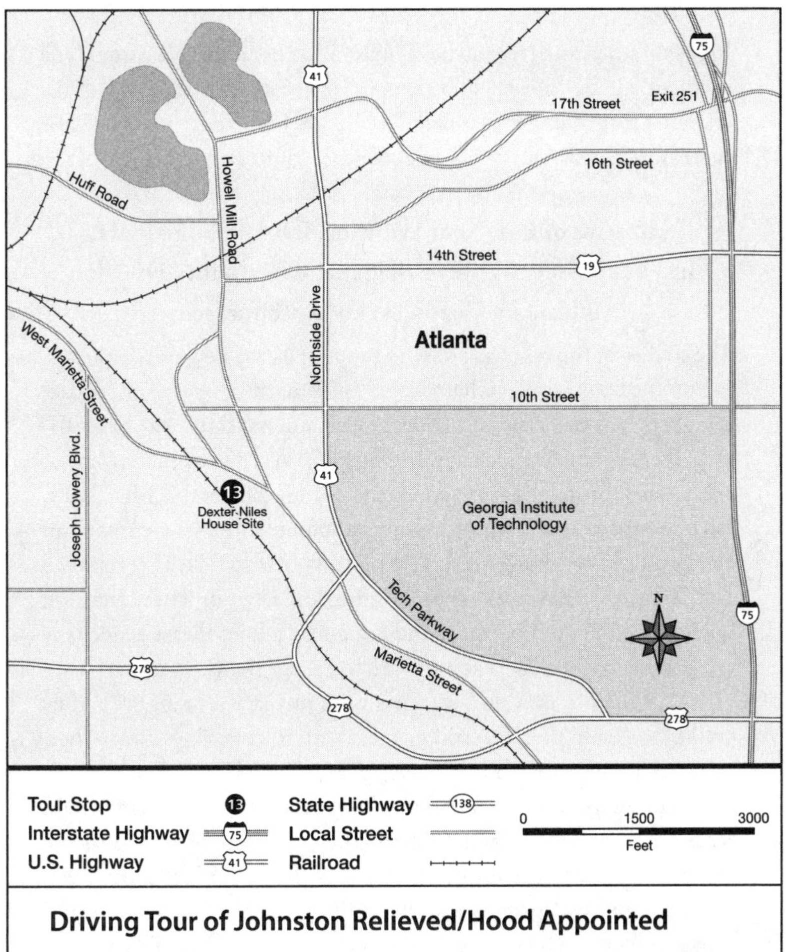

Driving Tour of Johnston Relieved/Hood Appointed

like children, others seemed speechless, and others poured forth denunciations and curses upon our deluded and infatuated President. In many commands, apparently, the address was not read at all. The fact was enough. Such formal mouthing would be a mocking of the uncontrollable grief and the tempest of indignation.

Mutiny, for the first time (and the last that I know of) lifted its ugly head. In our battery, Sgt. Thomas C. Allen, a superb soldier, mounted a stump and passionately advised going in a body to Johnston's headquarters to protest his leaving. A division was passing

Johnston's headquarters as he mounted his horse to ride away. One moment, all was silence, and then, as by one spontaneous impulse, a cry burst forth from every heart, "Johnston, Johnston, Johnston!" His successor, Hood, was by his side. Neither said a word.[35]

Narrative of Pvt. Sam Watkins, CSA, Company H, First Tennessee, Maney's Brigade, Cheatham's Division, Hardee's Corps, Army of Tennessee

The soldier of the relief guard who brought us the news while picketing on the banks of the Chattahoochee, remarked, by way of imparting gently the information, "Boys, we've fought all the war for nothing. There is nothing for us in store now." "What's the matter now?" "General Johnston is relieved, Generals Hardee and Kirby Smith have resigned, and General Hood is appointed to take command of the army [*sic*] of Tennessee." "My God! Is that so?" "It is certainly a fact." "Then I'll never fire another gun. Any news or letters that you wish carried home? I've quit, and am going home. Please tender my resignation to Jeff Davis as a private soldier in the C. S. Army."

Five men of that picket, there were just five, as rapidly as they could, took off their cartridge-boxes, after throwing down their guns, and their canteens and haversacks, taking out of their pockets their gun, wipers, wrench and gun-stoppers, and saying they would have no more use for "them things." They marched off and it was the last we ever saw of them. In ten minutes they were across the river, and no doubt had taken the oath of allegiance to the United States Government. Such was the sentiment of the army [*sic*] of Tennessee at that time.[36]

In fairness, memoirs like Watkins's were written after the war. Many soldiers had expressed at the time at least some concern about retreating prior to Johnston's removal.

Johnston's defensive strategy and tactics, combined with a few attempts at partial offense, had kept his army largely intact. However, the cost to the Confederacy had been the loss of much of northwestern Georgia. Every soldier knew that was about to change. After Davis's critical decision to place Hood in charge, several battles took place immediately.

Hood's headquarters, where he was notified of his promotion and elevation to command of the Army of Tennessee, was on the south side of the Chattahoochee River near where today's Veteran's Memorial Highway / Donald Lee Hollowell Parkway crosses the river. Nothing of the headquarters remains today, and no signage marks its former site.

Hood knew that he had been appointed to this command because he was expected to go on the offensive and protect Atlanta. As a direct result of his new responsibilities, he initiated the Battles of Peachtree Creek on July 20, Atlanta on July 22, and, indirectly, Ezra Church on July 28. While these were important engagements, all resulting in Confederate defeats, Hood fought them while following the mandate from Davis to resist Sherman.

Return to your vehicle and drive to Stop 14.

Turn southeast back onto Marietta Street, and drive about 0.8 mile to the intersection with Northside Drive. Turn right (southwest) onto Northside Drive and follow it as it turns southeast a short distance to the intersection with North Avenue. Turn left (east) onto North Avenue, and continue 0.7 mile or so under I-75 to Spring Street. Follow the signs to I-75 south. Drive south about 16.0 miles to Exit 233. Take Exit 233 to Jonesboro Road. Turn right (southwest) onto Jonesboro Road (State Road 54), and proceed about 3.2 miles to where Jonesboro Road becomes Main Street and parallels the railroad tracks. Continue south on Main Street 0.6 mile to the Jonesboro Depot on the left (east) side at 104 North Main Street. Park near the depot, leave your vehicle, and face west.

Stop 14: Jonesboro

Critical Decisions: (19) Sherman Destroys the Railroad, Not Hardee, (20) Sherman Ends the Pursuit of Hood, Captures Atlanta

The final two critical decisions of the Atlanta Campaign occurred in and around Jonesboro, south of Atlanta. Sherman and his men finally arrived at the surviving railroad and were ready to sever and destroy it.

Sherman's critical decision to cut the railroad supply lines to Atlanta, along with his critical decision to capture Atlanta, resulted in a series of movements around the city from the north, to the west, and then the south and east to strike the railroads. To sever the remaining railroad (near here), Sherman maneuvered with five corps toward Jonesboro. He and his men approached your position from the west. Hood, without most of his cavalry available for reconnaissance (Wheeler was raiding North Georgia and Tennessee), at first believed the Union movement was only a small raid, but he was incorrect. Within two days Sherman's troops had severely compromised the railroad to

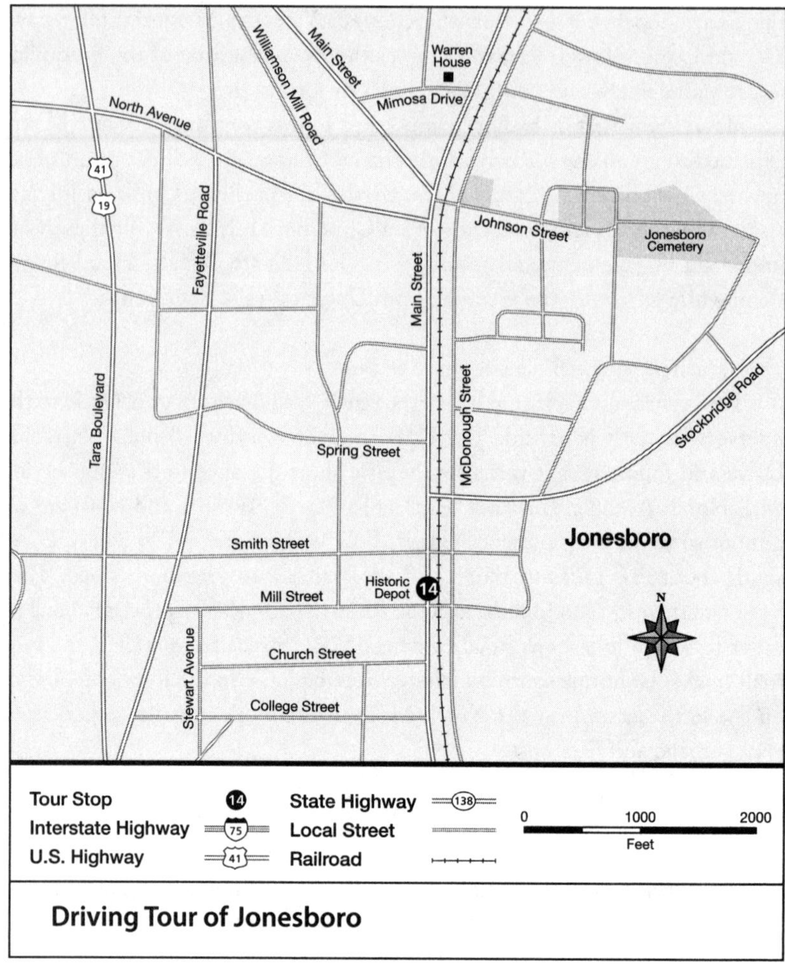

Driving Tour of Jonesboro

Montgomery and had begun to approach several locations on the remaining supply line from Macon.

Maj. Gen. Oliver O. Howard, commanding the Army of the Tennessee, and his troops were the first to cross the Flint River, a mile or so to the west of your position. A cautious general, Howard ordered his men to entrench on the high ground just east of the Flint River. Maj. Gen. "Blackjack" Logan's Fifteenth Corps was positioned on the left, and Brig. Gen. Thomas Ransom's Sixteenth Corps was positioned to the right (south) of the Fifteenth Corps, facing southeast. Part of Ransom's men still remained on the west side of the river. Maj. Gen. Francis Blair's Seventeenth Corps was stationed in reserve behind Logan's Fifteenth Corps.

The Union position was a formidable one, only about a mile from its intended target, the Macon and Western Railroad. Hood faced a desperate situation. Reacting to Sherman, he belatedly ordered Hardee's and Lee's Corps to Jonesboro to halt any further Union movement. After ordering an unsuccessful Confederate assault on August 31 just west of Jonesboro, the next day, September 1, Hood decided to withdraw Lee's Corps back to Atlanta. There, the troops would counter possible Union advances by Schofield and Thomas. Lee's withdrawal reduced Hardee's force to around twelve thousand men who had to contend with five Union corps of sixty thousand men. The odds of success were not good. Forced to spread out his corps to cover the loss of Lee's Corps, Hardee extended his position from the same location to the south up and around Tara Road and then east.

Report of Lieut. Gen. William J. Hardee, CSA, Commanding Hardee's Corps, Army of Tennessee

He [Hood] divided his force to attack a concentrated enemy. He in effect sent a detachment of his army to attack an enemy who was superior in numbers to his whole army.[37]

The Confederate line remained along the Fayetteville Road, about 0.2 mile west of your position, with the northern portion refused back to the right or east. At 4 p.m. Maj. Gen. Jefferson C. Davis's Fourteenth Corps attacked the northern end of the Confederate line. At the same time, Logan's Fifteenth Corps attacked from the west toward the Fayetteville Road. Davis overran Brig. Gen. Daniel Govan's brigade, which was defending the salient. Govan, most of his brigade (615 men), and eight cannon were captured. The timely arrival of Col. Michael Magevney's (formerly Vaughan's) brigade restored the Confederate line, and it held until darkness ended the Union assault.

Narrative of Pvt. Stanard C. Harley, CSA, 6th/7th Arkansas, Govan's Arkansas Brigade, Cleburne's Division, Hardee's Corps, Army of Tennessee

We were stretched one yard apart, trying to cover the enemy's front. The second assault was made in seven columns with fixed bayonets, guns atrail, and without firing a gun they ran over us like a drove of

Texas beeves by sheer force of numbers. We killed and wounded a great many of them, but our line was too weak.[38]

Overpowered by the Union hordes, Hardee was forced to retreat, hoping to escape almost certain annihilation or capture. After dark, he and what was left of his corps withdrew south down the railroad six miles to Lovejoy's Station. Sherman had an opportunity to cut Hardee off from the rest of the Confederates and possibly destroy his corps. Instead, Sherman made Critical Decision 20 to continue destroying the already severed Macon and Western Railroad. Elements of the Fourth and Fourteenth Corps had marched to and cut this railroad just south of Rough and Ready. This critical decision of Sherman's not to actively pursue and attack Hardee saved what was left of the Confederate corps to fight another day. Sherman had now eliminated all railroad supply lines to Atlanta, and Hood had no choice but to abandon the city he was placed in command to save. Faced with what many considered an impossible assignment, Hood blamed everyone but himself for Atlanta's loss, which was a telling blow to the Confederacy.

Narrative of Maj. Gen. William T. Sherman, USA, Commanding Military Division of the Mississippi

As he [Hardee] has a strong line, I do not wish to waste lives by an assault.[39]

Sherman made Critical Decision 21, the final one, to occupy Atlanta and not pursue the Confederate Army of Tennessee. Hood and his remaining men were thus allowed to escape. However, the capture of Atlanta assisted in giving President Lincoln the victory he needed for reelection in November. Atlanta's capture was the only major victory of Grant's proposed five-point plan, but it was enough to ensure a continuation of the Civil War until Union victory next spring.

Narrative of Maj. Gen. William T. Sherman, USA, Commanding Military Division of the Mississippi

I always expected to have a desperate fight to get possession of the Macon road, which was then the vital objective of the campaign. Its

> possession by us would, in my judgement, result in the capture of Atlanta, and give us the fruits of victory, although the destruction of Hood's army was the real object to be desired. Yet Atlanta was known as the "Gate-City of the South," was full of founderies (*sic*), arsenals, and machine shops, and I knew that its capture would be the death-knell of the Southern Confederacy.[40]

To return to I-75, turn right (north) onto Jonesboro Road. Drive 3.8 miles northeast back to I-75. This stop concludes the tour of the Jonesboro area and the critical decisions tour.

APPENDIX II

UNION ORDER OF BATTLE

MILITARY DIVISION OF THE MISSISSIPPI
Maj. Gen. William T. Sherman

Chief of Artillery
Brig. Gen. William F. Barry

Chief of Ordnance
Capt. Thomas G. Taylor

Chief of Engineers
Capt. Orlando M. Poe

Medical Director
Lieut. Col. Edward D. Kittoe

Headquarters Guard
7th Company, Ohio Sharpshooters, Lieut. William McCrory

ARMY OF THE CUMBERLAND
Maj. Gen. George H. Thomas

Chief of Artillery
Brig. Gen. John M. Brannan

Chief of Ordnance
Lieut. Otho E. Michaelis

Chief Engineer

Lieut. Henry C. Wharton

Medical Director

Surgeon George E. Cooper

Escort

Company I, 1st Ohio Cavalry, Lieut. Henry C. Reppert

FOURTH ARMY CORPS

Maj. Gen. Oliver O. O. Howard
Maj. Gen. David S. Stanley
Chief of Artillery, Capt. Lyman Bridges

First Division

Maj. Gen. David S. Stanley
Brig. Gen. William Grose
Brig. Gen. Nathan Kimball

First Brigade

Maj. Gen. Charles Cruft
Col. Isaac M. Kirby
21st Illinois, Maj. James E. Calloway
38th Illinois, Col. William T. Chapman
31st Indiana, Col. John T. Smith
81st Indiana, Lieut. Col. William C. Wheeler
1st Kentucky, Col. David A. Enyart
2nd Kentucky, Lieut. Col. John R. Hurd
90th Ohio, Lieut. Col. Samuel N. Yeoman
101st Ohio, Col. Isaac M. Kirby

Second Brigade

Brig. Gen. Walter C. Whitaker
Col. Jacob E. Taylor
96th Illinois, Col. Thomas E. Champion
115th Illinois, Col. Jessie H. Moore
35th Indiana, Maj. John P. Dufficy
84th Indiana, Col. Andrew J. Neff
21st Kentucky, Col. Samuel W. Price
40th Ohio, Col. Jacob B. Taylor
51st Ohio, Lieut. Col. Charles H. Wood

Third Brigade

Col. William Grose

Col. P. Sidney Post
59th Illinois, Col. P. Sidney Post
75th Illinois, Col. John E. Bennett
80th Illinois, Lieut. Col. William M. Kilgour
84th Illinois, Col. Louis H. Waters
9th Indiana, Col. Isaac C. B. Suman
30th Indiana, Lieut. Col. Orrin D. Hurd
36th Indiana, Lieut. Col. Oliver H. P. Carey
84th Indiana, Capt. John C. Taylor
77th Pennsylvania, Col. Thomas E. Rose

Artillery

Capt. Peter Simonson
Capt. Samuel M. McDowell
Capt. Theodore S. Thomasson
5th Indiana Light Battery, Capt. Alfred Morrison
Pennsylvania Light Battery B, Capt. Jacob Ziegler

Second Division

Brig. Gen. John Newton

First Brigade

Col. Francis T. Sherman
Brig. Gen. Nathan Kimball
Col. Emerson Opdycke
36th Illinois, Col. Silas Miller
44th Illinois, Col. Wallace W. Barrett
73rd Illinois, Maj. Thomas W. Motherspaw
74th Illinois, Col. Jason Marsh
88th Illinois, Lieut. Col. George W. Chandler
28th Kentucky, Col. J. Rown Boone
2nd Missouri, Col. Bernard Liabolt
15th Missouri, Col. Joseph Conrad
24th Wisconsin, Lieut. Col. Theodore S. West

Second Brigade

Brig. Gen. George D. Wagner
Col. John W. Blake
100th Illinois, Col. Frederick A. Bartleson
40th Indiana, Col. John W. Blake
57th Indiana, Lieut. Col. George W. Lennard
26th Ohio, Lieut. Col. William H. Squires

28th Kentucky, Col. J. Rowan Boone
97th Ohio, Col. John Q. Lane

Third Brigade

Brig. Gen. Charles G. Harker
Brig. Gen. Luther P. Bradley
22nd Illinois, Lieut. Col. Francis Swanwick
27th Illinois, Lieut. Col. William A. Schmitt
42nd Illinois, Lieut. Col. Edgar D. Swain
51st Illinois, Col. Luther P. Bradley
79th Illinois, Lieut. Col. Henry E. Rives
3rd Kentucky, Col. Henry C. Dunlap
64th Ohio, Col. Alexander McIlvain
65th Ohio, Lieut. Col. Horatio N. Whitbeck
125th Ohio, Col. Emerson Opdycke

Artillery

Capt. Charles C. Aleshire
Capt. Wilbur F. Goodspeed
1st Illinois Light Battery M, Capt. George W. Spencer
1st Ohio Light Battery A, Capt. Wilbur F. Goodspeed

Third Division

Brig. Gen. Thomas J. Wood
Col. P. Sidney Post

First Brigade

Brig. Gen. August Willich
Col. William H. Gibson
Col. Richard H. Nodine
Col. Charles T. Hotchkiss
25th Illinois, Col. Richard H. Nodine
35th Illinois, Lieut. Col. William P. Chandler
89th Illinois, Col. Charles T. Hotchkiss
32nd Indiana, Col. Frank Erdelmeyer
8th Kansas, Col. John A. Martin
15th Ohio, Col. William Wallace
49th Ohio, Lieut. Col. Samuel F. Gray
15th Wisconsin, Maj. George Wilson

Second Brigade

Brig. Gen. William B. Hazen
Col. P. Sidney Post

59th Illinois, Capt. Samuel West
6th Indiana, Lieut. Col. Calvin D. Campbell
5th Kentucky, Col. William W. Berry
6th Kentucky, Maj. Richard T. Whitaker
23rd Kentucky, Lieut. Col. James C. Foy
1st Ohio, Maj. Joab A. Stafford
6th Ohio, Col. Nicholas L. Anderson
41st Ohio, Lieut. Col. Robert L. Kimberly
71st Ohio, Col. Henry K. McConnell
93rd Ohio, Lieut. Col. Daniel Bowman
124th Ohio, Col. Oliver H. Payne

Third Brigade

Brig. Gen. Samuel Beatty
Col. Frederick Knefler
79th Indiana, Col. Frederick Knefler
86th Indiana, Col. George F. Dick
9th Kentucky, Col. George H. Cram
17th Kentucky, Col. Alexander M. Stout
13th Ohio, Col. Dwight Jarvis
19th Ohio, Col. Charles F. Manderson
59th Ohio, Lieut. Col. Granville A. Frambles

Artillery

Capt. Cullen Bradley
Bridges's Illinois Light Battery, Capt. Lyman Bridges
6th Ohio Light Battery, Lieut. Oliver H. P. Ayres

FOURTEENTH ARMY CORPS

Maj. Gen. John M. Palmer
Brig. Gen. Richard W. Johnston

First Division

Brig. Gen. Richard W. Johnson
Brig. Gen. John H. King
Brig. Gen. William P. Carlin

Provost Guard

Capt. Charles F. Trowbridge
Company D, 1st Battalion, 16th United States Regiment

First Brigade

Brig. Gen. William P. Carlin

Col. Anson G. McCook
104th Illinois, Lieut. Col. Douglas Hapeman
42nd Indiana, Lieut. Col. William T. B. McIntire
88th Indiana, Lieut. Col. Cyrus E. Briant
15th Kentucky, Col. Marion C. Taylor
2nd Ohio, Col. Anson G. McCook
33rd Ohio, Lieut. Col. James H. M. Montgomery
94th Ohio, Col. Rue P. Hutchins
10th Wisconsin, Capt. Jacob W. Roby
21st Wisconsin, Lieut. Col. Harrison C. Hobart

Second Brigade

Brig. Gen. John H. King
Col. William L. Stoughton
Col. Marshall F. Moore
Maj. John R. Edie
11th Michigan, Col. William L. Stoughton
15th US (6 companies), Maj. John R. Edie
15th US (9 companies), Maj. Albert Tracy
16th US (4 companies), Capt. Robert P. Barry
16th US (4 companies), Capt. Alexander H. Stanton
18th US (8 companies), Capt. George W. Smith
18th US (4 companies), Capt. William J. Fetterman
19th US (5 companies), Capt. James Mooney

Third Brigade

Col. Benjamin Scribner
Col. Josiah Given
Col. Marshall F. Moore
37th Indiana, Lieut. Col. William D. Ward
38th Indiana, Lieut. Col. Daniel F. Griffin
21st Ohio, Col. James M. Neibling
74th Ohio, Col. Josiah Given
78th Pennsylvania, Col. William Sirwell
79th Pennsylvania, Col. Henry A. Hambright
1st Wisconsin, Lieut. Col. George B. Bingham

Artillery

Capt. Lucius H. Drury
1st Illinois Light Battery C, Capt. Mark H. Prescott
1st Ohio Battery I, Capt. Hubert Dilger

Second Division

Brig. Gen. Jefferson C. Davis
Brig. Gen. James D. Morgan

First Brigade

Brig. Gen. James D. Morgan
Col. Robert F. Smith
Col. Charles M. Lum
10th Illinois, Col. John Tillson
16th Illinois, Col. Robert F. Smith
60th Illinois, Col. William B. Anderson
10th Michigan, Col. Charles M. Lum
14th Michigan, Col. Henry R. Mizner
17th New York, Col. William T. C. Grower

Second Brigade

Col. John G. Mitchell
34th Illinois, Lieut. Col. Oscar Van Tassell
78th Illinois, Col. Carter Van Vleck
98th Ohio, Lieut. Col. John S. Pearce
108th Ohio, Lieut. Col. Joseph Good
113th Ohio, Lieut. Col. Darius B. Warner
121st Ohio, Col. Henry B. Banning

Third Brigade

Col. Daniel McCook
Col. Oscar F. Harmon
Col. Caleb J. Dilworth
Lieut. Col. James W. Langley
85th Illinois, Col. Caleb J. Dilworth
86th Illinois, Lieut. Col. Allen L. Fahnestack
110th Illinois, Lieut. Col. E. Hibbard Topping
125th Illinois, Col. Oscar F. Harmon
22nd Indiana, Lieut. Col. William M. Wiles
52nd Ohio, Lieut. Col. Charles W. Clancy

Artillery

Capt. Charles M. Barnett
2nd Illinois Light Battery I, Lieut. Alonzo W. Coe
5th Wisconsin Light Battery and 2nd Minnesota Battery (detachment), Capt. George Q. Gardner

THIRD DIVISION
Brig. Gen. Absalom Baird

FIRST BRIGADE
Brig. Gen. John B. Turchin
Col. Moses B. Walker
19th Illinois, Col. Alexander W. Raffen
24th Illinois, Capt. August Mauff
82nd Indiana, Col. Morton C. Hunter
23rd Missouri, Col. William P. Robinson
11th Ohio, Lieut. Col. Ogden Street
17th Ohio, Col. Durbin Ward
31st Ohio, Col. Moses B. Walker
89th Ohio, Col. Caleb H. Carlton
92nd Ohio, Col. Benjamin D. Fearing

SECOND BRIGADE
Col. Ferdinand Van Dever
Col. Newell Gleason
75th Indiana, Col. William O'Brien
87th Indiana, Col. Newell Gleason
101st Indiana, Lieut. Col. Thomas Doan
2nd Minnesota, Col. James George
9th Ohio, Col. Gustave Kammerling
35th Ohio, Maj. Joseph L. Budd
105th Ohio, Lieut. Col. George T. Perkins

THIRD BRIGADE
Col. George P. Este
10th Indiana, Lieut. Col. Marsh B. Taylor
74th Indiana, Lieut. Col. Myron Baker
10th Kentucky, Col. William H. Hays
18th Kentucky, Col. Hubbard K. Milward
14th Ohio, Maj. John W. Wilson
38th Ohio, Col. William A. Choate

ARTILLERY
Capt. George Estep
7th Indiana Light Battery, Capt. Otho H. Morgan
19th Indiana Light Battery, Lieut. William P. Stackhouse

TWENTIETH ARMY CORPS
Maj. Gen. Joseph Hooker

Brig. Gen. Alpheus S. Williams
Maj. Gen. Henry W. Slocum

Escort
Company K, 15th Illinois Cavalry, Capt. William Duncan

First Division
Brig. Gen. Alpheus S. Williams
Brig. Gen. Joseph F. Knipe

First Brigade
Brig. Gen. Joseph F. Knipe
Col. Warren W. Packer
5th Connecticut, Col. Warren W. Packer
3rd Maryland Detachment, Lieut. Col. David Gove
123rd New York, Col. Archibald L. McDougall
141st New York, Col. William K. Logie
46th Pennsylvania, Col. James L. Selfridge

Second Brigade
Brig. Gen. Thomas H. Ruger
27th Indiana, Col. Silas Colgrove
2nd Massachusetts, Col. William Cogswell
13th New Jersey, Col. Ezra A. Carman
107th New York, Col. Nirom M. Crane
150th New York, Col. John H. Ketcham
3rd Wisconsin, Col. William Hawley

Third Brigade
Col. James S. Robinson
Col. Horace Broughton
82nd Illinois, Lieut. Col. Edward S. Salomon
101st Illinois, Lieut. Col. John B. Le Sage
45th New York, Col. Adolphus Dobke
143rd New York, Col. Horace Broughton
61st Ohio, Col. Stephen J. McGroarty
82nd Ohio, Col. David Thompson
31st Wisconsin, Col. Francis H. West

Artillery
Capt. John D. Woodbury
1st New York Light Battery I, Lieut. Charles E. Winegar
1st New York Light Battery M, Capt. John D. Woodbury

Second Division
Brig. Gen. John W. Geary

First Brigade
Col. Charles Candy
Col. Ario Pardee
5th Ohio, Col. John H. Patrick
7th Ohio, Lieut. Col. Samuel McClelland
29th Ohio, Col. William T. Fitch
66th Ohio, Lieut. Col. Eugene Powell
28th Pennsylvania, Lieut. Col. John Flynn
147th Pennsylvania, Col. Ario Pardee

Second Brigade
Col. Adolphus Buschbeck
Col. John T. Lockman
Col. Patrick H. Jones
Col. George W. Mindil
33rd New Jersey, Col. George W. Mindil
119th New York, Col. John T. Lockman
134th New York, Lieut. Col. Allan H. Jackson
154th New York, Col. Patrick H. Jones
27th Pennsylvania, Lieut. Col. August Riedt
73rd Pennsylvania, Maj. Charles C. Cresson
109th Pennsylvania, Capt. Frederick L. Gimber

Third Brigade
Col. David Ireland
Col. George A. Cobham
60th New York, Col. Abel Godard
78th New York, Lieut. Col. Harvey S. Chatsfield
102nd New York, Col. Herbert von Hammerstein
137th New York, Lieut. Col. Koert S. Van Voohis
149th New York, Col. Henry A. Barnum
29th Pennsylvania, Col. William Richards
111th Pennsylvania, Col. George A. Cobham

Artillery
Capt. William Wheeler
Capt. Charles C. Aleshire
13th New York Light Battery, Lieut. Henry Bundy
Pennsylvania Light Battery E, Capt. James D. McGill

Third Division
Maj. Gen. Daniel Butterfield
Brig. Gen. William T. Ward

First Brigade
Brig. Gen. William T. Ward
Col. Benjamin Harrison
102nd Illinois, Col. Franklin C. Smith
105th Illinois, Col. Daniel Dustin
129th Illinois, Col. Henry Chase
70th Indiana, Col. Benjamin Harrison
79th Ohio, Col. Henry G. Kennett

Second Brigade
Col. John Coburn
20th Connecticut, Lieut. Col. Philo B. Buckingham
33rd Indiana, Maj. Levin T. Miller
85th Indiana, Col. John P. Baird
19th Michigan, Col. Henry C. Gilbert
22nd Wisconsin, Col. William L. Utley

Third Brigade
Col. James Wood
20th Connecticut, Col. Samuel Ross
33rd Massachusetts, Lieut. Col. Godfrey Rider
136th New York, Lieut. Col. Lester B. Faulkner
55th Ohio, Col. Charles B. Gambee
73rd Ohio, Maj. Samuel H. Hurst
26th Wisconsin, Lieut. Col. Frederick C. Winkler

Artillery
Capt. Marco B. Gary
1st Michigan Light Battery I, Capt. Luther R. Smith
1st Ohio Light Battery C, Lieut. Jerome B. Stephens

Reserve Brigade
Col. Joseph W. Burke
Col. Heber Le Favour
10th Ohio, Col. Joseph W. Burke
9th Michigan, Lieut. Col. William Wilkinson
22nd Michigan, Lieut. Col. Henry S. Dean

Pontoniers
Col. George P. Buell

58th Indiana, Lieut. Col. Joseph Moore
Pontoon Battalion, Capt. Patrick O'Connell

Ammunition Train Guard
1st Battalion Ohio Sharpshooters, Capt. Gershom M. Barber

Siege Artillery
11th Indiana Battery, Capt. Arnold Sutermeister

ARMY OF THE TENNESSEE

Maj. Gen. James B. McPherson
Maj. Gen. John A. Logan

Chief of Artillery
Capt. Andrew Hickenlooper

Chief Engineer
Capt. Chauncey B. Reese

Medical Director
Surgeon John Moore

Escort
4th Company Ohio Cavalry, Capt. John S. Foster
Company B, 1st Ohio Cavalry, Capt. George F. Conn

FIFTEENTH ARMY CORPS

Maj. Gen. John A. Logan
Maj. Gen. Morgan L. Smith

First Division
Brig. Gen. Peter J. Osterhaus
Brig. Gen. Charles R. Woods
Col. Milo Smith

First Brigade
Brig. Gen. Charles R. Woods
26th Iowa, Col. Milo Smith
30th Iowa, Lieut. Col. Aurelius Roberts
27th Missouri, Col. Thomas Curly
76th Ohio, Col. William B. Woods

Second Brigade
Col. James A. Williamson
4th Iowa, Lieut. Col. Samuel D. Nichols

9th Iowa, Col. David Carskaddon
25th Iowa, Col. George A. Stone
31st Iowa, Col. William Smyth

Third Brigade
Col. Hugo Wangelin
3rd Missouri, Col. Theodore Meumann
12th Missouri, Lieut. Col. Jacob Kaercher
17th Missouri, Maj. Francis Romer
29th Missouri, Lieut. Col. Joseph S. Gage
31st Missouri, Lieut. Col. Samuel P. Simpson
32nd Missouri, Maj. Abraham J. Seay

Artillery
Maj. Clemens Landgraeber
2nd Missouri Light Battery, Capt. Louis Voelkner
4th Ohio Light Battery, Capt. George Froehlich

Second Division
Brig. Gen. Morgan L. Smith
Brig. Gen. Joseph A. J. Lightburn
Brig. Gen. William B. Hazen

First Brigade
Brig. Gen. Giles A. Smith
Col. James S. Martin
Col. Theodore Jones
55th Illinois, Lieut. Col. Theodore C. Chandler
11th Illinois, Col. James S. Martin
116th Illinois, Lieut. Col. Anderson Froman
127th Illinois, Lieut. Col. Frank S. Curtiss
6th Missouri, Lieut. Col. Delos Van Deusen
8th Missouri, Lieut. Col. David C. Coleman
30th Ohio, Lieut. Col. George H. Hildt
57th Ohio, Col. Americus V. Rice

Second Brigade
Brig. Gen. Joseph Lightburn
Col. Wells S. Jones
111th Illinois, Col. James S. Martin
83rd Indiana, Col. Benjamin J. Spooner
30th Ohio, Col. Theodore Jones
37th Ohio, Lieut. Col. Louis von Blessingh

47th Ohio, Col. Augustus C. Perry
53rd Ohio, Col. Wells S. Jones
54th Ohio, Lieut. Col. Robert Williams

Artillery
Capt. Francis De Gress
1st Illinois Light Battery A, Lieut. Samuel S. Smyth
1st Illinois Light Battery B, Capt. Israel P. Rumsey
1st Illinois Light Battery H, Capt. Francis De Gress

Third Division
Brig. Gen. John E. Smith
Deployed guarding the railroad; headquarters at Cartersville

Fourth Division
Brig. Gen. William Harrow

First Brigade
Col. Reuben Williams
Col. John M. Oliver
26th Illinois, Lieut. Col. Robert A. Gillmore
48th Illinois, Maj. Edward Adams
90th Illinois, Lieut. Col. Owen Stuart
12th Indiana Lieut. Col. James Goodnow
99th Indiana, Lieut. Col. John M. Berkey
100th Indiana, Lieut. Col. Albert Heath
15th Michigan, Lieut. Col. Frederick S. Hutchinson
70th Ohio, Capt. Louis Love

Second Brigade
Brig. Gen. Charles C. Walcutt
40th Illinois, Lieut. Col. Rigdon S. Barnhill
103rd Illinois, Col. Willard A. Dickerman
97th Indiana, Col. Robert F. Catterson
6th Iowa, Lieut. Col. Alexander J. Miller
46th Ohio, Maj. Henry H. Giesy

Third Brigade
Col. John M. Oliver
48th Illinois, Col. Lucien Greathouse
99th Indiana, Col. Alexander Fowler
15th Michigan, Lieut. Col. Austin E. Jaquith
70th Ohio, Maj. William B. Brown

Artillery
Maj. John T. Cheney
1st Illinois Light Battery F, Capt. Josiah H. Burton
1st Iowa Light Battery, Capt. Henry Griffiths

SIXTEENTH ARMY CORPS

Maj. Gen. Grenville M. Dodge
Brig. Gen. Thomas E. G. Ransom

Escort
1st Alabama Cavalry, Col. George L. Godfrey
Company A, 52nd Illinois, Capt. George E. Young

Second Division
Brig. Gen. Thomas W. Sweeny
Brig. Gen. John M. Corse

First Brigade
Brig. Gen. Elliott W. Rice
52nd Illinois, Lieut. Col. Edwin A. Bowen
66th Indiana, Lieut. Col. Roger Martin
2nd Iowa, Col. James B. Weaver
7th Iowa, Lieut. Col. James C. Parrott

Second Brigade
Col. Patrick E. Burke
Lieut. Col. Robert N. Adams
Col. August Mersy
Col. Robert N. Adams
9th Illinois Mounted Infantry, Lieut. Col. Jesse J. Phillips
12th Illinois, Lieut. Col. Henry Van Sellar
66th Illinois, Capt. William S. Boyd
81st Ohio, Lieut. Col. Robert N. Adams

Third Brigade
Col. Moses E. Bane
7th Illinois, Col. Richard Rowett
50th Illinois, Maj. William Hanna
57th Illinois, Lieut. Col. Frederick J. Harlbut
39th Iowa, Lieut. Col. Henry J. B. Cummings

Artillery
Capt. Frederick Welker

1st Michigan Light Battery B, Capt. Albert R. Arndt
1st Missouri Light Battery H, Lieut. Andrew T. Blodgett
1st Missouri Light Battery I, Lieut. John F. Brunner

Fourth Division
Brig. Gen. James C. Veatch
Brig. Gen. John W. Fuller
Brig. Gen. Thomas E. G. Ransom

First Brigade
Brig. Gen. John W. Fuller
Col. John Morrill
Lieut. Col. Henry T. McDowell
64th Illinois, Col. John Morrill
18th Missouri, Lieut. Col. Charles S. Sheldon
27th Ohio, Lieut. Col. Mendal Churchill
39th Ohio, Col. Edward F. Noyes

Second Brigade
Brig. Gen. John W. Sprague
35th New Jersey, Col. John J. Cladek
43rd Ohio, Col. Wager Swayne
63rd Ohio, Lieut. Col. Charles E. Brown
25th Wisconsin, Col. Milton Montgomery

Third Brigade
Col. William T. Grower
Col. John Tillison
10th Illinois, Capt. George C. Lusk
25th Indiana, Lieut. Col. John Rheinlander
17th New York, Maj. Joel O. Martin
32nd Wisconsin, Col. Charles H. De Groat

Artillery
Capt. Jerome B. Burrows
Capt. George Robinson
1st Michigan Light Battery C, Lieut. Henry Shier
14th Ohio Light Battery, Capt. Jerome B. Burrows
2nd United States Battery F, Capt. Albert M. Murry

SEVENTEENTH ARMY CORPS
Maj. Gen. Francis P. Blair

Escort

Company M, 1st Ohio Cavalry, Lieut. Charles H. Schultz
Company G, 9th Illinois Mounted Infantry, Capt. Isaac Clements
Company G, 11th Illinois Cavalry, Capt. Stephen S. Tripp

Third Division

Brig. Gen. Mortimer D. Leggett
Brig. Gen. Charles R. Woods

Escort

Company D, 1st Ohio Cavalry, Lieut. James W. Kirkendall

First Brigade

Brig. Gen. Manning F. Force
Col. George E. Bryant
20th Illinois, Lieut. Col. Daniel Bradley
30th Illinois, Col. Warren Shedd
31st Illinois, Col. Edwin S. McCook
45th Illinois, Lieut. Col. Robert P. Sealy
12th Wisconsin, Col. George E. Bryant
16th Wisconsin, Col. Cassius Fairchild

Second Brigade

Col. Robert K. Scott
Lieut. Col. Greenberry F. Wiles
20th Ohio, Lieut. Col. John C. Fry
32nd Ohio, Col. Benjamin F. Potts
68th Ohio, Lieut. Col. George E. Wells
78th Ohio, Lieut. Col. Greenberry F. Wiles

Third Brigade

Col. Adam G. Malloy
17th Wisconsin, Lieut. Col. Thomas McMahon
Worden's Battalion, Maj. Asa Worden

Artillery

Capt. William S. Williams
1st Illinois Light Battery D, Capt. Edgar H. Cooper
1st Michigan Light Battery H, Capt. Marcus D. Elliot
3rd Ohio Light Battery, Lieut. John Sullivan

Fourth Division

Brig. Gen. Walter Q. Gresham
Brig. Gen. Giles A. Smith

Escort

Company G, 11th Illinois Cavalry, Capt. Stephen S. Tripp

First Brigade

Col. William L. Sanderson
Col. Benjamin F. Potts
32nd Illinois, Col. John Logan
53rd Illinois, Lieut. Col. John W. McClanahan
23rd Indiana, Lieut. Col. William P. Davis
53rd Indiana, Lieut. Col. William Jones
3rd Iowa (3 companies), Capt. Daniel McLennan
32nd Ohio, Capt. William M. Morris
12th Wisconsin, Col. George E. Bryant

Second Brigade

Col. George C. Rodgers
Col. Isaac C. Pugh
14th Illinois, Capt. Carlos R. Cox
15th Illinois, Maj. Rufus C. McEathron
32nd Illinois, Lieut. Col. George H. English
41st Illinois, Maj. Robert H. McFadden
53rd Illinois, Lieut. Col. John W. McClanahan

Third Brigade

Col. William Hall
Brig. Gen. William W. Belknap
11th Iowa, Col. John C. Abercrombie
13th Iowa, Col. John Shane
15th Iowa, Col. William W. Belknap
16th Iowa, Lieut. Col. Addison H. Sanders

Artillery

Capt. Edward Spear
2nd Illinois Light Battery F, Lieut. Walter H. Powell
1st Minnesota Battery, Capt. William Z. Clayton
1st Missouri Light Battery C, Capt. John L. Matthaei
10th Ohio Light Battery, Capt. Francis Seaman
15th Ohio Light Battery, Lieut. James Burdick

ARMY OF THE OHIO (TWENTY-THIRD CORPS)

Maj. Gen. John M. Schofield
Maj. Gen. Jacob D. Cox

Escort

Company G, 7th Ohio Cavalry, Capt. John A. Asbury

Engineer Battalion

Capt. Charles E. McAlester
Capt. Oliver S. McClure

First Division

Brig. Gen. Alvin P. Hovey

First Brigade

Col. Richard Barter
120th Indiana, Lieut. Col. Allen W. Prather
124th Indiana, Col. James Burgess
128th Indiana, Col. Richard P. De Hart

Second Brigade

Col. John Q. McQuiston
Col. Peter T. Swaine
123rd Indiana, Lieut. Col. William A. Cullen
129th Indiana, Col. Charles Case
130th Indiana, Col. Charles S. Parrish
99th Ohio, Lieut. Col. John E. Cummins

Artillery

23rd Indiana Light Battery, Lieut. Luther S. Houghton
24th Indiana Light Battery, Capt. Alexander Hardy

Second Division

Brig. Gen. Henry M. Judah
Brig. Gen. Milo S. Hascall

First Brigade

Brig. Gen. Nathaniel C. McLean
Brig. Gen. Joseph A. Cooper
80th Indiana, Lieut. Col. Alfred D. Owen
91st Indiana, Lieut. Col. Charles H. Butterfield
13th Kentucky, Col. William E. Hobson
25th Michigan, Col. Benjamin F. Orcutt
45th Ohio, Col. Benjamin P. Runkle
3rd Tennessee, Col. William Cross
6th Tennessee, Col. Joseph H. Cooper

Second Brigade

Brig. Gen. Milo S. Hascall
Col. John R. Bond
Col. William E. Hobson
107th Illinois, Lieut. Col. Uriah M. Laurence
80th Indiana, Lieut. Col. Alfred D. Owen
13th Kentucky, Col. William E. Hobson
23rd Michigan, Lieut. Col. Oliver L. Spaulding
45th Ohio, Col. Benjamin P. Runkle
111th Ohio, Col. John R. Bond
118th Ohio, Lieut. Col. Thomas L. Young

Third Brigade

Col. Silas A. Strickland
14th Kentucky, Col. George W. Gallup
20th Kentucky, Lieut. Col. Thomas B. Waller
27th Kentucky, Lieut. Col. John H. Ward
50th Ohio, Lieut. Col. George R. Elstner

Artillery

Capt. Joseph C. Shields
22nd Indiana Light Battery, Capt. Benjamin F. Denning
1st Michigan Light Battery F, Capt. Byron D. Paddock
19th Ohio Light Battery, Capt. Joseph C. Shields

Third Division

Brig. Gen. Jacob D. Cox
Col. James W. Reilly

First Brigade

Col. James W. Reilly
Maj. James W. Gault
112th Illinois, Col. Thomas J. Henderson
16th Kentucky, Col. James W. Gault
100th Ohio, Col. Patrick S. Slevin
104th Ohio, Col. Oscar W. Sterl
8th Tennessee, Col. Felix A. Reeve

Second Brigade

Brig. Gen. Mahlon D. Mason
Col. John S. Hart
Col. Milo S. Hascall
Col. John S. Casement
Col. Daniel Cameron

65th Illinois, Col. William S. Stewart
63rd Indiana, Col. Israel N. Stiles
65th Indiana, Lieut. Col. Thomas Johnson
24th Kentucky, Col. John S. Hart
103rd Ohio, Capt. William W. Hutchinson
5th Tennessee, Col. James T. Shelley

Third Brigade
Brig. Gen. Nathaniel McLean
Col. Robert K. Byrd
Col. Israel N. Stiles
11th Kentucky, Col. Palace Love
12th Kentucky, Lieut. Col. Laurence H. Rousseau
1st Tennessee, Col. Robert K. Byrd
5th Tennessee, Col. James T. Shelley

Dismounted Cavalry Brigade
Col. Eugene W. Crittenden
16th Illinois, Capt. Hiram S. Hanchett
12th Kentucky, Lieut. Col. James T. Bramlette

Artillery
Maj. Henry W. Wells
15th Indiana Light Battery, Capt. Alonzo D. Harvey
1st Ohio Light Battery D, Capt. Giles A. Cockerill

CAVALRY CORPS, ARMY OF THE CUMBERLAND
Brig. Gen. Washington Elliott

Escort
Company D, 4th Ohio, Capt. Philip H. Warner

First Division
Brig. Gen. Edward M. McCook

First Brigade
Col. Joseph B. Dorr
Col. James P. Brownlow
Brig. Gen. John T. Croxton
8th Iowa, Lieut. Col. Horatio G. Barner
4th Kentucky Mounted Infantry, Col. John T. Croxton
2nd Michigan, Lieut. Col. Benjamin Smith
1st Tennessee, Col. James P. Brownlow

Second Brigade

Col. Oscar H. La Grange
Lieut. Col. James W. Stewart
Lieut. Col. Horace P. Lamson
Lieut. Col. William H. Torrey
2nd Indiana, Lieut. Col. James W. Stewart
4th Indiana, Lieut. Col. Horace P. Lamson
1st Wisconsin, Maj. Nathan Paine

Third Brigade

Col. Louis D. Watkins
Col. John K. Faulkner
4th Kentucky, Col. Wickliffe Cooper
6th Kentucky, Maj. William H. Fidler
7th Kentucky, Col. John K. Faulkner

Artillery

18th Indiana Horse Artillery Battery, Lieut. William B. Rippetoe

Second Division

Brig. Gen. Kenner Garrard

First Brigade

Col. Robert H. G. Minty
4th Michigan, Lieut. Col. Josiah B. Park
7th Pennsylvania, Col. William B. Sipes
4th United States, Capt. James B. McIntyre

Second Brigade

Col. Eli Long
Col. Beroth B. Eggleston
1st Ohio, Col. Beroth B. Eggleston
3rd Ohio, Col. Charles B. Seidel
4th Ohio, Lieut. Col. Oliver P. Robie

Third Mounted Infantry (Lightning Brigade)

Col. John T. Wilder
Col. Abram O. Miller
98th Illinois, Lieut. Col. Edward Kitchell
123rd Illinois, Lieut. Col. Jonathan Biggs
17th Indiana, Lieut. Col. Henry Jordan
72nd Indiana, Col. Abram O. Miller

Artillery

Chicago Board Of Trade Battery, Lieut. George Robinson

Third Division

Brig. Gen. Judson Kilpatrick
Col. Eli H. Murray
Col. William W. Lowe

First Brigade

Lieut. Col. Robert Klein
3rd Indiana, Maj. Alfred Gaddis
5th Iowa, Maj. Harlon Baird

Second Brigade

Col. Charles C. Smith
Maj. Thomas W. Sanderson
Lieut. Col. Fielder A. Jones
8th Indiana, Lieut. Col. Fielder A. Jones
2nd Kentucky, Lieut. Col. William H. Eifort
10th Ohio, Maj. William W. Sanderson

Third Brigade

Col. Eli H. Murray
Col. Smith D. Adkins
92nd Illinois Mounted Infantry, Col. Smith D. Adkins
3rd Kentucky, Maj. Lewis Wolfley
5th Kentucky, Col. Oliver L. Baldwin

Artillery

10th Wisconsin Battery, Capt. Yates V. Beebe

Cavalry Division, Army Of The Ohio

Maj. Gen. George Stoneman
Col. Horace Capron

Escort

Company D, 7th Ohio, Lieut. Samuel Murphy

First Brigade

Col. Israel Garrard
9th Michigan, Col. George S. Acker
7th Ohio, Lieut. Col. George G. Miner

Second Brigade

Col. James Biddle
16th Illinois, Capt. Hiram S. Hanchett
5th Indiana, Col. Thomas H. Butler
6th Indiana, Lieut. Col. Courtland C. Matson
12th Kentucky, Col. Eugene W. Crittenden

Third Brigade

Col. Horace Capron

14th Illinois, Lieut. Col. David P. Jenkins

8th Michigan, Lieut. Col. Elisha Mix

McLaughlin's Ohio Squadron, Maj. Richard Rice

Independent Brigade

Col. Alexander W. Holeman

Lieut. Col. Silas Adams

1st Kentucky, Lieut. Col. Silas Adams

11th Kentucky, Lieut. Col. Archibald J. Alexander

Artillery

24th Indiana Battery, Capt. Alexander Hardy

APPENDIX III

CONFEDERATE ORDER OF BATTLE

ARMY OF TENNESSEE
Gen. Joseph E. Johnston
Gen. John B. Hood

Chief of Staff
Brig. Gen. William W. Mackall
Brig. Gen. Francis A. Shoup

Chief Ordnance Officer
Capt. W. D. Humphries
Lieut. Col. James M. Kennard

Chief Engineer
Lieut. Col. Stephen W. Presstman
Maj. Gen. Martin L. Smith

Medical Director
Surgeon (Maj) A. J. Foard

HARDEE'S ARMY CORPS
Lieut. Gen. William J. Hardee
Maj. Gen. Patrick R. Cleburne

CHEATHAM'S DIVISION

Maj. Gen. Benjamin F. Cheatham
Brig. Gen. George E. Maney
Brig. Gen. John C. Carter

MANEY'S TENNESSEE BRIGADE

Brig. Gen. George E. Maney
Col. George C. Porter
Col. Francis M. Walker
1st & 27th Tennessee, Col. Hume R. Feild
4th Confederate, Lieut. Col. Oliver A. Bradshaw
6th & 9th Tennessee, Lieut. Col. John W. Buford
41st Tennessee, Col. James D. Tillman
50th Tennessee, Col. Stephen H. Colms

STRAHL'S TENNESSEE BRIGADE

Brig. Gen. Otho F. Strahl
Col. Andrew J. Kellar
4th & 5th Tennessee, Col. Jonathan J. Lamb
19th Tennessee, Col. Francis M. Walker
24th Tennessee, Col. John A. Wilson
31st Tennessee, Lieut. Col. Fountain E. P. Stafford
33rd Tennessee, Col. Warner P. Jones

WRIGHT'S TENNESSEE BRIGADE

Col. John C. Carter
8th Tennessee, Col. John H. Anderson
16th Tennessee, Maj. Benjamin Randals
28th Tennessee, Col. Sidney S. Stanton
38th Tennessee, Lieut. Col. Andrew D. Gwynne
51st & 52nd Tennessee, Lieut. Col. John W. Estes

VAUGHAN'S TENNESSEE BRIGADE

Brig. Gen. Alfred J. Vaughan, Jr.
Col. Michael Magevney
Col. George W. Gordon
11th Tennessee, Col. George W. Gordon
12th & 47th Tennessee, Col. William M. Watkins
13th & 154th Tennessee, Col. Michael Magevney
29th Tennessee, Col. Horace Rice

CLEBURNE'S DIVISION

Maj. Gen. Patrick R. Cleburne
Brig. Gen. Mark P. Lowrey

Polk's Brigade

Brig. Gen. Lucius Polk
1st & 15th Arkansas, Lieut. Col. William H. Martin
5th Confederate, Maj. Richard J. Person
2nd Tennessee, Col. William D. Robison
35th & 48th Tennessee, Capt. Henry G. Evans

Govan's Arkansas Brigade

Brig. Gen. Daniel C. Govan
2nd & 24th Arkansas, Col. E. Warfield
5th & 13th Arkansas, Col. John E. Murray
6th & 7th Arkansas, Col. Samuel G. Smith
8th & 19th Arkansas, Col. George F. Baucum
3rd Confederate, Capt. M. H. Dixon

Lowrey's Brigade

Brig. Gen. Mark P. Lowery
Col. John Weir
16th Alabama, Lieut. Col. Frederick A. Ashford
33rd Alabama, Col. Sam Adams
45th Alabama, Col. Harris D. Lampley
32nd Mississippi, Col. William H. Tison
45th Mississippi, Col. Aaron B. Hardcastle

Granbury's Texas Brigade

Brig. Gen. Hiram M. Granbury
Brig. Gen. James A. Smith
6th & 115th Texas Cavalry, Capt. Rhoads Fisher
7th Texas, Capt. C. E. Talley
10th Texas, Col. Roger Q. Mills
17th & 18th Texas Cavalry, Capt. George D. Manion
24th & 25th Texas Cavalry, Lieut. Col. William M. Neyland

Bate's Division

Maj. Gen. William B. Bate
Maj. Gen. John C Brown

Smith's Brigade

Brig. Gen. Thomas B. Smith
37th Georgia, Col. Joseph T. Smith
4th Georgia Sharpshooters, Maj. Theodore D. Caswell
15th & 37th Tennessee, Lieut. Col. Dudley R. Frayser
20th Tennessee, Lieut. Col. William M. Shy
30th Tennessee, Lieut. Col. James J. Turner

Lewis's Kentucky (Orphan) Brigade

Brig. Gen. Joseph H. Lewis
2nd Kentucky, Col. James W. Moss
4th Kentucky, Lieut. Col. Thomas W. Thompson
5th Kentucky, Lieut. Col. Hiram Hawkins
6th Kentucky, Col. Martin H. Cofer
9th Kentucky, Col. John W. Caldwell

Finley's Florida Brigade

Brig. Gen. Jessie J. Finley
Col. Robert Bullock
1st & 3rd Florida Cavalry (dismounted), Maj. Glover A. Ball
1st & 4th Florida, Lieut. Col. Edward Badger
6th Florida, Col. Angus D. McLean
7th Florida, Col. Robert Bullock

Walker's Division

Maj. Gen. William H. T. Walker
Brig. Gen. Hugh W. Mercer

Mercer's Georgia Brigade

Brig. Gen. Hugh W. Mercer
Lieut. Col. Morgan Rawls
Lieut. Col. Cincinnatus S. Guyton
Col. William Barkuloo
Col. Charles H. Olmstead
1st Georgia, Lieut. Col. Charles H. Olmstead
54th Georgia, Lieut. Col. Morgan Rawls
57th Georgia, Lieut. Col. Cininnatus S. Guyton
63rd Georgia, Col. George A. Gordon

Gist's Brigade

Brig. Gen. States R. Gist
Col. James McCullough
8th Georgia Battalion, Lieut. Col. Zachariah L. Watters
46th Georgia, Maj. Samuel J. C. Dunlap
16th South Carolina, Col. James McCullough
24th South Carolina, Col. Ellison Capers

Jackson's Brigade

Brig. Gen. John R. Jackson
47th Georgia, Col. A. C. Edwards
65th Georgia, Capt. William G. Foster

5th Mississippi, Col. John Weir
8th Mississippi, Col. John C. Wilkinson
2nd Georgia Sharpshooters, Maj. Richard H. Whiteley

Stevens's Georgia Brigade
Brig. Gen. Clement H. Stevens
Col. James C. Nisbet
Brig. Gen. Henry R. Jackson
1st Georgia Confederate, Col. George A. Smith
25th Georgia, Col. William J. Winn
29th Georgia, Maj. John J. Owen
30th Georgia, Lieut. Col. James S. Boynton
66th Georgia, Col. James C. Nisbet
1st Georgia Sharpshooters, Maj. Arthur Schaaff

HOOD'S ARMY CORPS

Lieut. Gen. John B. Hood
Maj. Gen. Carter L. Stevenson
Maj. Gen. Benjamin F. Cheatham
Lieut. Gen. Stephen D. Lee

Hindman's Division
Maj. Gen. Thomas C. Hindman
Brig. Gen. John C. Brown
Maj. Gen. Patton Anderson
Maj. Gen. Edward Johnson

Deas's Alabama Brigade
Brig. Gen. Zachariah C. Deas
Col. John C. Coltart
Brig. Gen. George D. Johnston
Lieut. Col. Harry T. Toulmin
19th Alabama, Col. George R. Kimbrough
22nd Alabama, Col. Benjamin R. Hart
25th Alabama, Col. George D. Johnston
39th Alabama, Col. William C. Clifton
50th Alabama, Col. John C. Coltart
17th Alabama Sharpshooters, Capt. James F. Nabers

Manigault's Brigade
Brig. Gen. Arthur M. Manigault
24th Alabama, Col. Newton N. Davis

28th Alabama, Lieut. Col. William L. Butler
34th Alabama, Col. Julius C. B. Mitchell
10th South Carolina, Col. James Pressley
19th South Carolina, Maj. James L. White

Walthall's Mississippi Brigade
Brig. Gen. Edward C. Walthall
Col. Samuel Benton
Col. William F. Brantley
24th & 27th Mississippi, Col. Robert P. McKelvaine
29th & 30th Mississippi, Col. William F. Brantley
34th Mississippi, Col. Samuel Benton

Tucker's Mississippi Brigade
Brig. Gen. William F. Tucker
Col. Jacob H. Sharp
7th Mississippi, Col. William H. Bishop
9th Mississippi, Lieut. Col. Benjamin F. Johns
10th Mississippi, Lieut. Col. George B. Myers
41st Mississippi, Col. J. Byrd Williams
44th Mississippi, Lieut. Col. R. G. Kelsey
9th Mississippi Sharpshooters, Maj. William C. Richards

Stevenson's Division
Maj. Gen. Carter L. Stevenson

Brown's Tennessee Brigade
Brig. Gen. John C. Brown
Col. Joseph C. Palmer
3rd Tennessee, Col. Calvin H. Walker
18th Tennessee, Lieut. Col. William R. Butler
26th Tennessee, Col. Richard M. Saffell
32nd Tennessee, Col. Edwin C. Cook
23rd & 45th Tennessee, Col. Anderson Searcy

Cumming's Georgia Brigade
Brig. Gen. Alfred Cumming
2nd Georgia State Line, Col. James Wilson
34th Georgia, Maj. John M. Jackson
36th Georgia, Maj. Charles E. Broyles
39th Georgia, Lieut. Col. J. E. B. Jackson
56th Georgia, Col. Elihu P. Watkins

Reynolds's Brigade

Brig. Gen. Alexander W. Reynolds
58th North Carolina, Maj. Thomas J. Dula
60th North Carolina, Col. Washington M. Hardy
54th Virginia, Col. Robert C. Trigg
63rd Virginia, Capt. Connally H. Lynch

Pettus's Alabama Brigade

Brig. Gen. Edmond W. Pettus
20th Alabama, Col. James M. Dedman
23rd Alabama, Col. Franklin R. Beck
30th Alabama, Col. Charles M. Shelly
31st Alabama, Col. Daniel R. Hundley
46th Alabama, Capt. George E. Brewer

Stewart's Division

Maj. Gen. Alexander P. Stewart
Maj. Gen. Henry D. Clayton

Stovall's Georgia Brigade

Brig. Gen. Marcellus A. Stovall
Col. Abda Johnson
Col. Robert J. Henderson
1st Georgia State Line, Col. Edward M. Galt
40th Georgia, Col. Abda Johnson
41st Georgia, Maj. Mark S. Nall
42nd Georgia, Col. Robert J. Henderson
43rd Georgia, Lieut. Col. Henry C. Kellog
52nd Georgia, Capt. John R. Russell

Clayton's Alabama Brigade

Brig. Gen. Henry D. Clayton
Brig. Gen. James T. Holtzclaw
Col. Bushrod Jones
18th Alabama, Col. Peter F. Hunley
32nd & 58th Alabama, Col. Bushrod Jones
36th Alabama, Col. Lewis T. Woodruff
38th Alabama, Col. A. R. Lankford

Gibson's Louisiana Brigade

Brig. Gen. Randall L. Gibson
1st Louisiana, Maj. S. S. Batchelor
13th Louisiana, Lieut. Col. Francis L. Campbell

16th & 25th Louisiana, Col. Joseph C. Lewis
19th Louisiana, Col. Richard W. Turner
20th Louisiana, Col. Leon von Zinken
14th Battalion Louisiana Sharpshooters, Maj. John E. Austin

Baker's Alabama Brigade
Brig. Gen. Alpheus Baker
37th Alabama, Lieut. Col. Alexander A. Greene
40th Alabama, Col. John H. Higley
42nd Alabama, Lieut. Col. Thomas C. Lanier
54th Alabama, Lieut. Col. John A. Minter

POLK'S ARMY CORPS

Lieut. Gen. Leonidas Polk
Maj. Gen. William W. Loring
Maj. Gen. Alexander P. Stewart
Maj. Gen. Benjamin F. Cheatham

Escort
Orleans Louisiana Light Horse Cavalry, Capt. Leeds Greenleaf

Loring's Division
Maj. Gen. William W. Loring
Brig. Gen. Winfield S. Featherston

Featherston's Mississippi Brigade
Brig. Gen. Winfield S. Featherston
3rd Mississippi, Col. Thomas A. Mellon
22nd Mississippi, Maj. Martin A. Oatis
31st Mississippi, Col. Marcus D. L. Stephens
33rd Mississippi, Col. Jabez L. Drake
40th Mississippi, Lieut. Col. George P. Wallace
1st Mississippi Sharpshooters, Maj. James M. Stigler

Adams's Mississippi Brigade
Brig. Gen. John Adams
6th Mississippi, Col. Robert Lowry
14th Mississippi, Lieut. Col. Washington L. Doss
15th Mississippi, Col. Michael Farrell
20th Mississippi, Col. William N. Brown
23rd Mississippi, Col. Joseph M. Wells
43rd Mississippi, Col. Richard Harrison

Scott's Brigade
Brig. Gen. Thomas M. Scott
27th Alabama, Col. James Jackson
35th Alabama, Col. Samuel S. Ives
49th Alabama, Lieut. Col. John D. Weeden
55th Alabama, Col. John Snodgrass
57th Alabama, Col. Charles J. L. Cunningham
12th Louisiana, Col. Noel L. Nelson

French's Division
Maj. Gen. Samuel G. French

Ector's Brigade
Brig. Gen. Matthew D. Ector
Brig. Gen. William H. Young
29th North Carolina, Col. Bacchus S. Proffit
39th North Carolina, Col. David Coleman
9th Texas, Col. William H. Young
10th Texas Cavalry, Col. C. R. Earp
14th Texas Cavalry, Col. John L. Camp
32nd Texas Cavalry, Col. Julius A. Andrews

Cockrell's Missouri Brigade
Brig. Gen. Francis M. Cockrell
Col. Elijah Gates
1st & 4th Missouri, Col. A. C. Riley
2nd & 6th Missouri, Col. Peter C. Fluornoy
3rd & 5th Missouri, Col. James McCowan
1st & 3rd Missouri Calvary, Col. Elijah Gates

Sears's Mississippi Brigade
Brig. Gen. Claudius W. Sears
Col. William S. Barry
4th Mississippi, Col. Thomas N. Adaire
35th Mississippi, Col. Reuben H. Shotwell
36th Mississippi, Col. William W. Witherspoon
46th Mississippi, Col. William H. Clark
7th Mississippi Battalion, Capt. W. A. Trotter

Walthall's Division
Maj. Gen. Edward C. Walthall

Reynolds's Arkansas Brigade

Brig. Gen. Daniel H. Reynolds
1st Arkansas Mounted Rifles, Col. Lee M. Ramsaur
2nd Arkansas Mounted Rifles, Col. James A. Williamson
4th Arkansas Mounted Rifles, Col. Henry Bunn
9th Arkansas Mounted Rifles, Col. Isaac L. Dunlop
25th Arkansas Mounted Rifles, Col. Charles J. Turnbull

Cantey's Brigade

Brig. Gen. James Cantey
Col. Edward A. O'Neal
17th Alabama, Col. Virgil S. Murphy
26th Alabama, Maj. David F. Bryan
29th Alabama, Col. John F. Conoley
37th Mississippi, Col. Orlando S. Holland

Quarles's Brigade

Brig. Gen. William A. Quarles
1st Alabama, Maj. Samuel L. Knox
4th Alabama, Col. Samuel E. Hunter
30th Louisiana, Lieut. Col. Thomas Shields
42nd Tennessee, Col. Isaac N. Hulme
46th & 55th Tennessee, Col. Robert A. Owens
49th Tennessee, Col. William F. Young
53rd Tennessee, Col. John R. White

Artillery

Brig. Gen. Francis A. Shoup
Col. Robert F. Beckham

Hardee's Corps Artillery

Col. Melancthon Smith

Hoxton's Battalion

Maj. Llewelyn Hoxton
Phelan's Alabama Battery, Capt. John Phelan
Perry's Florida Battery, Capt. Thomas J. Perry
Turner's Mississippi Battery, Capt. William B. Turner

Hotchkiss's Battalion

Maj. Thomas R. Hotchkiss
Capt. Thomas J. Key
Goldthwaite's Alabama Battery, Capt. Richard W. Goldthwaite

Key's Arkansas Battery, Capt. Thomas J. Key
Shannon's Mississippi Battery, Lieut. Harvey Shannon

MARTIN'S BATTALION
Maj. Robert Martin
Howell's Georgia Battery, Capt. Evan P. Howell
Bledsoe's Missouri Battery, Capt. Hiram M. Bledsoe
Beauregard's South Carolina Battery, Lieut. Rene Beauregard

COBB'S BATTALION
Maj. Robert Cobb
Gracey's Kentucky Battery, Capt. Frank P. Gracey
Washington Louisiana Battery, Capt. Cuthbert H. Slocomb
Mebane's Tennessee Battery, Capt. John W. Mebane

PALMER'S BATTALION
Maj. Joseph Palmer
Lumsden's Alabama Battery, Capt. Charles L. Lumsden
Anderson's Georgia Battery, Capt. Ruel W. Anderson
Havis's Georgia Battery, Capt. Minor W. Havis

HOOD'S CORPS ARTILLERY
Col. Robert F. Beckham
Lieut. Col. James H. Hallonquist

COURTNEY'S BATTALION
Maj. Alfred R. Courtney
Dent's Alabama Battery, Capt. Staunton H. Dent
Garrity's Alabama Battery, Capt. James Garrity
Douglas's Texas Battery, Capt. James P. Douglas

ELDRIDGE'S BATTALION
Maj. John W. Eldridge
Eufaula Alabama Battery, Capt. McDonald Oliver
Fenner's Louisiana Battery, Capt. Charles E. Fenner
Stanford's Mississippi Battery, Capt. Thomas J. Stanford

JOHNSTON'S BATTALION
Maj. John W. Johnston
Capt. Maximillian Van Den Corput
Georgia Light Battery, Capt. John B. Rowan
Cherokee Georgia Battery, Capt. Maximillian Van Den Corput
Marshall's Tennessee Battery, Capt. Lucius G. Marshall

Williams's Battalion

Lieut. Col. Samuel C. Williams
Capt. Reuben F. Kolb
Barbour Alabama Battery, Capt. Reuben F. Kolb
Jefferson Mississippi Battery, Capt. Putnam Darden
Jeffress's Virginia Battery, Capt. William C. Jeffress

Polk's Corps Artillery

Lieut. Col. Samuel C. Williams

Myrick's Battalion

Maj. John D. Myrick
Pointe Coupee Louisiana Battery, Capt. Alcide Bouanchard
Cowan's Mississippi Battery, Capt. James J. Cowan
Lookout Tennessee Battery, Capt. Robert L. Barry

Storrs's Battalion

Maj. George S. Storrs
Ward's Alabama Battery, Capt. John J. Ward
Hoskins's Mississippi Battery, Capt. James A. Hoskins
Guibor's Missouri Battery, Capt. Henry Guibor

Preston's Battalion

Maj. William C. Preston
Maj. Daniel Truehart
Tarrant's Alabama Battery, Capt. Edward Tarrant
Selden's Alabama Battery, Lieut. Charles W. Lovelace

Waddell's Battalion

Maj. James F. Waddell
Capt. Overton W. Barrett
Bellamy's Alabama Battery, Capt. Richard H. Bellamy
Emery's Alabama Battery, Capt. Winslow D. Emery
Barrett's Missouri Battery, Capt. Overton W. Barrett

CAVALRY CORPS

Maj. Gen. Joseph Wheeler

Martin's Division

Maj. Gen. William T. Martin

Allen's Alabama Brigade

Brig. Gen. William W. Allen
1st Alabama, Lieut. Col. D. T. Blakey

3rd Alabama, Col. James Hagan
4th Alabama, Col. Alfred A. Russell
7th Alabama, Capt. George Mason
51st Alabama, Col. M. L. Kirkpatrick
12th Alabama Battalion, Capt. Warren S. Reese

Iverson's Brigade
Brig. Gen. Alfred Iverson
1st Georgia, Col. Samuel W. Davitte
2nd Georgia, Col. Charles C. Crews
3rd Georgia, Col. Robert Thompson
4th Georgia, Col. Isaac W. Avery
6th Georgia, Col. John R. Hart

Kelly's Division
Brig. Gen. John H. Kelly

Anderson's Brigade
Brig. Gen. Robert H. Anderson
3rd Confederate, Lieut. Col. John McCaskill
5th Confederate, Col. Edward Bird
8th Confederate, Lieut. Col. John S. Prather
10th Confederate, Capt. W. J. Vason
12th Confederate, Capt. Charles H. Conner

Dibrell's Tennessee Brigade
Col. George G. Dibrell
4th Tennessee, Col. William S. McLemore
8th Tennessee, Capt. Jefferson Leftwich
9th Tennessee, Col. Jacob B. Biffle
10th Tennessee, Col. William E. De Moss
11th Tennessee, Col. Daniel W. Holman

Williams's Brigade
Brig. Gen. John S. Williams
2nd Kentucky, Maj. Thomas W. Lewis
3rd Kentucky, Col. J. R. Butler
9th Kentucky, Col. William C. P. Breckinridge
2nd Kentucky Battalion, Capt. John B. Dortch
Allison's Tennessee Squadron, Capt. J. S. Reese
Hamilton's Tennessee Battalion, Maj. Joseph Shaw

Hannon's Alabama Brigade
Col. Moses W. Hannon

53rd Alabama, Lieut. Col. John F. Gaines
24th Alabama Battalion, Maj. Robert B. Snodgrass

Humes's Division
Brig. Gen. William Y. C. Humes

Ashby's Tennessee Brigade
Col. Henry M. Ashby
1st Tennessee, Col. James T. Wheeler
2nd Tennessee, Capt. John H. Kuhn
5th Tennessee, Col. George W. McKenzie
9th Tennessee, Maj. James H. Akin

Harrison's Brigade
Col. Thomas H. Harrison
3rd Arkansas, Col. Anson W. Hobson
4th Tennessee, Lieut. Col. Paul F. Anderson
8th Texas, Lieut. Col. Gustave Cook
11th Texas, Col. George H. Reeves

Jackson's Division
Brig. Gen. William H. Jackson

Armstrong's Mississippi Brigade
Brig. Gen. Frank C. Armstrong
1st Mississippi, Col. R. A. Pinson
2nd Mississippi, Maj. John J. Perry
28th Mississippi, Col. Peter B. Starke
Ballentine's Mississippi Regiment, Lieut. Col. William L. Maxwell

Ross's Texas Brigade
Brig. Gen. Lawrence S. Ross
1st Texas Legion, Col. Edwin R. Hawkins
3rd Texas Legion, Col. Jiles S. Boggess
6th Texas Legion, Col. Peter F. Ross
9th Texas Legion, Col. Dudley W. Jones

Ferguson's Brigade
Brig. Gen. Samuel W. Ferguson
2nd Alabama, Col. Richard G. Earle
56th Alabama, Col. William Boyles
9th Mississippi, Col. Horace H. Miller

11th Mississippi, Col. Robert O. Perrin
12th Mississippi Battalion, Col. Robert M. Inge

Wheeler's Horse Artillery
Lieut. Col. Felix H. Robertson
Georgia Battery, Lieut. Nathan Davis
Huwald's Tennessee Battery, Lieut. D. Breck Ramsey
Huggins's Tennessee Battery Capt. Almaria L. Huggins
White's Tennessee Battery, Capt. Benjamin F. White
Wiggins's Arkansas Battery, Lieut. J. Wylie Callaway

Jackson's Division Artillery
Capt. John Waties
Columbus Georgia Battery, Capt. Edward Croft
Missouri Battery, Capt. Houston King
South Carolina Battery, Lieut. R. B. Waddell

First Division Georgia Militia
Maj. Gen. Gustavus W. Smith

First Brigade
Brig. Gen. Reuben W. Carswell
1st Regiment, Col. Edward H. Pottle
2nd Regiment, Col. James Stapleton
3rd Regiment, Col. Q. M. Hill

Second Brigade
Brig. Gen. Pleasant J. Phillips
4th Regiment, Col. James N. Mann
5th Regiment, Col. S. S. Stafford
6th Regiment Col. J. W. Burney

Third Brigade
Brig. Gen. Charles D. Anderson
7th Regiment, Col. Abner Redding
8th Regiment, Col. William B. Scott
9th Regiment, Col. J. M. Hill

Fourth Brigade
Brig. Gen. Henry K. McCay
10th Regiment, Col. C. M. Davis
11th Regiment, Col. William T. Toole
12th Regiment, Col. Richard Sims

MISCELLANEOUS UNITS

Youngblood's Battalion of Government Mechanics
Maj. E. H. Youngblood
Attached to Reynolds's Brigade of Walthall's Division at the Battle of Ezra Church

Samuel J. Gholson's Mississippi Brigade
Col. John McGuirk
Assigned to Reynolds's Brigade of Walthall's Division at the Battle of Ezra Church
Assigned to Granbury's Brigade of Cleburne's Division at the Battle of Jonesboro

NOTES

Preface

1. Lawrence K. Peterson, *Confederate Combat Commander: The Remarkable Life of Brigadier General Alfred Jefferson Vaughan Jr.* (Knoxville: University of Tennessee Press, 2013).
2. Alfred J. Vaughan Jr., *Personal Record of the Thirteenth Regiment, Tennessee Infantry, C.S.A.* (Memphis: S. C. Toof, 1897), 9–35; Stuart W. Sanders, "To Hell or to Victory: Confederate General Alfred J. Vaughan Jr.," in *Confederate Generals in the Western Theater*, ed. Lawrence Lee Hewitt and Arthur W. Bergeron Jr. (Knoxville: University of Tennessee Press, 2010), 2:25–51.
3. Ezra J., Warner, *Generals in Gray: Lives of the Confederate Commander* (Baton Rouge: Louisiana State University Press, 1959), 316–17.
4. Matt Spruill first introduced this concept in his *Decisions at Gettysburg: The Nineteen Critical Decisions That Defined the Campaign* (Knoxville: University of Tennessee Press, 2011).

Introduction

1. "One Nation, Divisible," in *The Civil War*, ed. William C. Davis (Alexandria, VA: Time Life Books, 1983), 1:25–47; James M. McPherson,

Battle Cry of Freedom: The Civil War Era (New York: Ballantine Books, 1988), 78–116.

2. McPherson, *Battle Cry of Freedom*, 234–75.
3. Ibid., 308–68, 502–10, 534–45.
4. Ibid., 392–417.
5. Ibid., 515–22, 579–83.
6. Ibid., 638–65.
7. Ibid., 636–37, 669–75.
8. Ibid., 626–38, 666–81. For the critical decisions at Chattanooga, see Larry Peterson, *Decisions at Chattanooga: The Nineteen Critical Decisions That Shaped the Battle* (Knoxville: University of Tennessee Press, 2018).
9. William R. Scaife, *The Campaign for Atlanta*, 4th ed. (Cartersville, GA: Civil War Publications, 1993), 4–6.
10. Albert Castel, *Decision in the West: The Atlanta Campaign of 1864* (Lawrence: University Press of Kansas, 1992), 14–15.
11. Ibid., 7–18; Scaife, *Campaign for Atlanta*, 7.
12. Castel, *Decision in the West*, 223, 259, 285.

Chapter 1

1. Richard M. McMurry, *Atlanta 1864: Last Chance for the Confederacy* (Lincoln: University of Nebraska Press, 2000), 5–11; Stephen Davis, *Atlanta Will Fall: Sherman, Joe Johnston, and the Yankee Heavy Battalions* (Wilmington, DE: Scholarly Resources, 2001), 17–18; US War Department, *The War of the Rebellion: A Compilation of the Official Records of the Union and Confederate Armies* (Washington, DC: United States Government, 1880–1901), series 1, vol. 31, pt. 3, 765, hereafter cited as *OR*. All references are to series 1 unless otherwise noted.
2. Steven E. Woodworth, *Jefferson Davis and His Generals: The Failure of Confederate Command in the West* (Lawrence: University Press of Kansas, 1990), 48, 60; McMurry, *Atlanta 1864*, 5.
3. McMurry, *Atlanta 1864*, 6–7; Stephen Davis, *A Long and Bloody Task: The Atlanta Campaign from Dalton through Kennesaw Mountain to the Chattahoochee River, May 5–July 18, 1864* (El Dorado Hills, CA: Savas Beatie, 2016), 6.
4. McMurry, *Atlanta 1864*, 7; Davis, *Atlanta Will Fall*, 17–18.
5. Davis, *Atlanta Will Fall*, 8–9.

6. Castel, *Decision in the West*, 29–30; McMurry, *Atlanta 1864*, 7. See Edward H. Bonekemper, *Grant and Lee: Victorious American and Vanquished Virginian* (Washington, DC: Regnery History, 2012), 264, 268, 423.
7. McMurry, *Atlanta 1864*, 7–8.
8. Davis, *Long and Bloody Task*, 6; Davis, *Atlanta Will Fall*, 18; Castel, *Decision in the West*, 30.
9. Castel, *Decision in the West*, 534; McMurry, *Atlanta 1864*, 186.
10. Castel, *Decision in the West*, 69–70; Richard M. McMurry, *John Bell Hood, and the War for Southern Independence* (Lincoln: University of Nebraska Press, 1982), 122–23.
11. McMurry, *Atlanta 1864*, 186.
12. Ibid., 5–11; Davis, *Atlanta Will Fall*, 18.
13. Castel, *Decision in the West*, 28.
14. McMurry, *Atlanta 1864*, 7–8.
15. Ibid., 7.
16. Ibid., 6.
17. Ibid., 1.
18. Scaife, *Campaign for Atlanta*, 3.
19. Ibid.
20. Castel, *Decision in the West*, 65.
21. Ibid., 62–64.
22. Wiley Sword, *Shiloh: Bloody April* (Dayton: Morningside House, 2001), 17–18. The three campaigns were Forts Henry-Donelson-Shiloh, Vicksburg, and Chattanooga.
23. Castel, *Decision in the West*, 65.
24. Ibid., 62-64; McMurry, *Atlanta 1864*, 1–2; *Davis, Atlanta Will Fall*, 19.
25. Castel, *Decision in the West*, 62–64.
26. Ibid., 62–66.
27. Davis, *Atlanta Will Fall*, 19–20.
28. McMurry, *Atlanta 1864*, 3–4.
29. Castel, *Decision in the West*, 22–24.
30. Ibid., 4–10.
31. Ibid., 65.
32. Ibid., 66–67.
33. Ibid., 65.

34. Ibid.

35. Ibid., 67.

36. Ulysses S. Grant, *Personal Memoirs of U. S.* Grant (1886; repr., Harrisburg, PA: Archive Society, 1997), 2:118; Castel, *Decision in the West*, 14–15, 67; McMurry, *Atlanta 1864*, 17.

37. Grant, *Memoirs*, 2:129–33; McPherson, *Battle Cry of Freedom*, 722–24.

38. Grant, *Memoirs*, 2:118.

39. McPherson, *Battle Cry of Freedom*, 725–43.

40. Ibid., 756–58.

41. Scaife, *Campaign for Atlanta*, 11.

42. McPherson, *Battle Cry of Freedom*, 722–23.

43. Scaife, *Campaign for Atlanta*, 25–26.

44. Bonekemper, *Grant and Lee*, 272–80.

45. McMurry, *Atlanta 1864*, 18–19.

46. Ibid.

47. Ezra J. Warner, *Generals in Blue: Lives of the Union Commanders* (Baton Rouge: Louisiana State University Press, 1964), 500–502; McMurry, *Atlanta 1864*, 19.

48. McMurry, *Atlanta 1864*, 18–19.

49. Castel, *Decision in the West*, 39–43; Warner, *Generals in Blue*, 441–44.

50. Castel, *Decision in the West*, 96–97.

51. Scaife, *Campaign for Atlanta*, 4; Davis, *Atlanta Will Fall*, 19; McMurry, *Atlanta 1864*, 18–19.

52. Scaife, *Campaign for Atlanta*, 120–21. For a very detailed description of Sherman's devastation of Atlanta, see Stephen Davis, *What the Yankees Did to Us: Sherman's Bombardment and Wrecking of Atlanta* (Macon, GA: Mercer University Press, 2012).

53. Noah Trudeau, *The Last Citadel, Petersburg, Virginia June 1864–April 1865* (Baton Rouge: Louisiana State University Press, 1991), 8–9, 401.

54. Gordon C. Rhea, "'Butcher' Grant and the Overland Campaign," *North and South* 4, no. 1 (November 2000): 44–55; Bonekemper, *Grant and Lee*, 317–18.

55. McMurry, *Atlanta 1864*, 19.

56. Scaife, *Campaign for Atlanta*, 4; Castel, *Decision in the West*, 93.

57. John E. Clark, *Railroads in the Civil War: The Impact of Management on Victory and Defeat* (Baton Rouge: Louisiana State University Press,

2001), 20 (map), 36–38; Tomas Weber, *The Northern Railroads in the Civil War, 1861–1865* (1952; repr., Bloomington: Indiana University Press, 1999), 195–96; McMurry, *Atlanta 1864*, 27–28.

58. McMurry, *Atlanta 1864*, 28–29.

59. Ibid., 30.

60. Castel, *Decision in the West*, 91–93.

61. Jack Coggins, *Arms and Equipment of the Civil War* (Wilmington, NC: Broadfoot, 1990), 121.

62. McMurry, *Atlanta 1864*, 30–31.

63. Castel, *Decision in the West*, 92, 191–93, 266.

64. McMurry, *Atlanta 1864*, 29–31.

65. Coggins, *Arms and Equipment of the Civil War*, 121.

66. Ibid., 121; Castel, *Decision in the West*, 117.

67. Davis, *Long and Bloody Task*, 6; Castel, *Decision in the West*, 31–34.

68. McMurry, *Atlanta 1864*, 48.

69. Ibid., 47–48.

70. *OR*, vol. 32, pt. 2, 698; McMurry, *Atlanta 1864*, 46–47.

71. McMurry, *Atlanta 1864*, 46, 59.

72. Ibid.

73. Ibid., 22.

74. *OR*, vol. 32, pt. 2, 698; McMurry, *Atlanta 1864*, 46–48.

75. Davis, *Atlanta Will Fall*, 28–29.

76. Ibid., 28–29.

77. Ibid., 47–48.

78. Ibid., 59; McMurry, *Atlanta 1864*, 61.

79. McMurry, *Atlanta 1864*, 28.

80. Davis, *Atlanta Will Fall*, 26.

81. McMurry, *Atlanta 1864*, 61–62.

82. Davis, *Atlanta Will Fall*, 33; Castel, *Decision in the West*, 127.

83. Davis, *Atlanta Will Fall*, 26.

84. McMurry, *Atlanta 1864*, 22.

85. Ibid.

86. Ibid., 62; Davis, *Atlanta Will Fall*, 39–40.

87. Davis, *Atlanta Will Fall*, 39–40.

88. Ibid., 64.

89. Ibid.

90. Gen. Joseph E. Johnston, *Narrative of Military Operations during the Civil War* (1874; repr., New York: Da Capo, 1959), 277–80.

Chapter 2

1. Attacks are categorized as main and supporting attacks. The main attack is the attack that the commander has designed to capture the enemy position or key terrain to achieve the overall objective. Usually, it has the majority of troops assigned to it, as well as priority of supporting artillery fire. The reserve is normally placed so as to reinforce the main attack or exploit success. The supporting attack(s) are designed to assist the main attack by causing the enemy to disperse his forces and fight in several locations. Supporting attacks also hold enemy forces in position, cause a premature or incorrect commitment of enemy reserve, and confuse the enemy as to which is the main attack. Department of the Navy, *Marine Corps Operations,* 7–21 (Washington, DC, 2011); Department of the Army, *Field Manual* 3-0 (Washington, DC, 2011), chapter 3; Department of the Army, *Field Manual* 3-90-1 (Washington, DC, 2013), chapters 1–5.

2. Scaife, *Campaign for Atlanta*, 17–18; McMurry, *Atlanta 1864*, 45–46.

3. McMurry, *Atlanta 1864*, 51.

4. Ibid., 43–45.

5. Ibid.

6. Ibid., 55–57; Davis, *Atlanta Will Fall*, 36.

7. McMurry, *Atlanta 1864*, 43–45.

8. Davis, *Atlanta Will Fall*, 36–38.

9. McMurry, *Atlanta 1864*, 55.

10. Ibid.

11. Ibid., 57–58; Davis, *Atlanta Will Fall*, 36–38. A turning movement is an offensive maneuver that avoids the enemy's principal defensive position by seizing an objective in the enemy rear area. The opposition is then forced to move out of its current position or direct major focus against a new threat. The presence of a friendly force in the enemy soldiers' rear area turns them out of their position. United States Marine Corps, *Operations Manual, 7-21*; Department of the Army,

Field Manual 3-0, chapter 3; Department of the Army, *Field Manual 3-90-1*, chapters 1–5.

12. William T. Sherman, *Memoirs* (1875; repr., New York: D. Appleton, 1997), 2:32; *OR*, vol. 38, pt. 4, 39–40; Scaife, *Campaign for Atlanta*, 18–19; McMurry, *Atlanta 1864*, 63–64; Davis, *Atlanta Will Fall*, 37–40; Castel, *Decision in the West*, 123.
13. Davis, *Atlanta Will Fall*, 36–38; Scaife, *Campaign for Atlanta*, 18, 22–23; McMurry, *Atlanta 1864*, 64. McMurry postulates on p. 207 that Johnston's failure to guard Snake Creek Gap portended Confederate failure to resist Sherman, and that Lincoln's reelection was likely thereafter.
14. McMurry, *Atlanta 1864*, 55.
15. See note 11 above. Peter Cozzens, *This Terrible Sound: The Battle of Chickamauga* (Chicago: University of Illinois Press, 1996), 53–60.
16. Scaife, *Campaign for Atlanta*, 18; McMurry, *Atlanta 1864*, 58.
17. McMurry, *Atlanta 1864*, 58; Castel, *Decision in the West*, 121.
18. Castel, *Decision in the West*, 80; Scaife, *Campaign for Atlanta*, table following 15.
19. Warner, *Generals in Blue*, 306–8; Scaife, *Campaign for Atlanta*, table following 15.
20. Scaife, *Campaign for Atlanta*, table following 15; David A. Powell, *The Chickamauga Campaign—Barren Victory: The Retreat into Chattanooga, the Confederate Pursuit, and the Aftermath of the Battle, September 21 to October 20, 1863* (El Dorado Hills, CA: Savas Beatie, 2016), 128.
21. Scaife, *Campaign for Atlanta*, table following 15.
22. McPherson, *Battle Cry of Freedom*, 640–41.
23. United States Marine Corps, *Operations Manual, 7-21*; Department of the Army, *Field Manual 3-0*, chapter 3; Department of the Army, *Field Manual 3-90-1*, chapters 1–5; Scaife, *Campaign for Atlanta*, table following 15.
24 *OR*, vol. 38, pt. 4, 39–40; Scaife, *Campaign for Atlanta*, 18–19; McMurry, *Atlanta 1864*, 73.
25. Castel, *Decision in the West*, 150.
26. Ibid.
27. Scaife, *Campaign for Atlanta*, table following 15.
28. Castel, *Decision in the West*, 79–80; Warner, *Generals in Blue*, 306–8.

29. Scaife, *Campaign for Atlanta*, 18, 22–23; McMurry, *Atlanta 1864*, 64; Davis, *Atlanta Will Fall*, 38–42.
30. Scaife, *Campaign for Atlanta*, 23–24.
31. Ibid., 23; McMurry, *Atlanta 1864*, 61, 64.
32. McMurry, *Atlanta 1864*, 59, 62, 64; *OR*, vol. 38, pt. 4, 681–84.
33. McMurry, *Atlanta 1864*, 45, 64–65; Scaife, *Campaign for Atlanta*, 23; Castel, *Decision in the West*, 135–39.
34. *OR*, vol. 38, pt. 4, 40.
35. Sherman, *Memoirs.* 2:34; Roland Cox, "Snake Creek Gap and Atlanta," in *The Atlanta Papers,* comp. Sydney C. Kerksis (Dayton, OH: Press of the Morningside Bookshop, 1980) 329–51.
36. *OR*, vol. 38, pt. 4, 40.
37. Castel, *Decision in the West*, 142–43; *OR*, vol. 38, pt. 4, 106.
38. McMurry, *Atlanta 1864*, 68.
39. Scaife, *Campaign for Atlanta*, 29–36, and two maps following 36; Castel, *Decision in the West*, 154–79.
40. Sherman, *Memoirs.* 2:34; Cox, "Snake Creek Gap and Atlanta," 19.
41. McMurry, *Atlanta 1864*, 68.
42. Author's speculation.
43. Scaife, *Campaign for Atlanta*, 42; McMurry, *Atlanta 1864*, 81; Castel, *Decision in the West*, 201–2.
44. Author's speculation.
45. McMurry, *Atlanta 1864*, 48.

Chapter 3

1. Scaife, *Campaign for Atlanta*, 27–29; McMurry, *Atlanta 1864*, 68–69.
2. McMurry, *Atlanta 1864*, 68–72; Scaife, *Campaign for Atlanta*, 35–36.
3. Davis, *Atlanta Will Fall*, 46.
4. Ibid., 47.
5. Ibid.
6. McMurry, *Atlanta 1864*, 68–72; Scaife, *Campaign for Atlanta*, 35–36.
7. Davis, *Atlanta Will Fall*, 46–49; McMurry, *Atlanta 1864*, 70–72; Scaife, *Campaign for Atlanta*, 34–36.
8. McMurry, *Atlanta 1864*, 68–72; Scaife, *Campaign for Atlanta*, 35–36.

9. McMurry, *Atlanta 1864*, 70–72.
10. Ibid., 194-95; Scaife, *Campaign for Atlanta*, tables following 15.
11. *OR*, vol. 38, pt. 4, 716.
12. Scaife, *Campaign for Atlanta*, 37–39, map following 45.
13. Davis, *Atlanta Will Fall*, 54 (map).
14. Ibid., 53; McMurry, *Atlanta 1864*, 77–80.
15. Davis, *Atlanta Will Fall*, 52–53.
16. Ibid.
17. Ibid.
18. Scaife, *Campaign for Atlanta*, 37; McMurry, *Atlanta 1864*, 78.
19. McMurry, *Atlanta 1864*, 79–80; Davis, *Atlanta Will Fall*, 52.
20. Scaife, *Campaign for Atlanta*, 42; McMurry, *Atlanta 1864*, 79–80.
21. Scaife, *Campaign for Atlanta*, 41.
22. Ibid., 42; Quote from *OR*, vol. 38, pt. 4, 728.
23. Scaife, *Campaign for Atlanta*, 42–43; McMurry, *Atlanta 1864*, 80–81.
24. Robert D. Jenkins Sr., *The Battle of Peach Tree Creek: Hood's first Sortie, 20 July 1864* (Macon, GA, Mercer University Press, 2013), 16; Robert R. Long, "*A Brief History of the Battle of Peachtree Creek, July 20, 1864*," personal papers of Robert D. Jenkins Sr., Dalton, GA, 8; John B. Hood, *Advance & Retreat*, (1880; repr., New York: Da Capo, 1993), 144.
25. Scaife, *Campaign for Atlanta*, 42–43; McMurry, *Atlanta 1864*, 80–81.
26. Scaife, *Campaign for Atlanta*, 43–45. Army engineer Walter J. Morris's June 24, 1874, statement confirms that Union artillery enfiladed Johnston's line at Cassville. Morris's account appears in Stephen M. Hood, *The Lost Papers of Confederate General John Bell Hood* (El Dorado Hills, CA: Savas Beatie, 2015), 89–95; also Stephen M. Hood, *The Rise, Fall, and Resurrection of a Confederate General* (El Dorado Hills, CA: Savas Beatie, 2013), 46–52. Some of Hood's actions were confirmed via emails with author Dr. Steven Davis, December–January 2015–16.
27. Davis, *Atlanta Will Fall*, 55–56.
28. Scaife, *Campaign for Atlanta*, 47; McMurry, *Atlanta 1864*, 85–86.
29. McMurry, *Atlanta 1864*, 85–86.
30. Davis, *Atlanta Will Fall*, 59; McMurry, *Atlanta 1864*, 85.
31. Davis, *Atlanta Will Fall*, 59; McMurry, *Atlanta 1864*, 85.
32. Davis, *Atlanta Will Fall*, 59; McMurry, *Atlanta 1864*, 85.

33. McMurry, *Atlanta 1864*, 86; Scaife, *Campaign for Atlanta*, 47.
34. Scaife, *Campaign for Atlanta*, 47–49.
35. Ibid., 49–53.
36. Ibid., 47–56; Davis, *Atlanta Will Fall*, 65–66.
37. Davis, *Atlanta Will Fall*, 63–65.
38. Scaife, *Campaign for Atlanta*, 53–56.
39. Ibid.
40. Ibid.
41. Davis, *Atlanta Will Fall*, 59.
42. Coggins, *Arms and Equipment of the Civil War*, 121; Cristopher Perello, *The Quest for Annihilation: The Role & Mechanics of Battle in the American Civil War* (Bakersfield, CA: Strategy and Tactics, 2009), 133.
43. Coggins, *Arms and Equipment of the Civil War*, 121.
44. McMurry, *Atlanta 1864*, 91, 104.

Chapter 4

1. Scaife, *Campaign for Atlanta*, 57; See McMurry, *Atlanta 1864*, 198–203 for an excellent discussion of this request by Johnston. Robert S. Henry, *First with the Most: Nathan Bedford Forrest* (New York: Konecky and Konecky, 1992), 277.
2. Warner, *Generals in Gray*, 92; *OR*, vol. 38, pt. 4, 480.
3. McMurry, *Atlanta 1864*, 198–203; Castel, *Decision in the West*, 274, 564–65; Davis, *Atlanta Will Fall*, 71.
4. McMurry, *Atlanta 1864*, 202–3; Davis, *Atlanta Will Fall*, 71.
5. McMurry, *Atlanta 1864*, 98–99; Castel, *Decision in the West*, 302–3. For an excellent discussion of Johnston's Railroad Strategy, see McMurry's appendix 3, 198–203, entitled the same.
6. Sherman, *Memoirs*, 2:103; Castel, *Decision in the West*, 302–3; McMurry, *Atlanta 1864*, 98–99.
7. Sherman, *Memoirs*, 2:103; Castel, *Decision in the West*, 302–3.
8. McMurry, *Atlanta 1864*, 98–99.
9. Ibid., 99.
10. Ibid.
11. Ibid. 177–80; Castel, *Decision in the West*, 543–45.

12. McMurry, *Atlanta 1864*, 86.
13. Scaife, *Campaign for Atlanta*, 9. For an interesting discussion concerning this topic, see Davis's *Atlanta Will Fall, chapter 17, "Hood Does What Joe Johnston Only Dreamed About: He Sends His Cavalry Out to Cut Sherman's Rail Lines, August 10," 167–73.*
14. *Davis, Atlanta Will Fall*, 73–81; McMurry, *Atlanta 1864*, 100–104.
15. Scaife, *Campaign for Atlanta*, 57–59.
16. Ibid., 60–62.
17. Ibid., 62; McMurry, *Atlanta 1864*, 107.
18. Scaife, *Campaign for Atlanta*, 62; McMurry, *Atlanta 1864*, 107.
19. McMurry, *Atlanta 1864*, 86, 107
20. Ibid.
21. McMurry, Atlanta 1864, 86, 107; Earl J. Hess, *Kennesaw Mountain: Sherman, Johnston, and the Atlanta Campaign*, (Chapel Hill: University of North Carolina, 2013), 51.
22. Scaife, *Campaign for Atlanta*, 63–64, map following 66; McMurry, *Atlanta 1864*, 107–8.
23. Scaife, *Campaign for Atlanta*, 63–64, map following 66; McMurry, *Atlanta 1864*, 107–8.
24. Scaife, *Campaign for Atlanta*, 63–66; Davis, *Atlanta Will Fall*, 86–87.
25. Scaife, *Campaign for Atlanta*, 66; quote from *OR*, vol. 38, pt. 4, 610.
26. Scaife, *Campaign for Atlanta*, 67; McMurry, *Atlanta 1864*, 110–11.
27. McMurry, *Atlanta 1864*, 110.
28. Scaife, *Campaign for Atlanta*, 67–69; Davis, *Atlanta Will Fall*, 92–95.
29. Scaife, *Campaign for Atlanta*, 68–74.
30. Ibid., 73. Interestingly, Sherman had planned, even before the campaign began, to outflank Johnston on his right at the Chattahoochee River. In Sherman, *Memoirs*, 2:28; Davis, *Long and Bloody Task*, 11–12.
31. Scaife, *Campaign for Atlanta*, 72, 74; Castel, *Decision in the West*, 336.

Chapter 5

1. *OR*, vol. 32, pt. 3, 245; *OR*, vol. 38, pt. 4, 607, 629; *OR*, vol. 40, pt. 2, 475.
2. Scaife. *Campaign for Atlanta*, 71–72. The Union had captured New Orleans in April 1862.

3. Clark, *Railroads in the Civil War*, 28–30, 88–94.
4. Castel, *Decision in the West*, 69–70.
5. *OR*, vol. 38, pt. 4, 629; Scaife, *Campaign for Atlanta*, 71–72.
6. Castel, *Decision in the West*, 69–70, 343–44.
7. *OR*, vol. 38, pt. 4, 629.
8. McMurry, *Atlanta 1864*, 14, 141–42. Also see McMurry's appendix 4, which provides an in-depth look at the possible capture of Atlanta and its possible effect on the November elections.
9. Sherman, *Memoirs*, 2:99; *OR*, vol. 38, pt. 4, 629; *OR*, vol. 38, pt. 1, 70; *OR*, vol. 39, pt. 5, 123, 149, 210.
10. Scaife, *Campaign for Atlanta*, 78.
11. Davis, *Atlanta Will Fall*, 97.
12. *OR*, vol. 32, pt. 3, 245.
13. Grant had suffered some 44,000 casualties during the Overland Campaign per McPherson, *Battle Cry of Freedom*, 733. According to Rhea, "'Butcher' Grant and the Overland Campaign," 55, Grant's losses numbered 55,000. Quoted in Bonekemper, *Grant and Lee*, 318.
14. Clark, *Railroads in the Civil War*, 20.
15. Davis, *Atlanta Will Fall*, 131; McMurry, *Atlanta 1864*, 146, 155–56.
16. McMurry, *Atlanta 1864*, 146.
17. Davis, *What the Yankees Did to Us*, 87.
18. Ibid.; Davis, *Atlanta Will Fall*, 149.
19. McMurry, *Atlanta 1864*, 155–56. For an in-depth review of the semisiege, see Davis, *What the Yankees Did to Us*.
20. McMurry, *Atlanta 1864, 155-56; Clark, Railroads in the Civil War*, 20 (map).
21. McMurry, *Atlanta 1864, 152-53; Scaife, Campaign for Atlanta*, 75, 85.
22. Clark, *Railroads in the Civil War*, 20 (map). The Atlanta and West Point Railroad paid the Macon and Western Railroad $3,000 per year for access from East Point to Atlanta. In *Annual Report*, Macon and Western Railroad, 1859; Robert C. Black, *The Railroads of the Confederacy* (Chapel Hill: University of North Carolina Press, 1998), 38, 251, 270; McMurry, *Atlanta 1864*, 91, 119.
23. McMurry, *Atlanta 1864*, 141–42.
24. Ibid., 118.

25. Ibid., 85.

26. Castel, *Decision in the West*, 352; McMurry, *Atlanta 1864*, 137–38; *OR*, vol. 38, pt. 5, 876; Davis, *Atlanta Will Fall*, 103.

27. Davis, *Atlanta Will Fall*, 102–6; McMurry, *Atlanta 1864*, 138–39.

28. Castel, *Decision in the West*, 358.

29. Davis, *Atlanta Will Fall*, 18.

30. McMurry, *Atlanta 1864*, 138–40; Castel, *Decision in the West*, 352–56; Joseph H. Parks, *General Edmund Kirby Smith, C.S.A.* (1954; repr., Baton Rouge: Louisiana State University Press, 1982), 380–82, 417–20; Douglas S. Freeman, *Lee's Lieutenants: A Study in Command*, one-volume abridgement by Stephen W. Sears (New York: Simon and Schuster, 1998), 716.

31. *OR*, vol. 52, pt. 2, 692; Davis, *Atlanta Will Fall*, 108–9.

32. Scaife, *Campaign for Atlanta*, 76; Davis, *Atlanta Will* Fall, 116; *OR*, vol. 38, pt. 3, 885.

33. One report of how the army privates responded is in Watkins, *Company Aytch, or, a Side Show of the Big Show*, ed. M. Thomas Inge (1882; repr., New York: Penguin Putnam, 1999), 144. See also Castel, *Decision in the West*, 364–65.

34. Castel, *Decision in the West*, 363–65; McMurry, *Atlanta 1864*, 140; Scaife, *Campaign for Atlanta*, 76–78. Per Scaife, Fabian policy was named for Roman dictator Quintus Fabius Maximus Cunctator, who successfully delayed Hannibal in the Second Punic War by constantly harassing him without committing to a pitched battle. William T. Sherman, "The Grand Strategy of the War of the Rebellion," *Century Magazine*, February 1888, 253.

35. McMurry, *Atlanta 1864*, 140; Castel, *Decision in the West*, 355. Evidence of Johnston's plan to attack is verified in Hood, *Advance & Retreat*, 144; and Jenkins, *Battle of Peach Tree Creek*, 11, 16.

36. Castel, *Decision in the West*, 355.

37. Scaife, *Campaign for Atlanta*, 78–83, and maps following 83; Davis, *Atlanta Will Fall*, 129–37; Robert D. Jenkins Sr., email to the author, August 26, 2016.

38. Castel, *Decision in the West*, 366.

39. McMurry, *Atlanta 1864*, 146; Davis, *Atlanta Will* Fall, 131.

40. McMurry, *Atlanta 1864*, 146–47.

41. Ibid., 152–53; Davis, *Atlanta Will* Fall, 138–39; Scaife, *Campaign for Atlanta*, 85.
42. Stephen Davis, *All the Fighting They Want: The Atlanta Campaign from Peachtree Creek to the City's Surrender, July 18–September 2, 1864* (El Dorado Hills, CA: Savas Beatie, 2017), 38–39.
43. Ibid., 39–41; Scaife, *Campaign for Atlanta*, 86.
44. Scaife, *Campaign for Atlanta*, 85–86; Davis, *Atlanta Will Fall*, 137–38.
45. Scaife, *Campaign for Atlanta*, 87–92, and map following 92; Davis, *Atlanta Will Fall*, 139–48.
46. Davis, *All the Fighting They Want*, 47.

Chapter 6

1. Scaife, *Campaign for Atlanta*, 93–94; Davis, *Atlanta Will Fall*, 148–50. Remember that the Montgomery and West Point Railroad had been rendered temporarily useless by Rousseau's cutting it at Opelika, Alabama. Thus traffic could not flow over the Atlanta and West Point into Atlanta. After the line briefly returned to service, on August 27, Sherman destroyed over twelve miles of the Atlanta and West Point Railroad. Davis, *All the Fighting They Want*, 104–5.
2. McMurry, *Atlanta 1864*, 156–57; Scaife, *Campaign for Atlanta*, 94–95.
3. Scaife, *Campaign for Atlanta*, 94–95; *OR*, vol. 38, pt. 5, 919; Davis, *Atlanta Will Fall*, 151.
4. Scaife, *Campaign for Atlanta*, 95–98, and map following 98; McMurry, *Atlanta 1864*, 157; Davis, *Atlanta Will Fall*, 153.
5. Davis, *Atlanta Will Fall*, 127–28; Scaife, *Campaign for Atlanta*, 98; McMurry, *Atlanta 1864*, 159, 197.
6. Scaife, *Campaign for Atlanta*, 99–107.
7. Ibid., 109–12, and map following 112; Davis, *Atlanta Will Fall*, 157.
8. McMurry, *Atlanta 1864*, 169–70; Scaife, *Campaign for Atlanta*, 117; Davis, *Atlanta Will Fall*, 141.
9. Scaife, *Campaign for Atlanta*, 117–19, and first map following 121; McMurry, *Atlanta 1864*, 171–73.
10. Scaife, *Campaign for Atlanta*, 119–20, and second map following 121; Castel, *Decision in the West*, 517–18; McMurry, *Atlanta 1864*, 187.

Vaughan had been wounded on July 4 on the Smyrna Line. See Peterson, *Confederate Combat Commander*, 184; Davis, *Atlanta Will Fall*, 183–87.

11. McMurry, *Atlanta 1864*, 175; Scaife, *Campaign for Atlanta*, 120.
12. McMurry, *Atlanta 1864*, 174–75; Castel, *Decision in the West*, 511–12.
13. Davis, *All the Fighting They Want*, 113–14.
14. Ibid., 111.
15. Ibid., 113–14; *OR*, vol. 38, pt. 5, 771; *OR*, vol. 38, pt. 1, 82; Scaife, *Campaign for Atlanta*, 119–20.
16. Scaife, *Campaign for Atlanta*, 120.
17. *OR*, vol. 38, pt. 5, 771.
18. For extensive coverage of Hood's Tennessee Campaign, see Wiley Sword, *The Confederacy's Last Harrah: Spring Hill, Franklin, & Nashville*, originally published as *Embrace an Angry Sword* (Lawrence: University Press of Kansas, 1992), 1–443.
19. *OR*, vol. 32, pt. 3, 245; Sherman, *Memoirs*, 2:26.
20. Scaife, *Campaign for Atlanta*, 120.
21. Ibid.
22. Castel, *Decision in the West*, 542, 552–53.
23. Ibid., 536.
24. McMurry, *Atlanta 1864*, 176.
25. *OR*, vol. 38, pt. 5, 777.
26. McMurry, *Atlanta 1864*, 177–78.
27. Ibid., 183; Castel, *Decision in the West*, 555–58.
28. Scaife, *Campaign for Atlanta*, 123–27; Thomas L. Connelly, *Autumn of Glory: The Army of Tennessee, 1862–1865* (Baton Rouge: Louisiana State University Press, 1971), 480–83.
29. Scaife, *Campaign for Atlanta*, 120.
30. Castel, *Decision in the West*, 565.
31. Ibid., 553–55.

Chapter 7

1. Jerry Korn, "Pursuit to Appomattox," in *The Civil War*, ed. William C. Davis (Alexandria, VA: Time Life Books, 1987), 25:160.

2. Castel, *Decision in the West*, 90–94; Sherman, *Memoirs* 2:151.
3. McMurry, *Atlanta 1864*, 194–97.
4. Ibid.
5. Ibid., 180, 204–8.
6. Castel, *Decision in the West*, 541, 553.
7. Ibid., 34–37; Bruce Levine, *Confederate Emancipation: Southern Plans to Free and Arm Slaves During the Civil* War (New York: Oxford University Press, 2006), 1–3, 79; James M. McPherson, *The Negro's Civil War: How American Blacks Felt and Acted During the War for the* Union (New York: Vintage Books, 2003), 241.

Appendix I

1. Johnston, *Narrative of Military Operations*, 275.
2. Grant, *Memoirs*, 2:115.
3. Ibid., 129.
4. *OR*, vol. 32, pt. 3, 245.
5. Sherman, *Memoirs*, 2:11.
6. Johnston, *Narrative of Military Operations*, 277–78.
7. Ibid., 275.
8. Sherman, *Memoirs*, 2:32.
9. Ibid.
10. *OR*, vol. 38, pt. 4, 106.
11. *OR*, vol. 38, pt. 3, 721.
12. Ibid., 92–93.
13. Sherman, *Memoirs*, 2:35.
14. Henry Stone, "Opening the Campaign," in *The Atlanta Papers*, comp. Sydney C. Kerksis (Dayton, OH: Press of the Morningside Bookshop, 1980), 11-162.
15. Sherman, *Memoirs*, 2:42.
16. *OR*, vol. 38, pt. 4, 299.
17. Johnston, *Narrative of Military Operations*, 320.
18. *OR*, vol. 38, pt. 4, 728.
19. Johnston, *Narrative of Military Operations*, 321.

20. Ibid., 322.
21. Ibid., 323–24.
22. Hood, *Lost Papers*, 89–95.
23. Bruce Catton, *Never Call Retreat* (New York: Washington Square, 1965), 318.
24. Johnston, *Narrative of Military Operations*, 359–60.
25. Davis to Gov. J. B. Brown, June 29, 1864, in ibid, 361.
26. Sherman, *Memoirs*, 2:43.
27. Ibid., 2:60.
28. John B. Gordon, quoted in John B. Lindsley, ed., *The Military Annals of Tennessee: Confederate* (Nashville: J. M. Lindsley, 1886), 299.
29. Vaughan, *Personal Record*, 33.
30. Watkins, *Company Aytch*, 132–33.
31. *OR*, vol. 38, pt. 4, 610.
32. Sherman, *Memoirs*, 2:99.
33. Maj. James A. Connally, *Three Years in the Army of the Cumberland: The Letters and Diary of Major James A. Connally*, ed. Paul M. Angle (Bloomington: Indiana University Press, 1959), 234.
34. *OR*, vol. 38, pt. 3, 885.
35. Philip Daingerfield Stephenson, *The Civil War Memoir of Philip Daingerfield Stephenson, D.D.*, ed. Nathaniel Cheairs, Jr. (Conway, AR: University of Central Arkansas Press, 1995), 208–9.
36. Watkins, *Company Aytch*, 144.
37. *OR*, vol. 38, pt. 3, 702.
38. Larry M. Strayer and Richard A. Baumgartner, eds., *Echoes of Battle, the Atlanta Campaign* (Huntington, WV: Blue Acorn, 2004), 310.
39. *OR*, vol. 38, pt. 5, 771.
40. Sherman, *Memoirs*, 2:99.

BIBLIOGRAPHY

Primary Sources

Connally, Maj. James A. *Three Years in the Army of the Cumberland: The Letters and Diary of Major James A. Connally*. Edited by Paul M. Angle. Bloomington: University of Indiana Press, 1996.

Department of the Army. *Field Manual* 3-0. Washington, DC: US Government Publishing Office, 2011.

———. *Field Manual* 3-90-1. Washington, DC: US Government Publishing Office, 2013.

Grant, Ulysses S. *Personal Memoirs of U. S. Grant*. 1886. Reprint. Harrisburg, PA: Archive Society, 1997.

Harley, Stanard C. "A Johnny Reb Writes." *National Tribune*. June 11, 1914.

Hood, John B. *Advance & Retreat*. 1880. Reprint. New York: Da Capo, 1993.

———. *The Lost Papers of Confederate General John Bell Hood*. Edited by Stephen M. Hood. El Dorado Hills, CA: Savas Beatie, 2015.

Jackman, John S. *Diary of a Confederate Soldier, John S. Jackman of the Orphan Brigade*. Edited by William C. Davis. Columbia: University of South Carolina Press, 1990.

Johnston, Gen. Joseph E. *Narrative of Military Operations during the Civil War*. 1874. Reprint. New York: Da Capo, 1959.

Long, Robert R. "A Brief History of the Battle of Peachtree Creek, July 20, 1864." Personal papers of Robert D. Jenkins Sr., Dalton, GA.

Manigault, Arthur. *A Carolinian Goes to War*. Edited by R. Lockwood Tower. 1983. Reprint. Columbia: University of South Carolina Press, 1992.

Nisbet, James Cooper. *Four Years on the Firing Line*. Edited by Bell Irvin Wiley. 1914. Reprint. Wilmington, NC: Broadfoot Publishing Co., 1987.

Sherman, William T. "The Grand Strategy of the War of the Rebellion." *Century Magazine*, February 1888.

———. *Memoirs*. 1875. 2 vols. Reprint. New York: D. Appleton, 1997.

Shoup, Francis A. "Recollections of Building Chattahoochee River Defenses." *Confederate Veteran* 3, no. 9 (September 1895).

Stephenson, Philip Daingerfield. *The Civil War Memoir of Philip Daingerfield Stephenson, D.D*. Edited by Nathaniel Cheairs, Jr. Conway, AR: University of Central Arkansas Press, 1995.

Stone, Henry. "From the Oostanaula to the Chattahoochee." In *The Atlanta Papers*, compiled by Sydney C. Kerksis, 65-97. Dayton, OH: Press of the Morningside Bookshop, 1980.

———. "Opening the Campaign." In *The Atlanta Papers*, compiled by Sydney C. Kerksis, 11-62. Dayton, OH: Press of the Morningside Bookshop, 1980.

Sykes, Columbus. Letter of May 29, 1864. Library, Kennesaw Mountain National Battlefield Park, Marietta, GA.

US Department of the Navy. *Marine Corps Operations*, 7-21. Washington, DC.

US War Department. *The War of the Rebellion: A Compilation of the Official Records of the Union and Confederate Armies*. 128 vols. Washington, DC: U.S. Government Publishing Office, 1880–1901. Hereafter cited as *OR*. All references are to Series 1 unless otherwise noted.

Vaughan, Alfred J., Jr. *Personal Record of the Thirteenth Regiment, Tennessee Infantry, C.S.A.* Memphis: S. C. Toof, 1897.

Watkins, Sam. *Company Aytch, or, a Side Show of the Big Show*. Edited by M. Thomas Inge. 1882. Reprint. New York: Penguin Putnam, 1999.

Secondary Sources

Baumgartner, Richard A., and Larry M. Strayer. *Kennesaw Mountain, June 1864: Bitter Standoff at the Gibraltar of Georgia*. Huntington, WV: Blue Acorn, 1998.

Black, Robert C. *The Railroads of the Confederacy*. Chapel Hill: University of North Carolina Press, 1998.

Bonds, Richard S. *War Like the Thunderbolt: The Battle and Burning of Atlanta*. Yardley, PA: Westholme, 2009.

Bonekemper, Edward H. *Grant and Lee: Victorious American and Vanquished Virginian*. Washington, DC: Regnery History, 2012.

Boritt, Gabor S., ed. *Jefferson Davis's Generals*. New York: Oxford University Press, 1999.

Clark, John E. *Railroads in the Civil War: The Impact of Management on Victory and Defeat*. Baton Rouge: Louisiana State University Press, 2001.

Castel, Albert. *Decision in the West: The Atlanta Campaign of 1864*. Lawrence: University Press of Kansas, 1992.

Catton, Bruce. *Never Call Retreat*. New York: Washington Square, 1965.

Coggins, Jack. *Arms and Equipment of the Civil War*. Wilmington, NC: Broadfoot, 1990.

Connelly, Thomas Lawrence. *Autumn of Glory: The Army of Tennessee, 1862–1865*. Baton Rouge: Louisiana State University Press, 1971.

Cozzens, Peter. *The Shipwreck of Their Hopes: The Battles for Chattanooga*. Chicago: University of Illinois Press, 1996.

———. *This Terrible Sound: The Battle of Chickamauga*. Chicago: University of Illinois Press, 1996.

Daniel, Larry J. *Soldiering in the Army of Tennessee: A Portrait of Life in a Confederate Army*. Chapel Hill: University of North Carolina Press, 1991.

———. *Days of Glory: The Army of the Cumberland, 1861–1865*. Baton Rouge: Louisiana State University Press, 2004.

Davis, Stephen. *All the Fighting They Want: The Atlanta Campaign from Peachtree Creek to the City's Surrender, July 18–September 2, 1864*. El Dorado Hills, CA: Savas Beatie, 2017.

———. *Atlanta Will Fall: Sherman, Joe Johnston, and the Yankee Heavy Battalions*. Wilmington, DE: Scholarly Resources, 2001.

———. *A Long and Bloody Task: The Atlanta Campaign from Dalton through Kennesaw Mountain to the Chattahoochee River, May 5–July 18, 1864*. El Dorado Hills, CA: Savas Beatie, 2016.

———. *What the Yankees Did to Us: Sherman's Bombardment and Wrecking of Atlanta*. Macon, GA: Mercer University Press, 2012.

Davis, William C., ed. *The Civil War*. 27 vols. Alexandria, VA: Time Life Books, 1983–87.

———. *Jefferson Davis: The Man and His Hour*. Baton Rouge: Louisiana State University Press, 1991.

Drake, Dr. Edwin L., Lieut. Col., CSA. *Annals of the Army of Tennessee and Early Western History*. 1878. Reprint. Jackson, TN: Guild Bindery Press, 1998.

Ecelbarger, Gary. *The Day Dixie Died: The Battle of Atlanta*. New York: St. Martin's, 2012.

Elliott, Sam Davis. *Doctor Quintard, Chaplain C.S.A. and Second Bishop of Tennessee*. Baton Rouge: Louisiana State University Press, 2003.

———. *Soldier of Tennessee: General Alexander P. Stewart and the Civil War in the West*. Baton Rouge: University of Louisiana Press, 1999.

Freeman, Douglas S. *Lee's Lieutenants: A Study in Command*. One-volume abridgement by Stephen W. Sears. New York: Simon and Schuster, 1998.

Grecian, Joseph. *History of the Eighty-Third Regiment Indiana Volunteer Infantry*. Cincinnati: John F. Uhihorn, Printer, 1865.

Hallock, Judith Lee. *Braxton Bragg and Confederate Defeat*. Vol. 2. Tuscaloosa: University of Alabama Press, 1991.

Henry, Robert S. *First with the Most: Nathan Bedford Forrest*. New York: Konecky and Konecky, 1992.

Hess, Earl J. *The Battle of Ezra Church and the Struggle for Atlanta*. Chapel Hill: University of North Carolina Press, 2015.

———. *Civil War Infantry Tactics: Training, Combat, and Small-Unit Effectiveness*. Baton Rouge: Louisiana State University Press, 2015.

———. *Kennesaw Mountain: Sherman, Johnston, and the Atlanta Campaign*. Chapel Hill: University of North Carolina Press, 2013.

Hewitt, Lawrence Lee, and Arthur W. Bergeron Jr., eds. *Confederate Generals in the Western Theater*. Vols. 1–2. Knoxville: University of Tennessee Press, 2010.

Hood, Stephen M. *The Lost Papers of Confederate General John Bell Hood*. El Dorado Hills, CA: Savas Beatie, 2015.

———. *The Rise, Fall, and Resurrection of a Confederate General*. El Dorado Hills, CA: Savas Beatie, 2013.

Horn, Stanley F. *The Army of Tennessee: A Military History*. New York: Bobbs-Merrill, 1941.

Hughes, Nathaniel Cheairs, Jr. *General William J. Hardee: Old Reliable*. Baton Rouge: Louisiana State University Press, 1965.

Jenkins, Robert D., Sr. *The Battle of Peach Tree Creek: Hood's First Sortie, 20 July 1864*. Macon, GA: Mercer University Press, 2013.

———. *To the Gates of Atlanta: From Kennesaw Mountain to Peach Tree Creek, 1–19 July 1864*. Macon, GA: Mercer University Press, 2015.

Jones, Archer. *Civil War Command & Strategy: The Process of Victory and Defeat*. New York: Free Press, 1992.

Levine, Bruce. *Confederate Emancipation: Southern Plans to Free and Arm Slaves During the Civil War*. New York: Oxford University Press, 2006.

Lindsley, John B., ed. *The Military Annals of Tennessee: Confederate*. Nashville: J. M. Lindsley, 1886.

McCarley, J. Britt. *The Atlanta Campaign: A Civil War Driving Tour of Atlanta-Area Battlefields*. Atlanta: Cherokee, 1989.

McDonough, James Lee. *Chattanooga—A Death Grip on the Confederacy*. Knoxville: University of Tennessee Press, 1984.

McMurry, Richard M. *Atlanta 1864: Last Chance for the Confederacy*. Lincoln: University of Nebraska Press, 2000.

———. *John Bell Hood and the War for Southern Independence*. Lincoln: University of Nebraska Press, 1982.

———. *Two Great Rebel Armies: An Essay in Confederate Military History*. Chapel Hill: University of North Carolina Press, 1989.

McPherson, James M. *Battle Cry of Freedom: The Civil War Era*. New York: Ballantine Books, 1988.

———. *The Negro's Civil War: How American Blacks Felt and Acted During the War for the Union*. New York: Vintage Books, 2003.

Miles, Jim. *Fields of Glory: A History and Tour Guide of the Atlanta Campaign*. Nashville: Rutledge Hill, 1989.

Parks, Joseph H. *General Leonidas Polk, C.S.A.: The Fighting Bishop*. 1962. Reprint. Baton Rouge: Louisiana State University Press, 1990.

Perello, Christopher. *The Quest for Annihilation: The Role & Mechanics of Battle in the American Civil War*. Bakersfield, CA: Strategy and Tactics, 2009.

Peterson, Lawrence K. *Confederate Combat Commander: The Remarkable Life of Brigadier General Alfred Jefferson Vaughan Jr*. Knoxville: University of Tennessee Press, 2013.

Peterson, Larry. *Decisions at Chattanooga: The Nineteen Critical Decisions that Defined the Battle*. Knoxville: University of Tennessee Press, 2018.

Powell, David A. *The Chickamauga Campaign—Barren Victory: The Retreat into Chattanooga, the Confederate Pursuit, and the Aftermath of the Battle, September 21 to October 20, 1863*. El Dorado Hills, CA: Savas Beatie, 2016.

Rhea, Gordon C. "'Butcher' Grant and the Overland Campaign." *North and South* 4, no. 1 (November 2000): 44–55.

Savas, Theodore P., and David A. Woodbury, eds. *The Campaign for Atlanta & Sherman's March to the Sea*. Vols. 1–2. Campbell, CA: Savas Woodbury, 1994.

Scaife, William R. *The Campaign for Atlanta*. 4th ed. Cartersville, GA: Civil War Publications, 1993.

———. *The Chattahoochee River Line: an American Maginot*. Cartersville, GA: Civil War Publications, 2004.

Scales, John R. *Sherman Invades Georgia*. Annapolis: Naval Institute Press, 2006.

Secrist, Philip L. *The Battle of Resaca*. Macon, GA: Mercer University Press, 1998.

Spruill, Matt. *Decisions at Gettysburg: The Nineteen Critical Decisions That Defined the Campaign*. Knoxville: University of Tennessee Press, 2011.

———. *Storming the Heights: A Guide to the Battle of Chattanooga*. Knoxville: University of Tennessee Press, 2003.

Strayer, Larry M., and Richard A. Baumgartner. *Echoes of Battle: The Atlanta Campaign*. Huntington, WV: Blue Acorn, 2004.

Stroud, David V. *Ector's Texas Brigade and the Army of Tennessee, 1862–1865*. Longview, TX: Ranger, 2004.

Sword, Wiley. *The Confederacy's Last Hurrah: Spring Hill, Franklin, & Nashville*. Originally published as *Embrace an Angry Sword*. Lawrence: University Press of Kansas, 1992.

———. *Mountains Touched with Fire: Chattanooga Besieged, 1863*. New York: Saint Martin's, 1995.

Symonds, Craig L. *Joseph E. Johnston: A Civil War Biography*. New York: W. W. Norton, 1992.

———. *Stonewall of the West: Patrick Cleburne & the Civil War*. Lawrence: University Press of Kansas, 1997.

Tanner, Robert G. *Retreat to Victory: Confederate Strategy Reconsidered*. Wilmington, DE: Scholarly Resources, 2001.

Trudeau, Noah. *The Last Citadel: Petersburg, Virginia June 1864–April 1865*. Baton Rouge: Louisiana State University Press, 1991.

Warner, Ezra J. *Generals in Blue: Lives of the Union Commanders*. Baton Rouge: Louisiana State University Press, 1964.

———. *Generals in Gray: Lives of the Confederate Commanders*. Baton Rouge: Louisiana State University Press, 1959.

Weber, Thomas. *The Northern Railroads in the Civil War, 1861–1865*. 1952. Reprint. Bloomington: Indiana University Press, 1999.

Woodworth, Steven E. *Decision in the Heartland: The Civil War in the West.* Westport, CT: Praeger, 2008.

———. *Jefferson Davis and His Generals: The Failure of Confederate Command in the West*. Lawrence: University Press of Kansas, 1990.

———. *Six Armies in Tennessee: The Chickamauga and Chattanooga Campaigns*. Lincoln: University of Nebraska Press, 1998.

INDEX

Page numbers in **boldface** refer to illustrations.